THINKING ABOUT GOD

REFLECTIONS ON CONCEPTIONS
AND MISCONCEPTIONS

Also by
STEPHEN M. LAMPE

The Christian and Reincarnation

Building Future Societies: The Spiritual Principles

THINKING ABOUT GOD

REFLECTIONS ON CONCEPTIONS
AND MISCONCEPTIONS

STEPHEN M. LAMPE

Millennium Press
Ibadan, Nigeria

Published by
Millennium Press
25, Moremi Street,
New Bodija
Ibadan
P.O. Box 38632, General Post Office, Dugbe
Ibadan

Tel: (+234)8091924774

Email: millenniumpress7@gmail.com
stephenlampe@gmail.com

First Published 2014

ISBN: 978-978-2751-06-5 (Hard Cover)
ISBN: 978-978-2751-07-2 (Paperback)

The truth is incontrovertible
Panic may resent it
Ignorance may deride it
Malice may distort it
But there it is ...
(Winston S. Churchill)

The right to search for truth
implies also a duty. One must
not conceal any part of what
one has recognized to be true.
(Albert Einstein)

Contents

Preface

With the word GOD, many different ideas arise and these depend on the individual's culture, religious exposure, education, and inner maturity. We often hear the question asked, "Do you believe in God?" The question is not really meaningful. And any answer is practically meaningless in the absence of clear elaboration of what conceptions of God the questioner has in mind. Therefore, those who call themselves believers in God need continually to clarify the nature and content of their beliefs. Serious-minded and well-intentioned atheists and agnostics similarly ought individually to review and ascertain, from time to time, the reasons for their unbelief or suspension of belief. They should want to know if wrong conceptions of God hitherto presented to them might be responsible for their position.

To get it right about the conception of God is to get it right about everything. False conceptions lead to false religions. False religions in turn reinforce various forms of unbelief. Worse still, false religions inevitably lead to hatreds, horrors, and all sorts of conflicts. And let it be said: seeking to acquire the right conception of God is not about religion; it is to follow the natural desire that is implanted in the human essence. Therefore, the search for the right conception of God is everybody's duty and it should be quite a personal matter, not dictated by other individuals or organizations. Following serious reflections, one should consciously adjust one's volition, thoughts, words, and deeds according to what one has become *personally* convinced are true.

Because the search for God is implanted in that which makes us human, it is not surprising that innumerable books and essays, ancient and modern, have been written on various aspects of the idea of God. In collaboration with *Encyclopaedia Britannica*, Professor Mortimer J. Adler led a project called Syntopicon in which he and colleagues at the University of Chicago identified and indexed the 102 "Great Ideas" of Western thought. The Syntopicon, published in 1952, showed that the discussion of the idea of God was by far the largest single discussion that has gone on in the intellectual tradition of the Western world. The same would be true of other cultures, including cultures in which discussions were not committed to writing but remained in the oral tradition.

Despite the intense intellectual discussions that have taken place it is safe to say that human beings still today do not have a clear and unequivocal conception of God. And this is despite what E. F. Schumacher calls centuries of 'theological imperialism'. Following those centuries we have now had, according to him, three centuries of an ever more aggressive 'scientific imperialism' and the result is a degree of bewilderment and disorientation, which can lead to the collapse of civilization. In Schumacher's opinion, many people, however learned they may be, know nothing about anything that really matters. No wonder the conversations about the idea of God continue unabated but with rather little to show in terms of real progress.

This book indicates the broad lines along which a non-sectarian and genuine truth-seeker might reflect in order to acquire a clear and self-consistent understanding of the greatness and sublimity of God as well as how He relates to Creation. My objective is to encourage individual spiritual contemplation, promote greater reflection about and deepen our understanding of God and how He relates to us creatures. By so doing one develops conviction about both what it means to be human and what the purpose of an earthly sojourn is. With that also comes an understanding of the great human potential as well as the duties and automatic privileges that go with being truly human.

I start from the premise that reality abounds in mysteries and extends beyond what is physical and material and, therefore, beyond the domain in which science can exercise authority. I indicate that revelation is part of reality and is encountered not only in religion and spirituality but in many different endeavours, including science. But revelation must always be tested. However, we do so not only with our intellectual tools but also with the help of the talents that are inherent in our human essence. Moreover, large-scale systematic revelations are not static but respond to changes in human and cosmic development. But a new revelation is not necessarily a negation of the old but may simultaneously clarify, modify as well as build on the old.

The emphasis of the book is the introduction into the contemplation of God knowledge that has been largely absent from the innumerable publications on the subject. Thus, a discussion of the nature of the human being features early in the book. Also addressed in an early Chapter of the book is the new knowledge of Creation and Subsequent Creation – what one might call an outline of a complete cosmology. It seems to me obvious that human beings cannot begin to think aright about God if they do not even know their own essence and in the absence of the knowledge of Creation.

In discussions about God, even those dealing specifically with the Will of God, one finds missing an explicit description of the unchanging laws by which God brought Creation into being and maintains it. This is because of the prevailing ignorance about these most important laws that are so fundamental to the right conception of God. I have discussed them in a whole chapter and applied them to the discussions of several other chapters. I believe that for these as well as for reasons of several pieces of new and key information, this book is an uncommon contribution to the contemplation of God. I have also pointed out the tendency unfairly to ascribe to God the problems that are of religion's making. It is wrong to presume that religions necessarily reflect the true Will of God. Any attempt to think about God relying exclusively on religions will very likely lead to false conceptions.

While I seek to stimulate and encourage forward movement in the age-old ideas about God and generally to help readers advance in the recognition of God, I hope that it will be evident to readers of this book that it is not my intention gratuitously to denigrate the viewpoints of any particular religions. But I should state that I have not been constrained by the dogmas and beliefs of any particular religion. I write out of deep personal conviction and with the objective of sharing my convictions with those of open mind.

I can embark on writing a book of this scope and depth only because of my good fortune in coming across and recognizing the unique significance of the work *In the Light of Truth, The Grail Message* by Abd-ru-shin (civil name Oskar Ernst Bernhardt). Oskar Ernst Bernhardt (1875-1941) wrote in his native German language; translations are now available in the major languages of the world. The work, which has become popularly known as "The Grail Message" is a unique source of knowledge that, in my view, is absolutely essential for truth seekers, regardless of current beliefs or unbelief.

The scope of The Grail Message is vast and extends well beyond traditional fields of religion and spirituality. It includes descriptions of the human being, its origin and purpose on earth, marriage and family, gender issues, ancient gods, the dangers of occult and psychic science, the evolution and development of material creation, the great untapped potentials as well as limitations of science, and indications of an emerging new world. It describes the real Act of Creation and outlines hitherto unknown realms of Creation and Subsequent Creation, thus presenting to humankind for the first time a complete cosmology. In addition to the work *In the Light of Truth, The Grail Message,* Abd-ru-shin published explanations of the Ten Commandments of God and of The Lord's Prayer. His written answers to some of the questions he was asked about his teachings have also been published as *Questions and Answers 1924-1937.* My own understanding of these sources of spiritual knowledge has guided my discussions and analyses of issues.

Not all the topics that some might legitimately consider pertinent to the subject of this book have been covered. The Grail Message would certainly provide answers to such missing topics. While I hope that the book will succeed in steering many on the right path to thinking about God, I am certain that God Himself, because of His very nature, will remain an eternal mystery to us His creatures. Any contrary impression in the book would be an unintended error.

Acknowledgments

This book has been in the making for a long time. My early thoughts on the topics that constitute some of the chapters of this book appeared in a series of nine essays in my newspaper column (*Millennium Wisdom*) as far back as 2003. Most of the work, however, has been done in the last three years. During this period, my wife and children were most encouraging, constantly wanting to know how far I had gone. Without them, this book may never have been completed. I thank them for the love and unflinching support. My grandchildren have also been a powerful stimulus as my ardent desire is that they grow up in a world in which there is much greater clarity about the conception of God.

Finally, I acknowledge the helpful comments and suggestions that Messrs Deji Haastrup, Festus Unuigbe, Femi Badaki, Kolawole Lawani, and Dr. Christian Fatokun provided on drafts of some of the chapters. My gratitude also goes to Dr. Kanayo F. Nwanze who, in several discussions while I was his guest in Rome, helped me clarify my thoughts on some ideas. Of course, I take full responsibility for this final product.

Stephen M. Lampe
August 17, 2014

Introduction and Overview

Some fundamental issues must first be settled if we are to put ourselves in a position to reflect on the idea of God in a logical and consistent manner. One is the matter of mystery. Is all reality fully knowable or at least potentially fully comprehensible using exclusively the tools of the human brain? In other words, is it right to think that there are no mysteries that our brains cannot unravel? Some people feel sure that any hints of mystery beyond human intellectual capacity (on which science depends) should be considered mere superstition. To them, everything must be intellectually provable. And the fact that there have always been many charlatans especially in the domain of religion and spirituality making a living on 'mysterious phenomena' tends to support their disdain for mysteries. They deride or at least disbelieve whatever the intellect seems unable to fathom. Many others think differently; their personal experiences have convinced them that mysteries abound in reality and ought not to be casually dismissed as superstition. Those two groups would, of course, have different dispositions to the idea of God.

Related to the issue of mystery is the subject of revelation. How would we know realities beyond the grasp of the human brain? This is where the idea of revelation comes in. But how do we know that a piece of revealed information is true? Those who believe in revelation suggest that one must have faith. But faith must not be blind but must be consistent with logic and other facts of experience.

I address the subject of mysteries and the interrelated issues of revelation and faith in Chapter 2 – *The Mystery of Reality*. I show that reality is mostly invisible and abounds in mystery. There are mysteries even in science but such are accepted as topics deserving of continuing contemplation and study; they are not dismissed as superstition. Indeed, it is true to say that the most important phenomena are mysteries to science. Science cannot explain the 'life force' (or simply *life*), which differentiates what is living from what is dead, such as a dead plant and a living plant. It is unable to explain *'consciousness'* that differentiates a living plant from any grown living animal. And the difference between a normal living animal and a normal living human being (*self-awareness*) remains a mystery to science. The dead plant, the living plant, the living animal, and the living human being represent different Levels of Being. We note that *life*, *consciousness*, and *self-awareness* responsible for the different fundamental possibilities and abilities at the different Levels of Being are invisible, mysterious, and incontestably real. Each of them can be destroyed but none can be created. All arguments against the existence of the invisible, the non-physical, and the mysterious are by implication debunked in the Chapter. And having thus undermined the position of the materialist, I find no need to rehash the traditional arguments for the existence of God.

Also in Chapter 2, I cite the experiences of many renowned scientists to indicate that revelation and faith feature in the practice of science just as they do in religion and spirituality. I continue the discussion on revelation with emphasis on the idea of God in Chapter 3 – *The Progressive Revelation of God*. The true revelations about God come through envoys and various prophets but from the same ultimate source – God. Therefore, such messages are mutually consistent, unless human beings have distorted them, wittingly or unwittingly. Each revelation was tailored to the stage of development and level of spiritual maturity of the target people and it was never intended to be the last word. New revelations are given to specific peoples as they develop further and to the entire humanity at definite turning points in the development of the whole of Creation. Such new revelations take into account the new needs that arise in the course of the further development of the parts of Creation in which the people reside. However, it should be stressed that a new revelation is not necessarily a negation of the old but may simultaneously clarify, modify as well as build on the old.

To think clearly, logically, and consistently about God one must also have knowledge of the nature of the human being. Is the human being merely the physical body that can be described and analysed by pure and applied science? Or is it the case that the physical body is only the outermost cloak of an essence that is called spirit or soul that is beyond the possibility of probing by science? Those two ideas necessarily lead to quite different conceptions of God. Thinking about God is of relevance to us as human beings first and foremost because of our need to know how God relates to us and what He expects of us. Therefore, it seems obvious to me that we should start from the basis of conviction about what we human beings really are, why we are here, and where we go at physical death. If as a seeker I do not even know for sure what I am, I am most unlikely to think aright about God. Surely, a great deal of wisdom lies in the admonition "Know Thyself". These and related issues are addressed in Chapter 4 entitled *The Human Being and Human Purpose*.

In anticipation of the discussions in Chapter 4, let me state that the nature of the human being is such that it has an unquenchable longing for the recognition of God. Religion and spirituality may wax and wane, human civilization may take whatever direction, and regardless of the wonders of new scientific discoveries and inventions, the idea of God will never go away, contrary to the imaginings of some philosophers and academics! And the longing is not a matter of mere DNA or genetics in general.

To think aright about God, who will forever be absolutely invisible to us, we should know something about Creation, which is at least in a small part visible to us. One who assumes that Creation consists of one universe of relatively small extent with our earth the only inhabited place would conceive of God, the presumed Creator, very differently from the person who knows of the vastness of our universe and of the possibility that there are other universes. Some within both groups might assume that everything is purely physical. Their thoughts about God would again differ from others who think that there is much more to the universe; who feel certain that Creation includes realities that are non-physical and that may never be accessible to science. I address these issues in Chapter 5 entitled *Creation and Subsequent Creation*. The Chapter may be described as a bare outline of what one may call the complete cosmology that includes the basic structure of material and non-material reality. In my opinion, it is impossible to have any meaningful conception of God without some knowledge, albeit meagre, of such complete cosmology.

There is a wide spectrum of views among those who contemplate the idea of God. I outline the broad categories of unbelief and belief in Chapter 6 entitled *Varieties of Unbelief and Belief*. Opinions vary from apparently total unbelief to complete conviction concerning the existence of God. We know, of course, that there are differences among believers, hence the many religions as well as sects and denominations within the same religion. But there are also differences among unbelievers. The issue to be highlighted in this respect is that the conception of God to which one is exposed would determine whether or not one believes as well as the nature of one's unbelief or belief. One might find certain conceptions of God (such as one who acts arbitrarily, feels free to contradict himself, and behaves like a magician) unreasonable and unbelievable while another conception might be exceedingly appealing and believable. It follows, therefore, that the question as to whether one believes or does not believe in God is really rather meaningless; the question acquires meaning only after a particular notion of God has been ascertained. Unfortunately most people have no clarity about the sort of God they accept or reject! An objective of this book is to help every reader, regardless of present orientation, clarify his or her own position.

Religious people frequently say "God's Will be done", "Thy Will be done", or "God Willing". All are references to the concept of *The Will of God*. However, some people say "God's Will be done" when something has happened that they wished did not happen, such as bereavement. The tone usually carries the clear implication that the speaker would have changed "God's Will" if he had the power, even though the statement is intended to suggest voluntary compliance with the Will of God. Thus, it is not always clear what people mean when they say "God's Will be done". And it suggests that many misunderstand the idea of *The Will of God*.

A further illustration of the misunderstanding is encountered in the Lord's Prayer, the prayer most commonly said by Christians. When in the Prayer it is said "Thy Will Be done on Earth as it is in Heaven", it is *not* intended as a plea with God to do something for us or for the earth as a whole. This is because it is the Will of God that brought Creation into being, supports and sustains it. God's Will rules the worlds. Therefore, no one needs specially to plead that the Will of God be done on earth. It is only human beings on earth who through the abuse of their Free Will act contrary to God's Will. A somewhat plausible interpretation of that statement might be that we are begging God to help us as we struggle to do His Will on earth.

Rightly understood, the Will of God is not a matter of religion and it does not depend on religious doctrines. Rather, religious doctrines and beliefs should derive from the Will of God; and so should the earthly laws by which societies govern themselves as well as the social, economic and political principles they adopt. The Will of God is expressed in eternal, immutable, and universal spiritual principles or laws. Those laws are the sole mechanism by which God relates to Creation and all creatures. Suppose one buys a new piece of equipment which comes with an operating manual. The right thing to do is to study the manual and follow the instructions. Doing so would not amount to doing the manufacturer a favour. Similarly, by doing the Will of God, we do not do God a favour; we would thereby simply be pursuing our own best interest. To do otherwise, is to create all sorts of problems for ourselves. Explanations and illustrations of the immutable laws are the subject of Chapter 7 entitled *The Will of God*.

In thinking about God, many people are content with the knowledge provided by particular ancient Scriptures. In this connection, let me first emphasize that all past messages of God should be considered the common heritage of humanity. While each message was given to particular peoples according to their state of maturity and their most urgent needs for further development, it was never intended to be an exclusive possession. Moreover, as explained in Chapter 3 on the progressive nature of the revelation of God, those messages were not meant to define all truths for all time. The expectations were that they would be integrated into new teachings made available as human beings matured spiritually and as the cycle of God's Creation advanced. Therefore, neither the peoples to whom the messages were first revealed nor later adherents of those teachings ought to feel obliged to take a position of infallibility with respect to particular Scriptures. And nobody should feel duty bound to defend ancient Scriptures to the hilt. Only careful weighing and examining of the old and whatever new teachings one comes across lead to genuine conviction. And with genuine conviction comes the ability really to embrace whatever is true regardless of its source. Moreover, the equanimity and inner stability of genuine conviction precludes desire to quarrel and fight with people who hold different beliefs. Only those whose beliefs are shaky and whose motives are impure employ violence and other vile means.

Some Scriptures present confusing and inconsistent pictures of the attributes and nature of God. In some passages we are told that no one can see Him and live and in another that a particular prophet speaks with God face to face as one speaks with a friend. The Scripture that describes God as love also narrates stories that suggest that He condoned series of genocides by ancient Israelites. He is even supposed to have demanded some of the atrocities. God is supposed to have subjected those He loved, such as Abraham and Job, to inhuman tests of loyalty – tests that one can only associate with earthly tyrants.

As the Creator of all Creation, He is a universal God and relates impartially to all creatures. But by and large, He is portrayed in some books of the Bible as one who was only concerned with the weal and woes of Israel. Such confused portrayal provides ammunition for atheists and shakes the faith of thoughtful believers. To think aright about God one must seek beyond traditional scriptures. Chapter 8 entitled *Beyond the Scriptural Portrayal of God* addresses the issue. In this and in some other Chapters, I have necessarily quoted from the Bible and the Koran. Unless where I indicate otherwise, Bible quotations are from the New Revised Standard Version, which is accepted by both Roman Catholic and Protestant denominations. Quotations from the Koran are from the Text, Translation, and Commentary by Abdullah Yusuf Ali published in Lahore, Pakistan, unless otherwise stated.

There is a tendency on the part of many to think about God as if He were a human being who happens to be the most perfect, most ideal, and loftiest of the human type. This is, of course, a misconception. The misconception is understandable on at least two grounds: the human language is severely limited when it comes to talking about something outside human experience and what the intellect cannot grasp; and secondly, knowledge of the place of humans in relation to God has been unknown until the relatively recent revelation of the structure of Creation and Subsequent Creation discussed in Chapter 5.

Consider a creative artist and his work. Even though, a close study of the art may permit one to say something about the artist, we know that the artist is quite different and distinct from his art. The artist and the art belong to quite different species. And it is self-evident that a piece of art cannot describe its own creator. The creative artist and his work faintly reflect the relation of God to Creation. If we think of Creation as a work of art of God, human beings would be only a minuscule element of that art. And that puts us in the position to which we belong in relation to God. This is not generally made quite clear in the Scriptures, especially because an overview of the structure of Creation was not known. Chapter 9 – *God is Unlike Human Beings* – deals with the misconception of thinking about God as if He were merely superhuman.

The next five chapters are contemplations of what are commonly considered the major attributes of God. They include Perfection, Omnipotence, Omniscience, Love, Justice, Omnipresence, and the Trinity. One could, of course, come up with more attributes. Indeed, based on the Koran and certain Hadiths, Islam speaks of ninety-nine 'beautiful names' or attributes of God. To discuss all those attributes is beyond me. However, I believe that most of those ninety-nine attributes can be subsumed in the ones discussed in this book.

In Chapter 10, *The Perfection and Omnipotence of God*, I discuss the attributes of both perfection and omnipotence. I have chosen to discuss them in the same Chapter because I consider them inseparable. Both are closely related since God exercises His Omnipotence only in the light of His Perfection. By ignoring this inseparable relationship, many believers accept and promote wrong conceptions of God's Omnipotence. In this Chapter, I explain how the Perfection of God should be understood as well as the implications for how we should understand God's Omnipotence. I indicate the errors that most people, including many philosophers, theologians, and religious leaders, make when they think about these attributes.

The Laws through which God operates in Creation and Subsequent Creation are perfect and immutable. Since God relates to us only through His Perfect Will as expressed in those Laws, the exercise of His Omnipotence is subject to the dictates of His perfect laws. God, as the Creator, is the sole and ultimate source of all power on which, in myriad transformations, everything depends. Whatever God wills for Creation always prevails ultimately, and the effects of all contrary volitions are ephemeral. This is the sense in which His omnipotence should be understood. It is a mistake to think that everything is possible with God. God cannot contradict Himself; He cannot act against His own nature; He cannot tell lies; He cannot make a stone so heavy that He would be unable to lift it; etc.

The Omniscience of God is the subject of Chapter 11. People ordinarily use the word omniscience to mean complete and exhaustive knowledge. Such knowledge would include actual facts, events, and possibilities relating to the past and the present as well as pertaining to the future. It is this popular meaning that most people have in mind when they think about the Omniscience of God, except that they presume that such all-knowing would be developed in God to the highest level imaginable. In line with the ordinary human conception of omniscience, God is presumed to know, for example, what each of the billions of individuals on earth is thinking, saying, and doing at all times. Such thinking about God's Omniscience is wrong!

We come close to the right understanding of Omniscience in relation to God if we think of God as *all-wise* rather than *all-knowing*. In other words, we should speak of *wisdom* not of knowledge when we think of the Omniscience of God. For omniscience, the German language uses the word *Allweisheit*, which literally means *All-wisdom*; this expression points directly to the correct conception of Omniscience as it relates to God.

The Omniscience of God has to do with infinite wisdom; it is *not* about earthly all-knowing. Technological advances in recent years, especially in remote control systems, make it much easier for human beings today to picture the working of God's Omniscience than it was for past generations. Human beings are now able to develop systems that work automatically and that have built-in self-correcting and self-adjusting features. Therefore, they can conceive of an infinitely more sophisticated system devised by God. In His Omniscience or infinite wisdom, God established from the very beginning of Creation mechanisms that ensure that His vision for Creation is fully accomplished. The mechanisms take into account all conceivable and even humanly inconceivable possibilities and include self-acting monitoring devices which restore order whenever disturbances are extraneously introduced.

Chapter 12 deals with how we should think about *the Love and Justice of God*. The two attributes of Love and Justice are discussed in the same Chapter to reflect the fact that they are inseparable. To use a rather crude analogy, they are like two sides of the same coin. The inseparable nature of the Love of God and the Justice of God helps to dispel some wrong conceptions. It follows, for example that, in the process of showering His Love on humanity, God cannot and will not commit an injustice, either to other creatures or to Himself. Any sacrifices made out of love cannot take the form of an obvious injustice. And God's Justice is always accompanied with Love.

In the Chapter, I explain that both the Love of God and the Justice of God rest in the Laws of Creation, which have existed since the very beginning of Creation. This fact implies that those two attributes of God are never dispensed in an arbitrary manner and they do not depend on the religions and the opinions of human beings. Moreover, there can be no contradictions in their expression and their manifestations on earth. Thus, in dispensing His Justice, God's Love cannot be and is never compromised.

The human notion of punishment is unknown to the Justice of God. God does not punish! Neither does God threaten and tempt. For us human beings on earth, God's Love and God's Justice have one common goal – spiritual benefit. God does not inflict suffering and tragedy on people. People bring them about purely by themselves, and by a process through which they could also ensure abundance, happiness and bliss for themselves. Furthermore, the fact that God's Justice is clear and unambiguous is stressed in Chapter 12. This is contrary to the impression that the Bible presents. In the Bible, we are told that God lets individuals reap whatever they sow, whether good or bad; and that is understandable justice. But He is also presumed to punish people for the sins of their parents and grandparents, which does not sound like, and is not, justice!

The Chapter also touches on the concept of reincarnation, which is fundamental to the right understanding of the Justice of God. It holds the key to the explanation of the many apparent injustices and seemingly undeserved misfortunes that befall people in what appears to be a haphazard, random and inexplicable manner.

Reincarnation is the fact that a human spirit, *in one continuous existence,* is given the opportunity to come to the earth more than once. The human spirit takes on a different human body on each occasion and the circumstances of each birth are determined by the Laws of Creation. This process is repeated until the human spirit attains that degree of maturity and of inner purity, which ensure that the earth no longer can hold it back from its ascent towards its spiritual home that is popularly called Paradise. Any benefits or disadvantages conferred on children by the circumstances of their birth are consequences of the Law of Sowing and Reaping and the Law of Homogeneity (discussed in Chapter 7) and they take into account the activities and predispositions of their past incarnations.

God's attribute of *Omnipresence* is the subject of Chapter 13. The idea that God is omnipresent seems straightforward and clear until one starts really to think about it. In most religious traditions, including Christianity, it is said that God is 'in heaven'. For example, in the Lord's Prayer, we say "Our Father who art in heaven." And in the Apostles' Creed, it is said that Jesus ascended into heaven, and is seated at the right hand of God the Father Almighty. The question arises: Is God 'in heaven' or is He everywhere as implied by the literal meaning of the word "omnipresent"?

In Chapter 14, under the title of *Making Sense of the Trinity,* I discuss the Trinity of God. The idea of the Trinity touches directly on the nature of God and must, therefore, be considered when thinking about God. For that reason, it should not be contemplated exclusively from the point of view of any particular religion neither should it be considered of interest only to members of particular sects. I focus almost exclusively on the Christian doctrine of the Trinity only because the Trinity is most prominent and most developed in Christianity.

Incomprehensibility is the recurrent theme of most serious discussions of the Trinity, even though it is a core concept for most Christian denominations.   Even leaders of Trinitarian churches agree that, as it is traditionally formulated, the Trinity is incomprehensible and even confusing. And yet to be saved members of such denominations are told that they must believe in it. The paradox is striking: one's salvation is said to depend on a mysterious idea whose comprehension is impossible! But true faith, which depends on personal conviction, is impossible where understanding is lacking. In that Chapter, I indicate how the Trinity should be understood and show that it does not have to be the incomprehensible mystery that it has historically been thought to be.

Praying and prayers are prominent aspects of most belief systems and are, therefore, invariably of interest in thinking about God. Among those who extol the importance of praying, there are differences in the understanding of what prayer is, how one should pray, what one should expect from prayers, why some prayers are apparently answered and some are not, and the nature of God's involvement in prayers. I address these and related issues in Chapter 15 entitled *Praying and Prayers*. Praying should be understood as an attempt to connect oneself invisibly with the Luminous Heights (as outlined in Chapter 5) and in doing so to open oneself to the holy streams of power that permeate all Creation and whose ultimate origin is God. Once connected, one may then make known one's desires, be they gratitude to God, specific requests on one's own behalf, or on behalf of other persons. If one succeeds in being linked to the Luminous Heights, one may not even need to utter any words, certainly not many words and the endeavor requires very little time. If, on the other hand, the attempt at connection does not succeed, one has not prayed, no matter how many hours or even days one devotes to petitions and praises, be they in silence, murmurs, or in ear-shattering shouts. In that case, there is no question of the prayer being answered.

And, above all, all prayers are subject to the mechanisms that God put in place from the beginning of Creation – the Laws of Creation, which express God's Will. Prayers cannot set aside those Laws. If a person (Jewish, Christian, Muslim, atheist, or pagan) sows rice, he can only reap rice. No amount of prayers, vigils, offerings, and fasting can make a planting of rice yield wheat.

Chapter 16 is on *God and Miracles*, a subject which, by implication, we have already touched upon in the Chapters on the *Perfection and Omnipotence of God* as well as in the Chapter on *Praying and Prayers*. Miracles are an important element in all religions, especially in Judaism and Christianity. In general, most religious people are predisposed to believe in miracles. But nothing can happen outside the Laws of Creation. Even God does not set aside His own Laws in order to make things happen. Therefore, what we call or think are miracles are happenings that we are unable to explain only because of deficits in our current state of knowledge.

In the Chapter, I explain the fact that some human beings have certain genuine abilities including that of healing, which the masses of humanity do not possess. In general, we would all be capable of doing much that would appear miraculous if we did not lag so far behind in our spiritual development. Unfortunately, many charlatans and frauds have made miracles a big money-making business at the expense of gullible and trusting individuals, taking advantage of the fact that unusually gifted people *do* exist. The Chapter discusses some miracles recorded in the Bible to indicate what is possible and what is not. And I stress the fact that *all* real miracles do comply with the Laws of Creation and that it is the gaps in human knowledge that lead to the presumption that events can occur outside or even in opposition to the Laws of Creation.

The problem of evil in relation to our understanding of God has been of interest for millennia. It is the subject of many books, treatises, and essays in ancient and modern times. Authors of such publications range from academic philosophers and theologians to fiction writers and playwrights. They include leaders and followers of various religions as well as agnostics and atheists of all shades. But the matter of God in relation to evil in the world remains perplexing even to the leading lights of most religions. How did evil come into the work of a perfect Creator? What sustains it in our world? Why would an omnipotent God not wipe out evil? In other words, why does God allow evil and catastrophes? Lack of answers to these and related questions provide support for atheism and agnosticism and shake the faith of many believers irrespective of religion. These are the topics covered in Chapter 17 entitled *God and the Problem of Evil*.

In the Chapter, I show that evil and suffering in the world need not be a mystery. Clarity is possible provided one is armed with the following pieces of knowledge: the immutable Laws of Creation that express the Will of God; the right understanding of the Perfection and Omnipotence of God; the correct conception of the Omniscience of God; and the right appreciation of the Love and Justice of God. In addition one must understand what the Free Will of the human being entails and the havoc that its misuse has caused. All of these pieces of essential knowledge have been presented in earlier Chapters. I apply them as appropriate in the context of the problem of evil and present additional information on 'hereditary sin', what it means, and how it brought in its wake the evils in the world.

Responding to New Knowledge
The new conceptions of spirituality and the attributes of God presented in this book suggest that we need to review our personal ideas about God and that most religions should

change their doctrines and dogmas. Each individual should do the review personally using the God-given ability to think and to reflect. The talent to reason is to be used and not buried. It is not a sin but a duty to use our reasoning faculties even in matters connected with God. But reason should be enlightened with rational spirituality. We should use our own healthy limbs rather than depend on crutches in the forms of opinions of other people, be they family members, friends, or religious leaders. Truth, shorn of superstitions, sets us free from the shackles of fanatical and commercialized religion, helps us to recognize the folly of crass materialism, and convinces us of the self-deception of half-hearted belief in God.

How might an individual proceed when confronted with new knowledge? First, one should ascertain that one really understands the new knowledge. Then one should individually and thoroughly reexamine one's past beliefs and weigh them carefully against the new knowledge. The premise for assessment should be what strikes one deeply as true. Finally, one should have the humility as well as the courage to acknowledge the truth. Indeed, it would be quite ironic for a genuine seeker to reject the truth; only a person of blind faith does so. On the question of how a genuine Christian should respond to new knowledge, Benjamin Warfield, a conservative Protestant theologian in the late nineteenth and early twentieth century, provided an answer that is pertinent. He wrote:

> We must not, then, as Christians, assume an attitude of antagonism toward the truths of reason, or the truths of philosophy, or the truths of science, or the truths of history, or the truths of criticism. As children of the light, we must be careful to keep ourselves open to every ray of light. Let us, then, cultivate an attitude of courage as against the investigations of the day. None should be more zealous in them than we. None should be more quick (sic) to discern

truth in every field, more hospitable to receive it, more loyal to follow it whithersoever it leads (B.B. Warfield, *Selected Shorter Writings*, Phillipsburg, PRR Publishing, 1970; Cited in *The Language of God: A Scientist Presents Evidence for Belief by* Francis S. Collins, p. 179).

Doctrines and Dogmas Do Change

As for religious leaders, they should note that adamantly defending illogical doctrines can only lead to retrogression spiritually, socially, and otherwise. No religion should let allegiance to evidently illogical dogmas and doctrines become its badge of identity. It does not make sense for any religion, denomination, or sect to keep carrying and waving flags of doctrines that patently contradict the correct conception of God, especially His Love and Justice. I realize that it takes a great deal of humility and courage on the part of religious leaders to acknowledge previous errors in their conception of God. But to be able to do so is a mark of nobility and true conviction. Those who lack humility will never benefit from new knowledge and will, therefore, be stuck and stagnate in ancient errors. And stagnation is retrogression.

The shepherd should be ever mindful of his duty to keep the sheep away from grazing where there is no more grass. He must make the extra effort to seek the lush grazing ground and lead his sheep there! To ignore the lush grazing ground for personal reasons is to commit a crime. Let me point out that religious leaders *can* demonstrate humility and courage and they *do* change their doctrines and dogmas. In this connection, I will cite recent positive developments in the Roman Catholic Church.

Galileo Galilei, the Italian physicist and astronomer, discovered and asserted that the sun and not the earth was the center of our solar system. The idea had been declared "false and erroneous" by a decree issued by the Church in March 1616 on the basis that it contradicted the doctrine of the Church. The position of the Church was based on the Bible from which it could be inferred (wrongly) that the earth, and not the sun, was the center of the solar system. In 1633, the Church authorities tried Galileo for his scientific view, found him guilty, and made him spend the rest of his life under house arrest. Everyone now knows that Galileo was right and the Church was wrong. The positive development is that in 1992 the Catholic Church, under the leadership of Pope John Paul II, formally acknowledged the gross error and injustice committed against Galileo in 1633, some 355 years earlier.

For centuries, it was the doctrine of the Roman Catholic Church that infants who died before receiving baptism (the sacrament the Church deemed necessary to wipe out original sin) would not go to Paradise but neither would they go to hell. They would be confined to 'the limbo of infants' (*Limbus infantium*). In 'the limbo of infants', they would enjoy happiness but not the bliss of heaven. Limbo, it should be noted, is a permanent condition, unlike purgatory. This doctrine implies that all non-Christians as well as all members of Christian sects (such as Quakers and Salvationists) who do not include baptism among their rites would be excluded from Paradise and be granted places only in limbo, even if their lives had been truly exemplary. This is, of course, an injustice that cannot possibly be compatible with the Will of God.

On April 20, 2007, Pope Benedict XVI authorized the publication of the results of several years of study by the Vatican's International Theological Commission on the matter of limbo of infants. The document, entitled *The Hope of Salvation for Infants Who Die Without Being Baptised,* declared that the teaching should no longer hold as it seemed to reflect an "unduly restrictive view of salvation." The report claimed that there was greater theological awareness today that God is merciful and "wants all human beings to be saved." "People find it increasingly difficult to accept that God is just and merciful if he excludes infants, who have no personal sins, from eternal happiness, whether they are Christian or non-Christian," the 41-page document stated. The report asserted that Grace has priority over sin, and that the exclusion of innocent babies from heaven does not seem to reflect Christ's special love for children.

Thus, the Catholic Church reversed the doctrine which it had held since the early 13th Century. This development in the Catholic Church is another welcome move away from rigid adherence to doctrines that are illogical or rest on shaky foundations. It took commendable courage and humility for Pope John Paul II and Pope Benedict XVI to change the positions of the Roman Catholic Church regarding Galileo and the 'limbo of infants'. Such reasoned changes of doctrines should be examples to religious leaders and ought to be the pattern of the future for all religions.

2 The Mystery of Reality

Reality comes in both visible and invisible forms and lies predominantly in the domain of human ignorance. That which is visible, known, and knowable is the tiny tip of the vast iceberg that constitutes reality. Reality abounds in what are commonly regarded as mysteries in ordinary life and in religion. And there are mysteries in science, although they are much less publicized. In this chapter, I suggest that most of reality is outside what science is capable of knowing or proving. God is part of such reality. For that reason, one should not look to science or scientists for matters concerning the conceptions of God.

In this Chapter, I outline some of what are, from both scientific and religious perspectives, acknowledged as mysteries. In scientific research such mysteries are accepted as realities deserving of further investigation, whereas there is a tendency on the part of many intellectuals to dismiss as superstitions analogous mysteries in the area of religion and spirituality. To think about God is to explore the ultimate and most important mystery conceivable. And yet God is the quintessential and ultimate reality. In the awareness of the vast realm of human ignorance, one should ignore those who scoff at the idea of God and who mock any talk of God.

What Do We Really Know?

The earth looks flat. But it is not; it is shaped rather like a ball with a somewhat bulging middle. The earth appears to stand still. But it is actually perpetually rotating on its axis at 1,680 km per hour and revolving around the sun at 107,640 km per hour. Thus, in a single hour, while sitting down in one place chatting or watching television, we have actually traveled 107,640 km in one direction and 1,680 km in another direction through space, as a consequence of two different motions of this earth. Just as we are being moved around by the earth, so is the earth itself being hurled around as part of the solar system at a speed of 792,000 km per hour. And it gets more mind-boggling. Our solar system is one of the billions of star systems in the galaxy called the Milky Way, which moves through space at about *two million* km per hour. Thus, despite what our physical senses may indicate, we human beings on earth are perpetual travelers traversing the cosmos at tremendous, dizzying speeds in various directions. We are, therefore, surely justified to say that our physical senses are inadequate to perceive *physical* reality. Shouldn't we then be humble enough to accept that there may be *non-physical* realities beyond our awareness and knowledge?

You would think that the broadest groupings of living things on earth have been known for several centuries, considering how much scientific research and observations have been carried out on living things since the seventeenth century. But that is not the case. Up until about 300 years ago only one group (now called Eukaryotes) that comprises animals (including humans), plants, and fungi was thought to exist. Antoni van Leeuwenhoek, a Dutch fabric merchant and civil servant discovered a second group, now known as Bacteria, more than 300 years ago (in 1674) when he looked at a drop of pond water through his single-lens microscope. For 300 years, the idea that all life on earth was either eukaryote or bacteria was considered an incontrovertible fact.

It was a huge surprise when in 1977 Carl Woese and his colleagues at the University of Illinois discovered a third domain of life on earth. In other words, for centuries, a whole group of organisms existed of which all scientists were unaware. The new group, called the Archaea, was initially thought to exist only in extreme environments where there was no oxygen and where temperatures can be near or above the normal boiling point of water. But the Archaea is now known to be a large and diverse group of organisms whose members are widely distributed in nature and which are significant players in the global carbon and nitrogen cycles.

Knowledge of the existence of this third group only became possible as a result of the development of molecular biology. Because of Woese's work, it is now widely agreed that there are three primary divisions of living systems – the Eukarya (Eukaryotes), Bacteria, and Archaea. Viruses lie in the grey area between living and non-living states and are not considered organisms in the same sense as eukaryotes, bacteria, and archaea. But viruses do have considerable medical importance. Who is to say that there are not more new groups of organisms waiting to be discovered if and when quite new biological techniques are developed? *The point is that since so much was not known until quite recently about material organisms which lie squarely in the domain of science, it should not be surprising to us that there are non-material entities of which scientists and the rest of us are completely ignorant.*

Schumacher's Guide for the Perplexed

Ernst Friedrich "Fritz" Schumacher (1911-1977), an internationally influential economist and development thinker, was best known for his book *Small Is Beautiful: a study of economics as if people mattered*. He conceptualized people-focused development strategies and promoted appropriate and environmentally sustainable technologies and small-scale industries. Societies and research institutes have been established to perpetuate his ideas. *The London Times Literary Supplement* of October 6, 1995 reported that a group of writers and scholars who wanted to create "a common market of the mind" to bridge the cultural divisions of post-war Europe included E. F. Schumacher's *Small Is Beautiful* among the hundred most influential books published in the 50 years since the Second World War. When he died in 1977, he was eulogized as "a prophet standing against the tide" and "a man who asks the right questions of his society and of all societies at a crucial time in their history." And a writer in *The Times* of London remarked that "he combined scientific thinking at its most vigorous with religious commitment at its most compassionate".

Schumacher wrote another book which may be considered a statement of the philosophical foundation for *Small Is Beautiful.* In the book, entitled *A Guide for the Perplexed*, Schumacher introduced the concept of *Adaequatio*. He asserts that nothing can be known without there being an appropriate "instrument" in the makeup of the knower. He states: "This is the Great Truth of *adaequatio* (adequateness), which defines knowledge as *adaequatio rei et intellectus* – the understanding of the knower must be adequate to the thing to be known" (p. 39). Schumacher remarks that with the rise of an exaggerated trust in the efficacy of the methods of natural science applied to all areas of investigation, the spirit and soul disappeared from the description of the human being. According to this false conception of science, whatever can neither be weighed nor measured is non-existent.

Schumacher argues that for all of us only those facts and phenomena "exist" for which we possess *Adaequatio*. "As we are not entitled to assume that we are necessarily adequate to everything, at all times, and in whatever condition we may find ourselves, so we are not entitled to insist that something inaccessible to us has no existence at all and is nothing but a phantom of other people's imaginations," declared Schumacher. *With respect to the subject of this book, I believe that it is safe to state that some people on earth today, regardless of their education and social standing, sadly no longer have the "adaequatio" for the recognition of God. And such are wrong in imagining that God is a figment of the imagination of believers.*

Schumacher observes that the mere mention of spirituality and spiritual phenomena in academic discussion is seen as a sign of 'mental deficiency'. He argues that where there is near total agreement, a subject becomes effectively dead; it is the subjects where there are doubts that deserve the most intense research. He laments the tendency of materialistic science to reject the validity of certain questions (such as spiritual phenomena), which ought to command the highest research priority. Schumacher says that science currently has a one-sided view of nature because of its rejection of the idea of Levels of Being.

In *A Guide for the Perplexed*, Schumacher develops a detailed and sophisticated explanation of the idea of Levels of Being. The presentation involves a little elementary algebra, which might be intimidating to some readers. I will, therefore, present only a rather oversimplified summary of the idea. Any dead plant is obviously different from any living plant; the difference is in what we might call *"life force"* or simply *life*, which the dead plant lacks. The living plant represents a higher Level of Being than the dead plant. We note that we can easily turn a living plant into a dead one but we cannot make a dead plant come alive. In other words, we can destroy *life* but we cannot make it. And it should be noted that science cannot explain or even describe what this *life* or life force is. Schumacher describes the jump in the Level of Being from a dead plant to a living one as an "ontological discontinuity."

Let us now move from a living plant to a living animal, both of which have *life*. We observe that the typical, fully developed animal is able to do things that are completely beyond the possibilities of a typical, fully developed living plant. We may say that the living animal has additional powers over and above the living plant. The additional powers may be designated as *consciousness*. We can sense what consciousness means for we know that any animal (such as a dog) may be knocked *unconscious* while it still retains *life*. The jump from the living plant to an adult living animal is another case of "ontological discontinuity".

Moving from the level of the living animal to the human level, we find additional new powers. The fact that a typical, fully developed human being can do, and does, innumerable things outside the range of possibilities of even the most highly developed animals cannot be disputed. Like the living plant, humans have *life*, and like living animals they have *consciousness*, and evidently something more. Schumacher notes that humans are not only able to think but are also able to be aware of their thinking. Consciousness and intelligence, as it were, recoil upon themselves. The human is not merely a conscious being, but a being capable of being conscious of its consciousness; not merely a thinker but a thinker capable of paying attention to his own thinking and studying his own thinking.

The additional power enables the human to be able to say "I" and to direct consciousness in accordance with its own purposes, a master or controller, a power at a higher level than consciousness itself. This power opens up unlimited possibilities of purposeful learning, investigating, exploring, and of formulating and accumulating knowledge. Schumacher calls it *self-awareness*; a word which he says does not fully capture the conception. Thus, there is another 'ontological discontinuity' between the Level of Being of Animals and that of Humans. It follows that the fundamental difference between humans and the most biologically evolved apes, for example, is *self-awareness* (or self-consciousness) in the sense illustrated by Schumacher. Anatomical and DNA similarities and differences are of absolutely secondary importance. Science can investigate these quite secondary factors but not the primary factor. The cause of the 'ontological discontinuity' between the Level of Being of the most highly developed animal and the Level of Being of Humans is beyond science.

Each Level of Being is a broad band within each of which there are gradations. For this reason, the precise determination of where one lower Level of Being ends and a higher Level of Being begins may sometimes be difficult to tell and be the subject of dispute. For example, we have already noted that viruses lie in the grey area between non-living and living organisms. We should note that *life* (or *life force*), *consciousness*, and *self-awareness* are invisible and extremely difficult to explain although their effects are real and obvious and are experienced routinely.

In the above discussion, we have taken dead matter (Mineral) as baseline and progressively added powers to it to get to Humans. One may proceed differently to the same conclusion by taking Humans as baseline and successively taking away powers from it to get to the Mineral level. Take away *self-awareness* from the Human Level of Being, you have the Animal Level of Being and when the Animal loses *consciousness* it descends to the Level of Being of Living Plants. Finally, when *life* is taken away from the Living Plant we get to the dead matter or Mineral Level of Being.

This scheme of progressively removing powers is easier to understand because it is closer to our practical experience. Each of the three factors *life, consciousness,* and *self-awareness* can in our experience be destroyed. *Self-awareness* can disappear while *consciousness* continues; *consciousness* can be lost while *life* continues; and *life* can be destroyed leaving behind inanimate matter. This is a process we can observe and in a sense feel. But we are not able to give *life* to inanimate matter, to give *consciousness* to living matter, and we cannot add the power of *self-awareness* to conscious creatures. Physics and chemistry deal with the lowest Level of Being – minerals (dead matter); they can tell us absolutely nothing about *life*, *consciousness*, and *self-awareness*. It is remarkable that the disciplines called the "Life Sciences," which involve the study of living organisms, do not deal with *life* as such, but devote infinite attention to the study and analysis of the physicochemical body, which is merely the carrier of *life* and not *life*. Schumacher remarks: "It may well be that modern science has no method for coming to grips with *life* as such. If this is so, let it be frankly admitted; there is no excuse for the pretence that *life* is nothing but physics and chemistry" (*A Guide for the Perplexed* p. 19).

It should be remarked that religious people take it for granted that *life* must have originated directly or indirectly through the Creator and they accept that it remains a mystery to us humans. An atheist on the other hand thinks that *life* originated by chance and that once it originated on earth, everything developed further by biological evolution through the mechanism of natural selection. Just how improbable it is that *life* would come into being by chance is expressed by no other person than a foremost chieftain of atheists, Richard Dawkins, who wrote: "We can allow it (the origin of *life*) to have been an extremely improbable event, many orders of magnitude more improbable than most people realize" (*The God Delusion*, p. 135). But it is not merely a question of infinitesimally low probability; the probability is simply *zero*. How can Dawkins show that it is not zero? His assertion that a chance origin of life is infinitesimally low but not zero seems to me, paradoxically, a case of blind faith on the part of an atheist! It would be surely more logical to say that the origin of life is a mystery and that those who assign a role to God may be right.

With respect to dead matter and anything that has no life, one speaks of "outer appearance" but not of "inner experience". Schumacher states that, in general, in the hierarchy of Being, "higher" always means and implies "more inner", "more interior", "deeper"; while "lower" means and implies "more outer", "more external", "shallower". He remarks that the progression from visibility to invisibility is just another facet of the great hierarchy of Levels of Being. The powers of *life, consciousness*, and *self-awareness* which come into play as we go up through the four Levels of Being are wholly invisible – without color, sound, skin, taste, or smell and also without extension or weight (*A Guide for the Perplexed*, pp. 32-33); and yet all three are obviously real.

It follows from the above discussion of Fritz Schumacher's Levels of Being that science does not know, and may never know, what the powers of life, consciousness, and self-awareness really are and how they came into being. In plain language, science does not know, and cannot know, what makes us human. In the light of this, why should anyone expect science to be able to tell whether or not the sublime God exists? Let me add that there is no reason to assume that only four Levels of Being exist. Higher Levels of Being would include, for example, creatures that have their origins in Realms that are higher than the Spiritual Realms, which we will discuss in Chapter 5.

Viewpoints of Some Scientists

Friedbert Karger, a plasma physicist at the Max Planck Institute of Plasma Physics in Garching, near Munich, Germany stated that, through his physical research of paranormal phenomena, he has come to the conclusion "that there must be more to existence than the matter which we can describe in terms of our physics, that there must be matter which is finer, more ethereal, even though this ethereal matter often seems paradoxical to physics" (*The Consequences of Non-Material Environmental Pollution*).

He adds that using the intellect exclusively to investigate the non-physical regions is like attempting to go to the moon with a balloon, something which is impossible. The balloon, no matter how sophisticated, cannot exceed the limit of the earth's atmosphere – a distance of about 40 km as compared with the 400,000 km that must be traveled to reach the moon. To get to the moon, a completely different principle, a rocket, is required. In an analogous manner, we can probe the non-physical regions only with the help of the spirit.

Arthur Eddington echoes this logic in his parable of a man who wished to study deep-sea life using a net that had a mesh size of three inches (about 7.6 cm). After catching many wild and wonderful creatures from the depths, the man concluded that there are no deep-sea fish that are smaller than three inches in length! If we are using the scientific net to catch our particular version of truth, we should not be surprised that it does not catch the evidence of spirit or anything beyond the physical (cited in *The Language of God* by Francis S. Collins, p. 229).

Consciousness

Many studies of "near-death experiences", that is, cases of people who had been certified clinically dead but who subsequently came back to life, prove that consciousness continues after clinical death. This means that after the brain has ceased to function, there is still a part of the human being, separate from the physical body, which continues to exist. Those who had near-death experiences are able to give detailed accounts of what transpired during the interval they were clinically dead. Even the blind among such people are able to describe visual events.

What those studies suggest is that the relationship between the brain and consciousness is not one of cause and effect; rather the brain functions as an intermediary between the spirit (the source of consciousness) and the physical body. In other words, the brain acts like a receiver-transmitter, passing messages from the body to the spirit and from the spirit to the body. The death of the brain would put a stop to reception but it would not mean that the source of consciousness ceases. This is analogous to the continued existence of transmission even though the receiver in one's possession no longer functions.

Faith and Revelation in Science

Science is a human enterprise and is, therefore, characterized by human strengths and weaknesses. Personal prejudices and even fraud do come into play in the practice of science. In this connection, Richard Lewontin, a Harvard University professor and renowned evolutionary biologist, has argued persuasively that science is in fact shaped and guided by social and political needs and assumptions. Such subjectivity is not always explicit in modern times, except for a period in the former Soviet Union during which scientific results that did not support an atheistic worldview were openly suppressed. For that reason, one should not allow oneself to be intimidated or carried away by individual scientists who mock the idea of God.

In his book, *The Demon-Haunted World: Science as a Candle in the Dark*, Carl Sagan, an atheist, argues that we exist as material beings in a material world, all of whose phenomena are the consequences of physical relations among material entities. Therefore, Sagan says we should dismiss non-material entities and beliefs such as demons, gods, extrasensory perceptions, prayers, etc. and instead accept the Scientific Method as the unique pathway to a correct understanding of the natural world. The following basic questions arise: Suppose reality extends far beyond what is material? Is the scientific method really adequate to the understanding of all phenomena? Why is science unable to explain non-material realities like *life*, *consciousness*, and *self-awareness* as Schumacher pointed out?

In his review of Sagan's book, Professor Lewontin made the following comments regarding the Scientific Method and materialism:

> Our willingness to accept scientific claims that are against common sense is the key to an understanding of the real struggle between science and the supernatural. We take the side of science *in spite* of the patent absurdity of some of its constructs, *in spite* of its failure to fulfill many of its extravagant promises of health and life, *in spite* of the tolerance of the scientific community for unsubstantiated just-so stories, because we have a prior commitment, a commitment to materialism. It is not that the methods and institutions of science somehow compel us to accept a material explanation of the phenomenal world, but, on the contrary, that we are forced by our *a priori* adherence to material causes to create an apparatus of investigation and a set of concepts that produce material explanations, no matter how counter-intuitive, no matter how mystifying to the uninitiated. Moreover, that materialism is absolute, for we cannot allow a Divine Foot in the door ("Billions and Billions of Demons", *New York Review of Books*, January 9, 1997).

Furthermore, Lewontin, a social activist, points out that some of the claims made in praise of the scientific method are in fact not true. He remarked that it is often claimed that science does not tolerate theories without data and assertions without supporting evidence; he says that is not the case. In practice there can be no scientific observations "without an immense apparatus of preexisting theory." Moreover, according to Lewontin, the literature of science is filled with assertions without adequate evidence, especially the literature of popular science writing. He wrote:

Carl Sagan's list of the "best contemporary science-popularizers" includes E.O. Wilson, Lewis Thomas, and Richard Dawkins, each of whom has put unsubstantiated assertions or counterfactual claims at the very center of the stories they have retailed in the market. Wilson's *Sociobiology* and *On Human Nature* rest on the surface of a quaking marsh of unsupported claims about the genetic determination of everything from altruism to xenophobia. Dawkins's vulgarizations of Darwinism speak of nothing in evolution but an inexorable ascendancy of genes that are selectively superior, while the entire body of technical advance in experimental and theoretical evolutionary genetics of the last fifty years has moved in the direction of emphasizing non-selective forces in evolution. Thomas, in various essays, propagandized for the success of modern scientific medicine in eliminating death from disease, while the unchallenged statistical compilations on mortality show that in Europe and North America infectious diseases, including tuberculosis and diphtheria, had ceased to be major causes of mortality by the first decades of the twentieth century, and that at age seventy the expected further lifetime for a white male has gone up only two years since 1950. Even *The Demon-Haunted World* itself sometimes takes suspect claims as true when they serve a rhetorical purpose as, for example, statistics on child abuse, or a story about the evolution of a child's fear of the dark. ("Billions and Billions of Demons", *New York Review of Books*, January 9, 1997).

Coming from a fellow evolutionary biologist, Lewontin's allegation that Professor Richard Dawkins is one of those who have "put unsubstantiated assertions or counterfactual claims at the very center of the stories they have retailed in the market" is particularly noteworthy and rather worrisome. This is because it means that Richard Dawkins has been misleading thousands of readers of his writings in which he uses what Lewontin calls "vulgarizations of Darwinism" as the foundation for the promotion of militant atheism. Dawkins might have been distorting the theory of evolution simply to suit his atheistic prejudices.

There are non-believers among respectable academics and scientists, just as in the general population. Some, like Carl Sagan mentioned above, are quite proud to call themselves materialists, meaning that they do not believe that anything exists outside what can be perceived with our five senses, with or without the aid of the technologies that enhance the powers of those senses. They reject the idea of faith and the possibility of revelations. But academics and scientists are far from being unanimous in such views; there are many incontestably distinguished scientists who are certain that the opposite is the case. They claim that faith and revelations have always been elements in the practice of science.

One such scientist is Professor Charles H. Townes, a 1964 Nobel laureate in physics and the inventor of the maser and the laser. The laser is now used in fiber optics communications, laser surgery, weapons systems, astronomical measuring tools, compact discs, and bar code scanners. In one of his many awards, the citation states inter alia: "His career in science has proven to be a remarkable trajectory of innovation, discovery and a lifetime of cutting-edge research." One of his students, Arno Allan Penzias, shared the 1978 Physics Nobel Prize for the co-discovery of the cosmic microwave background radiation, which helped to confirm the Big Bang Theory. Another student and collaborator, Arthur L. Schawlow, won the 1981 Physics Nobel Prize for the development of laser spectroscopy. Born in 1915, Townes became an Emeritus Professor at the University of California, Berkeley in 1986 and at the age of 98 (in the year

2013), he continued to be involved in research on the search for extraterrestrial intelligence and to promote a rational and harmonious accommodation between science and spirituality. He observes that there are fundamentalists in religion and fundamentalists in science, both narrow-minded.

Professor Townes points out that contrary to popular belief, there is faith in science just as in religion; that revelation plays an important role in science just as in religion; and that there are mysteries in science as there are in religion. With respect to faith, he remarks that science basically involves assumptions and faith and that nothing is absolutely proved. For example, to prove something in mathematics, there must be an overall set of assumptions but we can never prove that the assumptions are even self-consistent. He stated: "We must make the best assumptions we can envisage, and have faith. And wonderful things in both science and religion come from our efforts based on observations, thoughtful assumptions, logic, and faith!"

Moreover, Professor Townes believes that basic discovery is as much revelation as anything is. He cites his personal experience on the invention of the maser, and subsequently the laser. He had been working and worrying for many years trying to figure out how to produce shorter wavelengths, a prerequisite for the invention. One day, he got up early in the morning wondering why he and his colleagues had not found the answer. "I went outside in the park, it was a beautiful day, flowers were there and all of a sudden, hey wait a minute, it can be done; this is it. Where did the idea come from? Revelation?" The solution came to him in a flash as he sat on a bench at the park. He said that the incident reminded him of revelations to Moses as he worried about the people of Israel.

Friedrich August Kekulé had a similar experience in his discovery of the structure of benzene. He had been working on the problem for a long time without success. Then one night he had a dream of a snake that coiled around and grabbed its tail in its mouth, making a circle. That immediately gave him the idea of the correct structure of benzene, which in turn led to great advances in an important branch of chemistry. That would qualify as a revelation.

Mysteries in Science

Professor Townes further asserts that there are profound mysteries in science, just as there are in religion and spirituality. One area of mystery is quantum mechanics. According to Newtonian physics, everything is completely predictable from the laws of physics. But along came quantum mechanics showing that things are not deterministic. One can never measure precisely the position of an electron and its velocity at the same time (Heisenberg's Uncertainty Principle). Albert Einstein didn't want to believe that and insisted that there had to be a force that determines everything. It is now known and can be proved experimentally that there is nothing which can completely determine everything. Quantum mechanics philosophically revolutionized Newtonian physics but the latter is still taught in universities because it is an excellent approximation for large objects. Townes remarks that the lesson is that we should not worry about changes, but look forward to them and try to understand them increasingly deeply.

A related mystery is the relationship between quantum mechanics and general relativity. They are both important and famous scientific disciplines but quantum mechanics is inconsistent with general relativity. Professor Townes states: "They both work very well within their own domains. We trust them, we believe in them, but we can see there's a point where they are inconsistent with each other. We don't know what that means, but physicists accept this mystery, and they believe in both. And that's what we have to do in life, we have to recognize inconsistencies we don't understand, accept the mysteries, and proceed."

Another major mystery in science has to do with what makes up our universe. The universe that is visible using all the tools of science is made of protons, neutrons, and various subatomic particles bound in atoms. Perhaps one of the most surprising discoveries of the 20th century was that this ordinary matter makes up only about 5 per cent of the mass of the universe. Scientists are agreed that something is out there because of its effects on the motions of the various celestial bodies but they do not know what. The rest of the universe appears to be made of a mysterious, invisible substance designated as *dark matter* (27 percent) and *dark energy* (68 percent). Note that scientists have chosen the expression "dark" to indicate the unknown and mysterious nature of the invisible substance.

The United States National Aeronautic and Space Administration (NASA) states: "We are much more certain what *dark matter* is *not* than we are what it is." *Dark energy* is even more mysterious than *dark matter* and its discovery only as recently as in the 1990s astounded scientists. In an introduction to a write-up on *dark energy*, NASA states:

> More is unknown than is known. We know how much dark energy there is because we know how it affects the Universe's expansion. Other than that, it is a complete mystery. But it is an important mystery. It turns out that roughly 68 percent of the Universe is dark energy. Dark matter makes up about 27 percent. The rest — everything on earth, everything ever observed with all of our instruments, all normal matter — adds up to less than 5 percent of the Universe. Come to think of it, maybe it shouldn't be called 'normal' matter at all, since it is such a small fraction of the Universe.

In the light of these mysteries, is it not logical to have an open mind when presented with new sources of cosmological information, be they philosophical, religious, or spiritual? Surely, it would make sense to weigh and examine carefully and with humility any such sources of new knowledge. After all, science is telling us that it scores only 5 percent on questions of what the universe is made of; that the state of ignorance is 95 percent! Could *dark matter* and *dark energy* be indications of worlds beyond the physical?

Implications of the Big Bang Theory

Professor Charles Townes cites the Big Bang Theory as one of the modern developments in science that provide new depths of insight as it implies that there was a particular moment when the universe came into existence. According to Professor Townes, many scientists, including Albert Einstein, had presumed that our universe had always been the same and that it was ridiculous to think that it could have a beginning. But there is now evidence that there was a beginning to this universe about 13.7 billion years ago. The Big Bang Theory is that from a tiny little point (called a "singularity") the universe exploded, expanded, and developed. But what is a "singularity"? The singularity is postulated as an infinitesimally small, infinitely hot, infinitely dense something, and are thought to exist at the core of "black holes", which themselves are areas of intense gravitational pressure so intense that finite matter is actually squished into infinite density — a bewildering mathematical concept.

Professor Townes says that scientists do not know for sure what singularities are. "Where did the singularity of the Big Bang come from? We don't know. Why did it appear? We don't know. According to the Big Bang Theory, before the singularity, *nothing* existed, not time, neither matter, nor energy, nor space; there was simply nothing. So where and in what did the singularity appear if not in space? We don't know. We don't know where it came from, why it's here, or even where it is. Even today, the universe is still expanding. Since there should be no space where there is as yet no universe, into what is the universe expanding?" Presumably, into a void, of the character spoken of in the Biblical story of creation! Because many scientists did not want to admit to the possibility of a Divine Act of Creation, such as is alluded to in the Bible, the discovery of the Big Bang Theory shook up the scientific community. Professor Townes remarked that especially Sir Fred Hoyle (1915-2001), a famous British physicist, fought this discovery. Hoyle tried to provide different theories to show that the Big Bang didn't really happen. "But he finally had to give up, was convinced, and recognized yes, there was a unique moment of creation."

Initial Rejection of Truth
In religion, new revelations are initially rejected. Professor Townes says the same is true in science as scientists are sometimes also locked into their old ideas. He reported that his ideas, on the maser and the laser were initially doubted by important scientists. At first, Niels Bohr, after whom the Bohr Theory of atomic structure is named and who won the 1922 Physics Nobel Prize, said that the maser was not possible. The reaction was similar when Townes told another famous physicist, John von Neumann, that he had a working maser. "Oh no, that's not possible. You must misunderstand. It can't be." But he later came back to acknowledge that Townes was right on the invention. From his personal experience, Professor Townes concludes: "New ideas are new and we have to accept and recognize that. This is important, both in science and religion."

Because of people's tendency to reject new ideas, willingness to be different is important. Townes said he had shifted fields of research a number of times, moving on to new areas whenever a particular field had become popular. He said he went into astronomy and astrophysics because he felt that there were molecules up there in space but that people didn't realize it. He went to the University of California, Berkeley, which had good equipment that would enable him to investigate. But the chairman of the department of astronomy told him, "They can't be there, I can prove that molecules can't be there. You're crazy, you're just wasting time." Townes with his research students went ahead with the research anyway. One of his research students found molecules! First they looked for ammonia and found it and then they found water; the subject of molecular astronomy has since become quite important.

Professor Townes recalls the beginning of the Apollo space program. The Apollo program was, in the Cold War era, a way to prove that the United States was at least as good technically as the Soviet Union as well as to get ahead in worldwide recognition. The program had been proposed to President John F. Kennedy by German rocket scientists who had been brought over to the United States after the Second World War and not by American scientists and engineers. Maybe that was part of the reason why most of the important scientists and engineers in the United States were against it, some of whom came out publicly against it.

A friend of Professor Townes who happened to be in charge of the Apollo program complained to him that opponents of the program were making unfair comments. President Kennedy wanted a moon landing achieved within a decade. The critics said that it could not be done in that time frame and with anything like the money that was being proposed. They were saying that it would take five times longer than that and a lot more money. Townes suggested that his friend should get together with the critics "and if they have good points maybe you'll understand them and if they don't, maybe they'll understand you". A week later the management of the program invited Townes to form a committee of proponents and critics and to chair the committee.

He accepted and put together a committee of scientists, many of whom were doubters. Many of the critics later became convinced. The Apollo program was an outstanding success, was on time, and cost slightly less than the proposed budget. Townes remarks that the Program was another case where skeptics were wrong but he cautioned that it does not mean that people are always realistic; we always have to be careful.

Anthropic Principle

Several types of evidence indicate that our universe is what it is only because of a confluence of a number of finely tuned factors. If any of such factors were different, however slightly, our universe would not have existed and would certainly not have provided us a living space. Francis Collins, for example, cites three observations which I paraphrase below (Francis Collins, *The Language Of God*, pp. 71-75).

In the early moments of the universe following the Big Bang, matter and antimatter were created in almost equal amounts. From these, at one millisecond of time following the Big Bang, quarks and antiquarks were formed. When a quark encounters an antiquark, both are annihilated and energy is released. It so happened that for about every billion pairs of quarks and antiquarks, there was an extra quark; it is this tiny deviation from absolute equality that made it possible for matter to form and to give rise to the universe as we know it. Was this just pure chance or the outcome of design by agents of a Superior Being? Some say it was pure chance; others say it is evidence of design.

Whether or not the universe continued to expand or collapsed again after the Big Bang depended critically on the values of some physical factors. As Stephen Hawking put it, "If the rate of expansion one second after the Big Bang had been smaller by even one part in 100 thousand million million, the universe would have re-collapsed before it ever reached its present size"

(Stephen Hawking, *A Brief History of Time*, p. 138). On the other hand, if the rate of expansion had been greater by even one part in a million, stars and planets would not have been able to form. How did this incredible degree of fine-tuning come about? Was it by pure chance or design?

The formation of heavier elements, so essential to nature as we know it, depended on the fine-tuned value of what physicists call 'the strong nuclear force', which holds together protons and neutrons. If it had been just slightly stronger, carbon which is critical to life on earth would not have been formed but would have been converted to oxygen. In other words, there would have been no life in the universe. The British physicist, Fred Hoyle, who discovered how carbon and oxygen could both occur due to nuclear reactions was so surprised by the extent of fine-tuning involved that he wrote: "Would you not say to yourself, 'some super-calculating intellect must have designed the properties of the carbon atom?' Of course you would. A common sense interpretation of the facts suggests that some super intellect has monkeyed with physics – and there are no blind forces worth speaking about in nature." It should be recalled that Fred Hoyle had been skeptical about the Big Bang, preferring to believe that the universe had always been in existence and was not created.

Francis Collins says there are altogether fifteen physical constants that have values fine-tuned to make our universe the way it is. They include the speed of light, the strength of the weak and strong nuclear forces, the force of gravity, and various parameters associated with electromagnetism. It seems highly improbable that these constants would, by pure chance, have the values required to result in a stable universe that can support complex life forms. These unusual characteristics of our universe lead to the conclusion that our universe is purposely finely tuned to permit human existence. This is the Anthropic Cosmological Principle.

Atheists agree that the probability that such fine-tuning happened by chance is incredibly low but it is not zero. Therefore, they stick with the belief that it all happened by chance. Do they have proof that the probability is not zero? Of course, they don't.

Some Comments on the Anthropic Principle. The anthropic principle is another case of the mystery of reality with which science is confronted. I do not believe that all the fine-tuning necessary to form the universe as we know it came about by pure chance or through a process of trial and error. I believe that the same power that gave rise to the Big Bang ensured that the physical constants were such as to bring about a suitable abode (the universe) for various creatures including humans. Just as the earth is so positioned relative to the sun and to the other planets and the moon, I believe that it is *possible* that there are other planets similarly located to permit human life; in other words, we are not *necessarily* the only humans in our universe. Whether or not we will ever be able to communicate with human beings on other planets is quite another matter.

Moreover, in my view, there is no logical reason to believe that the agency that formed our universe cannot replicate it. Therefore, it is possible that there are other universes with the same or closely similar laws, physical constants, and structures. This seems to me more plausible than to assume that only other kinds of universes with different laws and physical constants might exist, as dictated by the mathematics of theoretical physicists. Our current knowledge of the universe shows that its size is so inconceivably large that there is no question of scientifically probing beyond it. As long as we restrict ourselves to intellectual investigation and exclude revelations, we will remain confined to our own physical universe in terms of our knowledge. Cosmological research has probably reached a stage at which only revelations can provide the vision necessary for the next revolutionary breakthroughs in scientific theorizing, as has happened in the past.

Higgs Particle — the so-called God Particle

The 2013 Nobel Prize in Physics was awarded to François Englert and Peter W. Higgs for a theory formulated to explain the origin of the mass of subatomic particles. The theory predicted the existence of a particle that became known as the Higgs particle or Higgs Boson. Higgs Boson was confirmed to exist in experiments conducted in 2012 at the Large Hadron Collider of the European Laboratory for Particle Physics (CERN) located in Geneva, Switzerland. The theory independently discovered by Englert and Higgs is important because it provides the missing piece in what is called the Standard Model of particle physics.

The Higgs particle is theorized to originate in an invisible field, the Higgs field, which is supposed to permeate all of space and to confer mass upon particles. A Higgs field endorses the idea that apparently empty space may contain the seeds of all existence because without it nothing can acquire mass and, therefore, there would be no universe. It is this unusual characteristic that led to the phrase "the God Particle" that has been much hyped by the media. The nickname was created for a popular science book (*The God Particle: If the Universe Is the Answer, What Is the Question?*) by the Nobel Laureate Leon Lederman and the science writer Dick Teresi. Both Lederman and Higgs say they are atheists and now deplore the use of the term as misleading.

It should be noted that the Standard Model to which the Higgs particle provides support is not fully satisfactory and still leaves the cosmic mystery unsolved. The Model assumes that certain particles such as neutrinos are virtually massless, whereas recent research shows that they do have mass. Moreover, the Standard Model only applies to visible matter; it does not deal with *dark matter* that, as earlier discussed, accounts for most of the matter in the universe. Furthermore, the theory of François Englert and Peter W. Higgs cannot explain why the Higgs field happens to have the peculiar properties it is supposed to have. And if the Higgs field is supposed to solve the problem of mass, it creates a new mystery; how did the Higgs field itself originate? Ignorance about the origin of mass is replaced by ignorance of the Higgs field, as Martinus J.G. Veltman, who shared the 1999 Physics Nobel Prize is reported to have noted. The cosmic mystery remains! No matter how hard we try intellectually, we cannot run away from the mystery of the origin of the universe.

Survival Physics
Some scientists armed with facts and concepts in quantum physics have studied the idea of an invisible world parallel to our own (what one might perhaps call 'worlds of the immediate Beyond'). They have speculated about the form that such world might take. Conclusions arising from this area of investigation (sometimes called "Survival Physics") include the following: The invisible part of the universe (which they term the ethereal world) occupies the same space as the visible part. The ethereal world is invisible to us because of different "universal" constants such as the speed of light, c, and Planck's constant, h, while their product, $c \times h$, which determines the elementary charge, is unchanged. The speed of light in the ethereal world is much higher than the speed of light on earth, and Planck's constant is much smaller. This leads to higher frequencies, which makes the ethereal world invisible to us. Gravitational interaction exists between the ethereal world and our world, but this interaction is very small because of the very small masses of ethereal bodies.

Henry P. Stapp, born in 1928, received his PhD in particle physics at the University of California, Berkeley, under the supervision of Nobel Laureates Emilio Segrè and Owen Chamberlain and did post-doctoral work in Europe with two other scientific giants — Wolfgang Pauli and Werner Heisenberg. Henry Stapp specializes in the mathematical and logical foundations of quantum mechanics and is a member of the Theoretical Physics Group at the Lawrence Berkeley National Laboratory. He has published extensively on the subject of mind, matter, and quantum theory. He wrote a paper entitled "Compatibility of contemporary physical theory with personality survival". Summarizing the paper, he stated:

> The central point of this paper is merely to point out that the elaboration of orthodox quantum mechanics that achieves the most commonsensical solution to the biocentrism problem parallels an elaboration that naturally accommodates personality survival. Neither of these elaborations appears to require any basic change in the orthodox theory. But both require a relaxing of the idea that physical and mental events occur only when paired together.

> In light of these considerations, strong doubts about personality survival based solely on the belief that post-mortem survival is incompatible with the laws of physics are unfounded. Rational science-based opinion on this question must be based on the content and quality of the empirical data, not on a presumed incompatibility of such phenomena with our contemporary understanding of the workings of nature (http://www-physics.lbl.gov/~stapp/Compatibility.pdf, pp. 15-16).

Let's translate the technical jargon into ordinary English language: Dr. Henry Stapp concludes that life after death is perfectly compatible with the state of knowledge in theoretical physics as at the year 2010. He joins others in supporting the possibility of non-physical worlds in which that which survives the death of the physical body (the soul) might reside. That being the case, the position held in common by atheists and so-called 'sober materialists' is completely undermined.

The results of survival physics and the various pieces of information presented in this Chapter lead to the conclusion that the non-physical world, the so-called Beyond is part of our reality – part of the mystery of reality. Our concern should no longer be whether there is a Beyond but of what the Beyond might consist. And proceeding from there, the existence of God becomes conceivable. The focus shifts to how we should and should not think about God. In other words, our task becomes one of deciding which ideas of God make sense and which do not. But we would surely be justified to pronounce those who scoff at the idea of God as uninformed, certainly not sophisticated.

3 The Progressive Revelation of God

Many people consider the idea of revelation a religious superstition. It is not. I indicated in the last Chapter, The Mystery of Reality, that revelation is real and is experienced commonly, even in science. I continue that discussion in this Chapter.

Among religious people, many misconceptions arise from the assumption that everything that can be known about God has been revealed centuries, if not millennia, ago. How long ago the last revelation happened usually varies according to the religion of the believer. Based on this assumption, many believers feel obliged to defend ancient revelations about God that might have been appropriate at a particular stage of a people's spiritual maturity but which clearly fall short of the present stage in the cycle of development of Creation. It should be obvious that what can reasonably be revealed must depend on the state of maturity of the target audience. As the audience matures, we should expect new revelations to be given, adapted in both content and manner of presentation to the higher ability to understand. Such new revelations also take into account the new needs that arise in the course of the further development of the parts of Creation in which the people reside. However, it should be stressed that a new revelation is not necessarily a negation of the old but may simultaneously clarify, modify as well as build on the old. That, after all, is how rational earthly educational systems work.

The true revelations about God come through envoys and various prophets but from the same ultimate source – God. Therefore, the messages are mutually consistent, unless human beings have distorted them, wittingly or unwittingly. In the light of historical and contemporary problems posed by religious fanaticism, politicized religion as well as religious commercialism, the following statement by Abd-ru-shin, the author of the work *In the Light of Truth, The Grail Message,* is especially significant:

> For what comes from God, or what is carried out in purity at His behest, knows neither hate nor enmity, nor any contradictions.
>
> *Wherever* you find intolerance and malice, or even enmity and stirring up strife against others who are not of the same faith, wherever men seek to harm those of different belief, either *the teaching is not from God* or it has been falsified! And such people serve only the Darkness, *never the Light!*

Revelation is not as strange a phenomenon as it may at first appear. It occurs regularly and in all fields of knowledge and endeavour, including in scientific research. Of course, our attitude to revelations should be: "trust but verify" to the utmost extent possible. The trusting and verifying must be done by each individual, so that whatever one believes is not merely out of habit or hearsay but a matter of personal conviction. The necessary verification demands that we be active both intellectually and spiritually. We are all endowed with the ability to do so and we can do so if we would listen to our inner voice and provided that we have not destroyed our inherent spiritual abilities through superficial and careless living.

Abd-ru-shin, the author of The Grail Message, discourages thoughtless acceptance of new knowledge. In the last paragraph of his one-page preface to his work, he wrote: "Genuine faith lies only in conviction, and conviction comes solely through an inflexible weighing and examining!" Elsewhere he declared: "He who accepts important matters *without question* and professes them as his own conviction shows boundless indifference and no true belief!"

The Idea of Revelation

In Chapter 2, I outlined a few of the ideas of the renowned Professor Charles H. Townes on mysteries in science. Professor Townes thinks that basic discovery is as much revelation as anything is. He cites his personal experience on the invention of the maser, and subsequently the laser. He had been working and worrying for many years trying to figure out how to produce shorter wavelengths. One day, he went to the park early in the morning wondering why he and his colleagues had not found the answer. While in the park, the answer came to him in the form of a sudden visualization of what might be done to produce electromagnetic waves. In his opinion, it was somewhat parallel to what we normally call revelation in religion. He wrote:

> Whether the inspiration for the maser and the laser was God's gift to me is something one can argue about. The real question should be: where do brand new human ideas come from anyway? To what extent does God help us? I think He's been helping me all along. I think He helps all of us — that there's a direction in our universe and it has been determined and is being determined. How? We don't know these things. There are many (unanswered) questions in both science and religion and we have to make our best judgment. But I think spirituality has a continuous effect on me and on other people.

Intuition is a faculty of the human spirit, which is able to probe beyond earthly conceptions of space and time, and can receive totally new knowledge and understanding (revelation), which the intellect may then adapt to the conditions on earth. Major breakthroughs in knowledge (resulting in what are sometimes called paradigm shifts) are quite often the product of intuition, inspiration or revelation.

Students of the history of science and invention know the significant role that intuition has played in achieving major scientific and technological breakthroughs over the centuries. Henri Poincare (1854-1912), a famous French mathematician stated in his 1908 publication (*Science and Method*): "It is by logic that we prove, but by intuition that we discover." Albert Einstein strongly believed in the significance of intuition in scientific discovery and in general. He said that the intuitive mind is a sacred gift and the rational mind is a faithful servant but that we have created a society that honours the servant and has forgotten the gift. He believed that it is not intellect but intuition that advances humanity and that all great achievements must start from intuitive knowledge. About his own personal experience, Einstein said: "At times I feel certain I am right while not knowing the reason."

William Hermanns (1895-1990) had a 34-year relationship with Albert Einstein during which they had four formal conversations: in Germany in 1930, and in the United States in 1943, 1948, and 1954 (shortly before Einstein's death in 1955). The 1943 conversation inevitably included discussion of the Nazis and the Second World War that was raging. Hermanns stated that at one point, Einstein leaned back in his chair and said, "I have no doubt that the Allies will win the war." Hermanns responded with a smile, "Oh, you are my prophet again." Einstein scratched his head and said: "Prophet or not, what I say is more often *felt* through intuition than *thought* through intellect." In his 1983 book, *Einstein and the Poet – In Search of the Cosmic Man*, Hermanns quoted Einstein as saying:

Many people think that the progress of the human race is based on experiences of an empirical, critical nature, but I say that true knowledge is to be had only through a philosophy of deduction. For it is intuition that improves the world, not just following the trodden path of thought. Intuition makes us look at unrelated facts and then think about them until they can all be brought under one law... Intuition is the father of new knowledge, while empiricism is nothing but an accumulation of old knowledge. Intuition, not intellect, is the 'open sesame' of yourself. (p. 16).

In 1983, William Hermanns in collaboration with Kenneth Norton and Ulf Sjödin incorporated the Einstein-Hermanns Foundation to foster reliance on intuition for intercultural exchange and understanding.

Debunking traditional ideas about the formulation of scientific hypotheses and theories, Sir Fred Hoyle (1915-2001), the eminent English astronomer stated:

It is often held that scientific hypotheses are constructed, and are to be constructed, only after a detailed weighing of all possible evidence bearing on the matter, and that then and only then may one consider, and still only tentatively, any hypotheses. This traditional view, however, is largely incorrect, for not only is it absurdly impossible of application, but it is contradicted by the history of the development of any scientific theory. What happens in practice is that *by intuitive insight, or other inexplicable inspiration*, the theorist decides that certain features seem to him more important than others and capable of explanation by certain hypotheses. Then basing his study on these hypotheses the attempt is made to deduce their consequences. The successful pioneer of theoretical science is he whose intuitions yield hypotheses on which satisfactory theories can be built, and conversely for the unsuccessful (as judged from a purely scientific standpoint). (F. Hoyle and R.A. Lyttleton, "Internal Constitution of the Stars", p. 90, italics added).

What Hoyle calls "intuitive insight or other inexplicable inspiration" might simply be called "revelation."

Andrew K. Geim and Konstantin Novoselov were awarded the Nobel Prize in Physics in 2010 for ground-breaking experiments regarding graphene, the thinnest material in the world and which has highly unusual characteristics that are now being industrially exploited. In his Nobel Lecture (*Random Walk to Graphene*), Prof. Geim mentioned his other outstanding accomplishments while pursuing an unstructured research agenda in physics. One of them was his research which led to the understanding that the magnetism of 'nonmagnetic things' including humans and water is not negligible. He wrote:

I poured water inside the lab's electromagnet when it was at its highest power. Pouring water in one's equipment is certainly not a standard scientific approach, and I cannot recall why I behaved so 'unprofessionally.' Apparently, no one had tried such a silly thing before, although similar facilities existed in several places around the world for decades. To my surprise, water did not end up on the floor but got stuck in the vertical bore of the magnet.

Instead of the water falling on the floor, it turned into balls of levitating water, staying up against the force of gravity. Geim explained that the phenomenon (technically called diamagnetic levitation) was due to the feeble magnetism of water, which although billions of times weaker than that of iron, was sufficient to compensate the earth's gravity. And he remarked: "Many colleagues, including those who worked with high magnetic fields all their lives were flabbergasted, and some of them even argued that this was a hoax."

The levitation was subsequently demonstrated for other 'nonmagnetic' entities including live frogs. The fact that high magnetic fields could have such a dramatic effect on what have always been regarded as nonmagnetic has important possibilities of application and significant implications, possibly even for the understanding of certain paranormal phenomena. Professor Andrew Geim's achievements again show that major discoveries are not always the result of carefully thought-out research programmes.

R. Buckminster Fuller (1895-1983), American inventor, scientist, architect, cosmologist, futurist, philosopher, and poet has been described as one of the 20th century's most notable "Renaissance Man". He earned 25 patents including one for the Geodesic Dome and was awarded 47 honorary doctorates. He wrote that he became aware of his own intuitive gift at the age of nine, and declared that intuition is the most important faculty of the human being. He says that intuition is a uniquely human quality, which we should use to develop long-range solutions for survival of life and the planet. Among his many writings is a book entitled "Intuition", which has gone through several editions.

The point of these stories is that breakthroughs, discoveries, and inventions are often not the product of sheer, sharp intellect alone. Sometimes, they are simply revelations.

The Theory of Evolution
The theory of evolution by means of natural selection is of great importance in biology and many have considered its validity a

basic argument in support of atheism. But the manner in which the theory came into being contains the element of revelation. It is in itself an interesting story. The two individuals who are most closely associated with the theory are Charles Darwin and Alfred Russel Wallace. It turns out that both of them were independently influenced by a short essay published by Thomas Malthus in 1798. Malthus was an English economist and clergyman who theorized that population tends to increase faster than the means of subsistence and that this will result in an inadequate supply of goods supporting life unless war, famine, or disease reduce the population or the increase of population is purposely checked.

The mechanism of natural selection, which is central to the theory of evolution, came to them in a manner that can be described as a revelation. I quote below statements about how each of them came about the idea. Charles Darwin wrote:

> In October 1838, that is, fifteen months after I had begun my systematic enquiry, I happened to read for amusement 'Malthus on Population' and being well prepared to appreciate the struggle for existence which everywhere goes on from long-continued observation of the habits of animals and plants, it at once struck me that under these circumstances favorable variations would tend to be preserved, and unfavorable ones to be destroyed. The result of this would be the formation of new species. Here then I had at last got a theory by which to work (Cited in Francisco J. Ayala, *The Big Questions: Evolution,* p. 39).

Alfred Wallace writing on his source of inspiration stated:

> At the time (February 1858) I was suffering from a rather severe attack of intermittent fever at Ternate in the Moluccas … and something led me to think of the positive checks described by Malthus in his 'Essay on Population', a work I

had read several years before, and which had made a deep and permanent impression on my mind. These checks – war, disease, famine, and the like – must, it occurred to me act on animals as well as on man. Then I thought of the enormously rapid multiplication of animals, causing these checks to be much more effective in them than in the case of man; and while pondering vaguely on this fact *there suddenly flashed upon me the idea of the survival of the fittest* – that the individuals removed by these checks must be on the whole inferior to those that survived (Cited in Francisco J. Ayala, *The Big Questions: Evolution*, p. 40, italics added).

Following the publication of Darwin's book in 1859 (*On the Origin of Species by Means of Natural Selection*) there was a lot of excitement and controversy because it was thought that the implication of the theory was that God had no hand in the creation of the different plant and animal species, including human beings. If that were so, many reasoned that there would be no basis to believe in God and, indeed, even to this day, the theory forms the backbone of atheistic arguments. The truth, however, is that the theory is perfectly compatible with the idea of God as the Creator. Evolution through the mechanism of natural selection is one of the consequences of the Law of Movement, which we will discuss in Chapter 7. Also in consequence of this immutable Law, any species that has reached the peak of its development and stagnates eventually becomes extinct.

Charles Darwin did not interpret his work in atheistic terms neither did he commit himself to the atheistic implication. He thought that natural selection (chance) could have been the mechanism by which God created the various species; but, obviously, this did not happen in six earthly days. In a May 22, 1860 letter to Asa Gray, a Harvard Professor and one of the most influential botanists of the period, Darwin wrote:

With respect to the theological view of the question; this is always painful to me. I am bewildered. I had no intention to write atheistically. But I own that I cannot see, as plainly as others do, and as I should wish to do, evidence of design and beneficence on all sides of us. There seems to me too much misery in the world. I cannot persuade myself that a beneficent and omnipotent God would have designedly created the Ichneumonidæ (wasp-like insects) with the express intention of their feeding within the living bodies of caterpillars, or that a cat should play with mice. Not believing this, I see no necessity in the belief that the eye was expressly designed. On the other hand I cannot anyhow be contented to view this wonderful universe and especially the nature of man, and to conclude that everything is the result of brute force. I am inclined to look at everything as resulting from designed laws, with the details, whether good or bad, left to the working out of what we may call chance. Not that this notion *at all* satisfies me. I feel most deeply that the whole subject is too profound for the human intellect. A dog might as well speculate on the mind of Newton. Let each man hope and believe what he can. Certainly I agree with you that my views are not at all necessarily atheistical. (Darwin Correspondence Project, www.darwinproject.ac.uk/letter/entry-2814)

We can say to Charles Darwin, 'How correct!' Indeed, certain subjects are too profound for the human intellect and we must thank inspiration and revelation for human progress! The mention of the implication of evolution for religious belief is somewhat of a digression here. The real point I wish to make is that the manner in which the two distinguished scientists, Charles Darwin and Alfred Wallace, arrived at the theory of evolution by natural selection indicates that in considering the sources of new knowledge, one ought not to dismiss the possibility of revelation. Revolutionary knowledge does not always come through experimentation and intellectual rigor.

On the question of inspiration, let me state in passing one mechanism by which it comes about. When one seriously contemplates a subject, the thought takes on an invisible form. Depending on the strength of contemplation, the invisible thought-form is able to attract similar thoughts or is attracted by centres at which similar thought-forms are already concentrated. Such centres of concentration of the thought-forms on that particular topic might be called a "power-centre" for that topic. The power-centre may already contain the answer that one seeks. Inspiration occurs when one is able to connect with the appropriate power-centre and draws the answer that already exists there. It is obviously possible for several people to access the same power-centre at about the same period. This is one explanation for the phenomenon of major discoveries being made by investigators working quite independently; they obtain the inspiration from the same power-centre.

The Air Composition Analogy
With respect to revelations about God, it should be emphasized that the process is in stages. It is wrong to assume that all truths are to be found in the extant ancient Scriptures. It is simply not so. Truths are revealed to humankind according to humanity's state of spiritual preparednes; that is, revelation is progressive. Some truths may not have been given at some particular point in time because the people were not yet ready for such truths. Even the way a particular truth is presented depends on how mature or otherwise the audience is perceived to be. We find that this makes sense in our educational system; why should it not make sense in the school of spiritual life?

When a child has finished drinking her bottle of fruit juice, we may tell her that the bottle is empty. She will agree, and this is true for her age. But we may tell an older child that the bottle is not really empty, that nature does not permit a vacuum. The bottle is full of air. And again, this is true. And we can go on to tell a yet more mature person that the empty bottle contains more than one item; that it contains a mixture of many gases including nitrogen, oxygen, hydrogen, and carbon dioxide. It is in an analogous manner that spiritual truths have been revealed to humankind over millennia. It should be remarked that, as in this analogy, the progressively new knowledge does not necessarily negate the old, which remains valid at some level.

Jesus, for example, spoke explicitly only of the most urgent things that people of His time needed to know to enable them make spiritual progress. He did not teach all there was to know. And so Paul could say:

> For our knowledge is imperfect and our prophecy is imperfect; but when the perfect comes, the imperfect will pass away. When I was a child, I spoke like a child, I thought like a child, I reasoned like a child; when I became a man, I gave up childish ways. For now we see in a mirror dimly, but then face to face. Now I know in part; then I shall understand fully ... (1 Corinthians 13: 9-12).

Moreover, by implication, Jesus endorsed the idea of progressive revelation when he made statements such as the following:

> You have heard that it was said, 'You shall not commit adultery.' But I say to you that everyone who looks at a woman with lust has already committed adultery with her in his heart (Matthew 5:27-28).

> Again, you have heard that it was said to those of ancient times, 'You shall not swear falsely, but carry out the vows

you have made to the Lord.' But I say to you, do not swear at all, either by heaven, for it is the throne of God, or by the earth, for it is his footstool, or by Jerusalem, for it is the city of the great King. And do not swear by your head, for you cannot make one hair white or black. Let your word be 'Yes, Yes' or 'No, No'; anything more than this comes from the evil one (Matthew 5:33-36).

You have heard that it was said, 'You shall love your neighbour and hate your enemy.' But I say to you, Love your enemies and pray for those who persecute you, so that you may be children of your Father in heaven; for he makes his sun rise on the evil and on the good, and sends rain on the righteous and on the unrighteous (Matthew 5:43-45).

The teachings of Jesus were new revelations and constituted a natural spiritual progression relative to those of the prophets of the Old Testament.

Revelations are given to humankind to facilitate achievement of the purpose of their existence on earth, which requires understanding of how they should conduct themselves and face the varying challenges at different stages in the cycle of development of the World of Matter. This involves understanding that the World of Matter is only an arena for their development, whereas their permanent home is located in the Spiritual Realm. Revelations, among other things, also serve to help satisfy the natural longing of the human spirit for the recognition of God, which is necessary for its ascent out of the World of Matter to the Spiritual Realm. Thus, at very definite stages in the maturing of Creation, new revelations about the working of God in Creation are given to human spirits. And human spirits are expected to strive constantly for progress in spiritual knowledge; for as in everything, stagnation is retrogression.

Revelations of God's Will

Revelations about God come through a long chain beginning from the highest heights of Creation and descending through the spiritual spheres to humans who are spiritually prepared to receive the revelations. The contents depend on the level of spiritual maturity and the specific needs of the people for whom the revelations are intended. But the contents of revelations addressed to human beings also depend on the stage in the cycle of development of the World of Matter in which we must sojourn in order to mature spiritually.

The World of Matter is presently at an advanced stage and in the process, it will at some point, become increasingly uninhabitable for human spirits and eventually will "disintegrate" and cease to be an abode for human spirits. Any human spirits that would not have left the World of Matter and returned to their non-material home in the spiritual part of Creation (Paradise) will suffer disintegration, which is the permanent death of the essence of the human being. This is the death of the human spirit that should really be dreaded. In contrast, physical death is the process whereby the spirit merely sheds off its outermost physical cloak and finds itself in other realms, as determined not by religious beliefs but by unchanging Laws discussed in Chapter 7. The one who sheds his physical body may have the opportunity to reincarnate on earth again.

Revelations for the New Time

On account of the advanced stage in the development of the World of Matter and the consequent urgency for us human spirits to get out of Matter and find our way to Paradise, God has now made full revelation of His Will to humankind. Those who seek genuinely and in humility will find. In this connection, it should be stated that at this present stage of development of the World of Matter all previous revelations as well as the revelation for the new spiritual millennium should be considered the common heritage of all humanity. It should no longer be (and should never have been) a matter of religion. No groups should behave as if a particular set of revelations belong to them exclusively. Moreover, it is now a question of what accords with the true Will of God and not a matter of religious doctrines and dogmas. Therefore, the greatest individual challenge we face is to rouse ourselves from spiritual indolence and seek the truth beyond the boundaries of established religions, sects, and related organizations. In doing so, we must, of course, carefully examine and rigorously question whatever new revelations we come across or are offered to us. We should do so individually and should not merely rely on the opinions of others, especially those who have a vested interest in the status quo.

Following the great Cosmic Turning-Point some decades ago, a reshaping of the world has been taking place and for this reason, there is an absolute necessity for a further extension of spiritual knowledge. The Revelation for our time is the work *In the Light of Truth, The Grail Message*. Its author, Abd-ru-shin (civil names Oskar Ernst Bernhardt) states:

> In the knowledge of Creation which I have given in my Message, and in the related explanation of all the Laws automatically working in Creation, which may also be called the Laws of Nature, the whole weaving of Creation is displayed without a gap; it allows every process to be clearly recognised, and therewith the purpose of man's whole life. With unassailable logic it also unfolds his "whence" and his "whither", thus giving an answer to every question, provided man seriously seeks for it. (*In the Light of Truth, The Grail Message*, Volume I, Lecture "Rigidity.")

And in response to a question, Abd-ru-shin wrote: "I offer to the seekers, but I do not solicit. He who truly seeks *will* find! He will find because it is so willed by God, and helping forces from the Luminous Heights lead every serious seeker to it."

As part of the grace of enlightenment for the New Time (which is continually unfolding) the pure, undistorted teachings of all the past Truth Bringers are restored. Through them, genuinely seeking individuals are able to recognize the continuity of the great guidance that sought to lead humanity step by step to the true recognition of God, which was the common purpose of all the teachings. Differences and, in some cases, even contradictions have arisen only because of human weaknesses, pettiness, and vanities. The teachings should never have led to division, much less enmity and violence.

By past Truth Bringers, I mean personages such as Jesus, Mohammed (or Muhammad, as written in the Koran), Krishna, Buddha, Zoroaster, and Lao-Tse (or Lao-Tzu) among others. Take the case of the Lord Jesus Christ. He did not Himself write anything about His own life, mission, and teachings. The accounts contained in the Bible were written years after His earthly departure and these were selections from among the many accounts written by different authors. It is not surprising, therefore, that there are gaps in the accounts of His life and teachings and even inconsistencies. Gaps of a related nature exist with respect to other Truth Bringers.

The Forerunner Book Series

The gaps have been filled in the *Forerunner Book Series* that is an unusual source of spiritual knowledge. The books of the Series shine light on the lives and authentic teachings of all the major past Truth Bringers and collectively demonstrate the essential unity of their original and true teachings and point strongly to the fact that they all came from the same source – the Almighty Creator. That the teachings have resulted in exclusive, mutually antagonistic, religions is simply the result of human faults and limited understanding of Divine purpose.

The *Forerunner Book Series* came into being in the 1930's in connection with the activities of Abd-ru-shin. Some individuals who were closely associated with him were gifted with unusual abilities such as perceiving, seeing, and hearing past events as they unfolded in connection with the lives and works of specific Truth Bringers. They wrote down what they perceived, saw, and heard as would a living witness to the events. But these "seer-reporters" were even better than any contemporary witnesses in that they did not only see the events as they unfolded and heard what was being said, they also perceived the thoughts and volitions of all the physically visible and invisible participants.

These unusually gifted persons did not consider themselves authors in the traditional sense, as they were merely transcribers or recorders of events of past eras, some of which date back to many millennia. For this reason, the books were published (and are still published) without any indication of authors; rather, under the title of each book appears the following statement: *"Received in the proximity of Abd-ru-shin through the special gift of one Called for the purpose."* Although the origins of the books may be considered highly unusual, anyone who reads them objectively is inwardly struck by their uniform ring of authenticity and truth.

This kind of writing is possible because everything (including thoughts, words, and actions) is recorded indelibly in the annals of time; nothing has ever been or will ever be truly lost or destroyed. But it takes unusual spiritual abilities and special spiritual environments to "retrieve" such records. Because of the wider range and scope of the perceptions of the "seer-reporters", the accounts in the *Forerunner Book Series* are more authentic and are from a far more comprehensive standpoint than would have been possible for ordinary contemporary witnesses.

This whole process should not be so inconceivable to the 21st century citizen familiar with current communication technologies. We are aware of what is already possible with digital audio-visual recording, preservation, and dissemination within security agencies and, to some extent, even on the Internet. What it should suggest is that there are, indeed, infinitely more sophisticated mechanisms in Creation by which all sorts of records (including recordings of thoughts, words, actions, visible and invisible entities) may be created, preserved, and made accessible to individuals with the requisite abilities under certain circumstances.

The Forerunner Book Series includes the following:

EPHESUS: Life and Work of the Forerunner Hjalfdar in Prehistoric Times. 222 pages

LAO-TSE/LAO-TZU: Life and Work of the Forerunner in China. 283 pages

BUDDHA: Life and Work of the Forerunner in India. 276 pages

ZOROASTER: Life and Work of the Forerunner in Persia. 254 pages

MOHAMMED: Life and Work of the Forerunner in Arabia. 240 pages

FROM PAST MILLENNIA (347 pages)
The contents are: Moses (pages 11-86); The Life of Abd-ru-shin on Earth (pages 87-186); Mary (pages 187-248); and The Life of Jesus on Earth (pages 249-342).

PAST ERAS AWAKEN, *Volume I* (291 pages)
The contents are: Krishna (pages 11-92); Nahome (pages 95-156); Cassandra (pages 159-212); and Mary of Magdala (Mary Magdalene) (pages 215-288).

PAST ERAS AWAKEN, *Volume II* (512 pages)
The contents are: Atlantis (pages 11-55); The Realm of the Incas (pages 57-99); The First Earthly Fulfillment from out of the Light – Abd-ru-shin (pages 101-281); The Second Grace from out of the Light – Cassandra (pages 283-389); John the Baptist (pages 391-437); and For the Third Time the Love of God Inclines – Jesus of Nazareth (pages 439-503).

PAST ERAS AWAKEN, *Volume III* (426 pages)
The contents are: Part One – The Struggle for the Truth 1. Egypt (pages 13-27); 2. Nemare (pages 29-76); 3. Pharaohs (pages 77-188). Part Two – And When the Word of Truth Came 1. Unknown Events from the Life of Jesus, The Son of God (pages 191-269); 2. The Apostles (pages 271-417).

The books in the Forerunner Series were all originally written in German. They have been translated into English and French and some of the books have been translated into additional languages. They are available through the regular book trade channels as well as via the Internet. The books listed above are *not* the only books *"received in the proximity of Abd-ru-shin through the special gift of one Called for the purpose"*; some are in typescript form and are yet to be published. It should be noted, however, that the published ones include the lives and works of most of the bringers of the teachings on which virtually all the present-day major religions and belief systems are based. *The Forerunner Book Series* thus constitutes a truly unique record and history of humankind's spiritual heritage. It will be noted that accounts about some Truth Bringers and personages occur in more than one volume; these are not necessarily repetitions but different aspects of the lives and activities of those concerned, perhaps written by different seers.

Serious seekers, regardless of religion, will find a study of these books richly rewarding and they will have a new appreciation of the inconceivable Grace of God throughout the ages. But they will also be appalled by the gross distortions that human beings have introduced into the teachings brought by the faithful messengers. Abd-ru-shin emphasized the uniform wisdom that runs through the original, unadulterated teachings of all the Truth Bringers. He wrote:

> If in the course of thousands of years men had not *always* acted as they still do *today*, if they had not time and again distorted everything that was intended to help them, in order to adapt it to their human way of thinking and their earthly desires, there would now be only *one uniform* teaching here on earth, issuing from the Will of God. There would not be so many kinds of denominations.

> All the teachings that have come to earth in the past would, *united*, form *a single flight of steps* to the pedestal on which the Truth is to stand, as it has so often been proclaimed to mankind in various promises.

> There would be no differences in the interpretations, much less differences in the teachings themselves!

> For all teachings were at one time willed by God, precisely adapted to the individual peoples and countries, and formed in complete accord with their actual spiritual maturity and receptivity.

Originally they all led in a straight line to the Truth, which you find in the Message. Even then everything was leading up to the time of the Final Judgment. The Bringers of all the individual teachings were Forerunners of the Word of Truth Itself.

And these Forerunners have made great efforts, very often amid intense inner struggles, loyally to fulfill their tasks, despite all the obstructions that men sought again and again to put in their way.

4 The Human Being and Human Purpose

It is remarkable that after millennia of human existence, we cannot boast of a clear and unanimous understanding of what human beings really are, where they come from, why they are on earth, and where they are headed after their short or relatively long sojourns on earth. Any ideas and opinions about God the Creator formed on the foundation of such ignorance are bound to be flawed. If we have no answers to those questions about ourselves, how can we begin to think aright about the forever invisible and most sublime God? We must first ascertain what makes us human, for it is in this that the instrument to the true recognition of God lies. Therefore, it is right to admonish: know yourself before attempting to know about God! This chapter outlines the nature of the human being, highlighting what makes us human and what endows us with the potential ability to think aright about God.

In the long history of human existence, many ideas have been formulated and many thoughts presented in attempts to answer the questions: what really is a human being, where does he come from, where does he go on leaving the earth, and why is he on earth? It is true to say that the questions remain baffling to all but a relatively few people. Answers offered are often unclear, difficult to understand, illogical, and unconvincing. Of course, millions of people do not even think about these questions; they are unable to see the relevance to their lives, which consist only of material pursuits with no spiritual content. They consider themselves too busy, or paradoxically, too "enlightened" to worry about such knowledge.

Others, who find the answers unsatisfactory for one reason or another, tend to conclude that these questions cannot be answered, that nobody knows. They are right to the extent that their position implies that the right answers cannot be ordinarily "thought out"; that such answers can only come through inspiration or revelation. However, the truth is that the right answers have now been revealed to interested humanity. They are simple and logical. And they help to clear various mysteries in human life, in their relationships among themselves, and in the relationship of human beings to God. The answers indicate the general direction in which we must look as we search for a new set of values and new lifestyles that are called for by the new and rapidly changing situations in the world.

A Person is a Spirit

The fact that a person is much more than the physical body is the belief of millions of people around the world. A basic tenet in most religions is the existence of spirit and soul, although the understanding of what they are may differ. But there are many people who do not accept the idea of spirit and soul, who imagine that physical death marks the end of the individual and that human beings come into existence only at the point of birth. This means that for such people the physical world constitutes the entire Creation. This severely limited view of Creation must in turn affect their notions of God, of what the purpose of human existence is, what the needs of human beings are, how one should relate to other people, etc.

The existence of the soul, the spirit and the non-material realms is central to the explanations in this Chapter and, indeed, of this whole book. But it is not my purpose to prove their existence. They are parts of the mystery of reality as discussed in Chapter 2. However, each person can come to a personal conviction of this reality, if he or she seeks genuinely, and provided the search is conducted not only with the intellect but also with the intuitive faculties. However let me mention a few pieces of evidence.

Wilder Penfield, a neurosurgeon, came to the scientific conclusion that the human being is more than the physical body. In his book, *Mystery of the Mind: A Critical Study of Consciousness and the Human Brain,* Penfield wrote:

> I worked as a scientist trying to prove that the brain accounted for the mind (consciousness) and demonstrating as many brain-mechanisms as possible hoping to show how the brain did so. In presenting this monograph, I do not begin with a conclusion and I do not end by making a final and unalterable one. Instead, I reconsider the present-day neurophysiological evidence on the basis of two hypotheses: (a) that man's being consists of one fundamental element, and (b) that it consists of two. In the end I conclude that there is no good evidence, in spite of new methods such as the employment of stimulating electrodes, the study of conscious patients, and the analysis of epileptic attacks, that the brain alone can carry out the work that the mind does. I conclude that it is easier to rationalize man's being on the basis of two elements than on the basis of one.

Like Wilder Penfield, Sir John Eccles, who won the Nobel Prize for Medicine in 1963, came to the conclusion that the mind (consciousness) is separate from the brain. And like Penfield, Eccles also thinks that consciousness may conceivably exist without the brain. Eccles postulated a two-way interaction between brain and mind, with "brain receiving from conscious mind in a willed action and in turn transmitting to mind in a conscious experience." In his book, *How the Self Controls Its Brain,* Eccles derides the position of materialists as "impoverished and empty" and states that materialists fail to account for "the wonder and mystery of the human self with its spiritual values, with its creativity, and with its uniqueness for each of us." In short, these distinguished brain researchers are convinced that the human being is more than the physical body; that life after death is a possibility and, therefore, those who think that existence is confined to this physical world are wrong.

Benito F. Reyes, an academic philosopher and the first President of the University of the City of Manila, wrote a book which may well appeal to academics and scientists who may be sceptical about non-physical phenomena. In the book entitled *Scientific Evidence of the Existence of the Soul*, Reyes marshals results of academic research on consciousness, memory, sleep, dreams, death and the process of dying, hypnotism, psychical and parapsychological research to prove the existence of the soul.

It would seem to me that even without reading any books, there must be many experiences in our individual lives which should lead us to at least an occasional sensing that we must be more than our physical selves and more than the emotions that can be attributed to our brains. All we need do is reflect on our individual experiences. Moreover, consider: I speak of my body. To whom do "I" and "my" refer? In speaking about "my body" (like everybody does), am I not suggesting that the body belongs to something other than the body? Am I not acknowledging that I am more than my body and that the body belongs to my real self (the spirit) — no matter what word is used to express the concept of this real self? Surely, I am not suggesting that my body belongs to my brain!

Let us also recall the discussion of Chapter 2 on survival physics in which researchers in theoretical physics conclude that there exist invisible, non-physical worlds parallel to our own. And that what survives the death of the physical body (spirit or soul) might reside in such non-physical worlds. It must, of course, be admitted that what amounts to sufficient proof varies from individual to individual. It is conceivable that as a result of a long period of suppression of one's inner self, the organs of perception of one's non-physical bodies have completely ceased to function, making it extremely difficult for one to sense non-physical phenomena.

The driving force in the individual, that which makes her or him a human being, is the spirit. The physical body is simply the outermost covering of the spirit which it needs to operate on earth. In other words, it is not that a person has spirit, but that a person *is* spirit and the physical body with all its senses and features is the spirit's tool while it is on earth. In addition to the physical body, the spirit has other non-physical bodies and sense organs that are appropriate for the non-material parts of Creation in which it spends time during its existence. The physical body is alive only as long as it is linked with the spirit; when the spirit detaches itself from the body, death of the physical body occurs. This implies that earthly death is not the end of human existence; the soul moves on to another realm of existence.

The process of dying may be compared to the process of undressing, of changing one's clothes, which we all do every day. Undressing may be easy and painless or difficult and painful, depending on the fabric of the dress, whether or not it fits too tightly, and the condition of the person undressing (whether a child or an adult, ill or handicapped, etc.). In an analogous manner, the process of dying may be painless or painful. The most physically violent death may be completely painless for the spirit concerned; conversely, an apparently painless death (for example, through euthanasia) may be extremely painful to the spirit. The more noble and less materialistic a person is, the easier and less painful it is for the spirit to detach itself from the physical body, regardless of the earthly circumstances leading to the major malfunctioning of the physical body. Thus, the spirits of victims of the same tragedy experience it differently.

Spirit and Soul

It is necessary to distinguish between body, soul, and spirit. When the spirit drops its physical body, which is its outermost cloak, it is still left with other cloaks; this condition of the human being is called the soul. That is, the soul is the spirit with all its cloaks except the physical body. These other cloaks are derived from, and are adapted to, the non-physical planes of existence situated between the earth (the gross material plane) and the spiritual part of Creation. We will discuss the various parts of the non-material worlds in the next Chapter, which deals with Creation and Subsequent Creation.

In anticipation of that discussion, I will make the following statements about the spirit and its cloaks. When the spirit starts its journey from its point of origin in the spiritual part of Creation, which is commonly called Paradise, it is purely spiritual. As it descends towards the gross material plane of the earth, it acquires the coverings of those planes through which it passes. Thus, while passing through the planes in which the souls of animals have their origin it acquires substantiate cloaks, and from the ethereal matter, it acquires ethereal cloaks. Finally through incarnation in a pregnant woman at a particular stage of maturity of the fetus, the spirit acquires a physical body. Thus, the spirit exists before birth and lives on after "shedding" its physical body (after death).

Next to the physical body (the outermost cloak of the spirit) is the astral body which is finer than the coarse physical body. The astral body is an important link between the physical body and the other cloaks of the spirit. Whatever happens to the astral body affects the physical body but the experiences of the physical body affect the astral body to a much lesser extent. For example, if some part of the physical body, such as a leg or an arm is lost, the leg or the arm of the astral body is not simultaneously lost but remains in place. Thus, an amputee might actually still feel pain or a pressure periodically on the leg or arm which he no longer possesses; hence the medical term "phantom pains". But the pains are not due to imagination; they are quite real and are the sensations from the astral body, which is still intact. In other words, phantom pains point to the existence of astral bodies which in turn suggests that human beings are more than their gross physical bodies.

I should state here that the spirit and all its cloaks have human form, a form which is characteristic of the spirit. Thus the physical body has only been shaped in accordance with the spiritual prototype. Any correct picture of a human soul must, therefore, also have human form.

More about Spirit

Because the spirit and all its non-physical cloaks are invisible to our physical eyes, many people ask where these various coverings are. How are they located in relation to the physical body? It should be remarked that each cloak differs in consistency from the other cloaks. These cloaks are held together by their radiations; radiations that act in a manner analogous to magnets. When, for example, the condition of the physical body is such that its radiation becomes weak because of illness, the strength of magnetic attraction is reduced, and if the radiation is weaker than a certain minimum, the body and soul will fall apart – that is, earthly death occurs.

The idea of the human spirit and its various coverings may be illustrated, in a somewhat crude way, by reference to water and the basic forms it takes. Scientists tell us that water is a compound whose molecule consists of two atoms of hydrogen and one of oxygen. Water in the form of ice is solid. It can be held, thrown up, and caught; thrown against glass, the glass might break. When the ice is heated, when it absorbs heat radiation, it becomes regular water. It can no longer be held, thrown up, and caught in the hand. Unlike ice, it flows; it can be swallowed readily. Apply more heat to water, and it gradually vaporizes, until it finally becomes invisible. It can no longer be held; its character has changed. But in each of the three states, the substance we are dealing with remains the same – two atoms of hydrogen joined to an atom of oxygen. The rate of vibration of the constituent molecules of a substance increases as it absorbs more heat. Thus, the fundamental difference among the three states (solid, liquid, and gas) is the vibration frequency. As the vibration increases, the substance becomes less tangible and finally, beyond a certain rate, it becomes invisible.

Just as at a certain rate of vibration, two atoms of hydrogen joined to an atom of oxygen make a relatively hard substance called ice, and at a faster rate of vibration, they form an invisible gas, so it is that the human spirit in the world of gross matter has a visible covering known as the human body which vibrates at a somewhat sluggish rate. At rates of vibration different from that prevailing on earth, the outermost cloak of the human spirit is no longer visible to earth dwellers. But the spirit certainly continues to exist, just as water that has vaporized continues to exist. It should, however, be emphasized that this analogy is only a crude one. The cloaks of the spirit belong to different species, whereas all the various forms of water belong to the same gross material species and can all be studied and observed using gross material instruments. Naturally, the non-material cloaks of the spirit cannot be studied with material instruments.

In Paradise where the rate of vibration is exceedingly fast, the human spirit is "at home" and it would have dropped all its non-spiritual cloaks. Because of the vastly increased vibration, things happen very fast indeed. So fast that events and experiences that would require one thousand years on earth, can be packed into one day in Paradise. Hence, the following statement in the Bible:

> But do not ignore this one fact, beloved, that with the Lord one day is like a thousand years, and a thousand years are like one day (2 Peter 3:8).

The different realms of Creation have different rates of vibration. The spirit has cloaks appropriate to each of the realms through which it must pass, and such cloaks vibrate in tune with the realms. It should be clear that all spirits and creatures at the same rates of vibration are mutually tangible and can interact directly, just as people on earth do. It makes no difference whether the equal vibrational rate occurs on earth or in the Beyond. In other words, the experiences of the soul in non-physical realms are as real as they are on earth. Thus, the human being in its non-physical cloaks knows happiness and feels pain, it relates to other souls, sees other creatures and landscapes, and lives in communities. The existence of the spirit is continuous and unbroken.

Spirit and Spiritual

In order to clarify how the word 'spirit' as it relates to the human being should be understood, it is appropriate here to jump ahead to outline a topic that will be discussed fully in Chapter 5. There is a part of Creation known as the Spiritual Sphere or Spiritual Realm, which may also be called the Spiritual Plane. This Sphere or Realm is, of course, non-material and has many sections. Each section has its indigenous inhabitants; the indigenes are called spirits. We may, therefore, say that a human spirit is a native, an indigene, of one of the sections of the Spiritual Realm, in the sense in which a native inhabitant of Europe is a European. The section of the Spiritual Realm from which human spirits on earth originated is commonly called Paradise. When it is said that a human being is a spirit, it means that he is a stranger on earth and that he is an indigene of a non-material Spiritual Realm to which it should aspire to return.

Those in the Spiritual Realm communicate and interact just as human beings and other creatures do on earth, except that interactions are much more intense. All sections of the Spiritual Realm are characterized by much faster rates of vibration and the environment is infinitely finer and more luminous than the World of Matter.

The word 'spiritual' refers to whatever is connected with the Spiritual Realms. Thus, spiritual values refer to higher, sublime, and lasting values that we can associate with the luminous Spiritual Realms. Love, justice, beauty, lawfulness, peace and happiness are necessarily associated with spiritual values on account of their origin.

The word 'spiritual' has been distorted and misunderstood in certain circles that speak, for example, of 'spiritual attacks'. Such attacks, where they are real, can only come from the dark regions of the World of Matter and are experienced only by those whose volition, thoughts, and activities are impure. They have nothing to do with the truly spiritual. People who recognize their spiritual origin and strive to live accordingly, by first and foremost keeping their thoughts pure, naturally and quite unconsciously repel forces of darkness. This is because goodness repels evil, while evil attracts evil. One should distance oneself from those who are preoccupied with so-called 'spiritual attacks,' as they are connected with the regions of darkness. The biblical statement, 'let the dead bury their dead', applies.

The Purpose of Human Existence

We now have the gist of an answer to two of the questions we raised: What is man, and whence does he come? A person is a spirit and originates in the spiritual part of Creation commonly called Paradise. But to appreciate why we are on earth, we need to know why we had to leave Paradise, our home. Why did the human spirit embark on a journey from a realm of peace, love, and joyful activity to a world that has sadly become characterized by chaos, hatred, distrust, and sorrow?

In the Spiritual Realm, there are spirits that are unconscious although they have life; they are called spirit-germs. In that Realm, everything that has life strives to develop. When the desire to develop reaches a certain stage, the spirit-germs are allowed to descend away from the Spiritual Realm into the World of Matter in order through experiencing to gain consciousness and self-consciousness. At maturity, a spirit-germ becomes a fully self-conscious spirit, able to adjust to the environment of the Spiritual Realm and to participate in the activities there in accordance with the Will of God, with which it would have become quite familiar in the long process of its development. Each human spirit on earth started its journey from Paradise as one of such unconscious spirit-germs (or spirit-seeds). As an unconscious spirit-germ, it could not participate in the joyful activities of the self-conscious, mature spirits in Paradise. But it carried with it the potential and the strong desire to become self-conscious and mature, and thus qualify to be a full and active member of the community in Paradise. To achieve this objective is the reason for the journey of us human spirits to the World of Matter, which includes the earth.

This phenomenon is a somewhat familiar one. Take the seed of any crop, for example, that of maize (corn). The maize seed, small and lifeless as it appears, does, in fact, have the potential of becoming a good sized plant, up to two metres tall, with many long leaves and looking obviously alive. But to achieve this potential, it must first be given an opportunity to germinate by being planted in the soil. For the human spirit-seed, the World of Matter is the soil in which it must be "planted", if it is to attain its potential. It gradually acquires consciousness, self-consciousness, and maturity in the course of its journey; the successful end of which is a return to Paradise as a self-conscious, fully mature spirit.

How did the first human spirit-germs come to the earth since there were no human mothers on earth at the time? They used the bodies of the most developed anthropoid ape species of that time as temporary bridges. Normally, an ape soul would incarnate in the developing fetus of a pregnant female ape during the middle of the pregnancy. But at the highest point of ape evolution, the earliest human spirit-germs were able to incarnate in the developing fetuses of pregnant apes. Thus, these most evolved ape species provided the temporary bridge for the human spirit-germs to enter the World of Matter. Even today, the process of incarnation still takes place; an appropriate human soul incarnates in the developing fetus of a pregnant woman when the fetus has reached a particular stage of development. As for the most evolved anthropoid apes, members of the species in which spirit-germs did not incarnate gradually died out and the species became extinct. The 'missing link' between apes and human beings lies in the fact that apes have their origin in a Realm that is lower than the Spiritual Realm in which the human spirit-germs originated. In other words, humans and apes have different innermost cores; there is a fundamental discontinuity in the evolutionary development between the ape and the human.

I should point out in passing that fresh spirit-germs continue to descend from the Spiritual Realm to the World of Matter for the purpose of development, but they no longer incarnate on our earth because the earth is already too far gone in the cycle of its development. The new spirit-germs incarnate in other material globes that are in an earlier stage of development than our earth. This implies that there must be communities of human beings in other parts of the World of Matter.

Under the influence of the spirit-germs, the inherited ape bodies were modified considerably and quite rapidly in evolutionary terms. For example, the original bent posture of the ape species gave rise to the erect walking posture of modern humans. The "the descent of the larynx", the gradual sinking downwards of the larynx took place and allows a space to be formed at the back of the throat. It is "the descent of the larynx" and the simultaneous adjustment of the shape of the mouth and the nose that made it possible for human beings to vocalize and speak clearly. At every stage of the development of the maturing human spirits, more mature human spirits and specially incarnated ones progressively guided them and revealed to them the knowledge they required for advancement. As the spirit-germ developed from its state of unconsciousness to self-consciousness, it was able more effectively to control its physical body and its environment.

In short, the real purpose of human existence is spiritual development. This cycle of development starts and ends in a section of the Spiritual Realm, commonly called Paradise. This spiritual purpose of existence, therefore, defines the real needs of the individual and thereby the goal to which all activities of human beings should be directed, as individuals or as members of groups, whether small or large. This means that the ultimate goal of all individual and collective actions should be the facilitation of spiritual development. The goal should be the same for large and small groups, nation-states and the global community. The strategy for development may vary from community to community, from nation to nation, but the goal should be the same everywhere – the facilitation of spiritual development.

This, of course, has nothing to do with promoting religion, as will become obvious in later Chapters.

Spiritual development is a personal, individual matter; each one has to develop himself. No 'gurus' are called for. And membership of organizations may or may not be helpful, depending on the individual and the true character of the organization. But in any case, each one must take personal responsibility. Spiritual development entails constantly extending our knowledge of the Creator, the Creation of which our world is a part as well as what the Creator expects of us (His creatures). Furthermore, one should strive genuinely to live in accordance with the Creator's expectations in thought, word, and deed if one wishes to develop spiritually. The Creator's expectations are more properly referred to as the Will of God, which is discussed in Chapter 7. Perhaps a valid starting point for spiritual growth is to cultivate purity in our innermost being so that our volitions and thoughts are always pure.

One Earth-life is Insufficient
The earth offers unique opportunities for the development of the human spirit. It is one plane of existence in which human spirits of different degrees of maturity and with differing volitions may come together, teach and influence one another. In other planes, human spirits are separated according to their maturity and dispositions. Thus, the opportunities for rapid progress are greatest on earth. Therefore, every earth-life is an immense blessing, offering great possibilities for spiritual polish, refinement, and growth.

It should not be surprising that one earth-life is insufficient to achieve the necessary maturity. We should note that some earth-lives are very short indeed, perhaps only a few days or even less and some are stillborn. Some have what may be considered long lives, but their experiences are so limited that they cannot be said to have lived anything like a full life. And we should not forget those who are born with severe handicaps. That is one reason reincarnation is necessary. Reincarnation is the process whereby a human spirit, *in one continuous existence*, returns to the earth repeatedly in different human bodies. We will not deal with the subject of reincarnation here except to note that, given the varied circumstances of birth of human individuals, without reincarnation one could not reasonably speak about the justice of the Creator. Those unfamiliar with the subject or as yet unconvinced may wish to read my book, *The Christian and Reincarnation,* in which I discuss reincarnation rather comprehensively. It is available from Amazon.com both in print and Kindle versions.

Human spirit-germs all have equal endowments on leaving Paradise and they are supposed to develop those endowments. But here on earth individual endowments and life experiences are bound to be different, because of the various actions and inactions of each person in the immediate Beyond and during many past incarnations. This applies even to so-called identical twins. Recent research in human genetics has shown that even though identical twins supposedly share their entire DNA, they acquire hundreds of genetic changes early in development, which could set them on different paths. When a human spirit has acquired all the experiences it requires on earth and has at the same time broken all its ties with the earth, it ceases to reincarnate on earth. The spirit's experiencing is then confined to the intervening realms between the physical world and the Spiritual Realm.

As the human spirit matures, it becomes finer and lighter and rises automatically towards the Spiritual Realm, in accordance with the Laws which express the Will of God, as will be discussed in Chapter 7. On successful completion of its journey, it arrives in

Paradise as a fully self-conscious human spirit. It has graduated from a state of unconscious seed to a mature, personally conscious human spirit capable of co-operating in the continual development of Creation in accordance with the Will of God. Such a human spirit has accomplished its purpose of coming into the worlds of matter. Paradise is a realm of intense joyful activity; therefore, the human spirit there does not "rest in perfect peace." Indeed, any spiritually mature human spirit does not wish to rest perpetually but rather to engage in constructive work, which gives him or her deep joy whether here on earth or in the Beyond.

The Spirit and Free Will

One attribute of the human spirit that is particularly important in discussions of human beings in relation to God is Free Will. Free Will is an inseparable part of the spirit as distinct from the physical body (in which the intellect resides). When we think of a human being on earth, a picture that includes a head, two legs, two arms, etc. arises within us. Just as we do not picture a human being without a head, so there can be no human spirit without Free Will.

What does this Free Will entail? It means simply that the human spirit is endowed with the ability to choose, to decide. It may choose to act or not to act, to do good or evil, to love or to hate, to assist or hinder, to obey or break the law, etc. Free Will lies in the freedom of decision and no more. The consequence of each decision rests exclusively on the immutable Laws of Creation; laws that existed before the creation of the human spirit and against which it can do nothing. A man holding a loaded gun has the Free Will, the ability to decide whether or not to turn the gun on another person. If he does so, he is still free to decide whether or not to pull the trigger. Once he pulls the trigger, he has no control over what happens to his victim. We as human spirits are free to decide, but we are irrevocably subject to the consequences of every one of our decisions. And the rewards and punishments stipulated by earthly legal provisions do not substitute for the consequences of our choices as determined by the Laws of the Creator.

In this connection, it is important to stress that whether or not a decision is made in a personal or official capacity, the decision-maker will personally experience the consequence, in accordance with the Laws of Creation. This is one of the many reasons why we must strive for conviction in everything we do, so that we may gladly accept the consequences of all our decisions — whether they are made on behalf of a government, a corporation, a club or on our own behalf. Given that all the consequences of the exercise of our Free Will must fall upon us, we owe a duty to ourselves to be sure that we always make decisions which accord with the Will of God as expressed in the Laws of Creation (see Chapter 7). Whether we decide in ignorance or in full knowledge, the consequences will fall upon us. Thus, we should never permit ourselves to make decisions thoughtlessly or carelessly; we should always weigh matters carefully and with all the tools of our being, including our intellectual and spiritual faculties. I will have more to say about Free Will in Chapter 17 on God and the Problem of Evil.

Intuition

One of the abilities of the human being as a human spirit is intuitive perception or intuition. The more well-connected the physical body is with the spirit, the more intuitive the individual would be. What is intuition? Webster's Collegiate Dictionary defines it as "the power or faculty of attaining to direct knowledge or cognition without evident rational thought and inference." In other words, the intuition, also called the inner voice, permits one simply to know; without conscious thinking, without racking the brain. It is as if a piece of information or idea simply drops into one's consciousness, or flashes across one's inner horizon. We have already mentioned this phenomenon in Chapters 2 and 3 on "The Mystery of Reality" and "The Progressive Revelation of God", respectively.

One international satellite television channel had a programme on which highly successful businessmen and women were interviewed. Each of them commented on the major factors responsible for his or her success. In one interview, an American woman, who had built a highly successful fresh flower mail-order business, said she attributed her success to her habit of depending on her "gut feelings" (her intuition) in decision-making. Even though she was a graduate of Harvard Business School, she said that she did not rely on traditional analytical tools in the management of her business. She said that she found that decisions based on her "gut feelings" always turned out right. A characteristic of true intuition, the voice of the spirit, is that it is always right!

On another occasion, one of America's most successful oil businessmen was interviewed on the same television program. He stressed his love of nature and his belief in a "sixth sense". Asked the secret of the man's success, the wife said she believed it could be stated in one word: "intuition". Steve Jobs of Apple fame (makers of Apple computer and iPhone) in his biography by Walter Isaacson expressed an opinion on intuition. He stated: "Intuition is a very powerful thing, more powerful than intellect, in my opinion. That's had a big impact on my work."

All human beings, as human spirits, can develop the gift of intuition. But to become intuitive, we must become spiritual in the sense of keeping our thoughts pure, living simply, interacting with nature, and always striving to do that which would be pleasing to God. We should cultivate the habit of saying only what is useful and we should embrace noble silence and refrain from superficial chatter. Moreover, we should note that intuition travels on the path of purity and humility.

The Metro Section of *The Washington Post* of November 20, 1999 carried the story of how one man happened *not* to have travelled on the ill-fated Egyptian plane that plummeted into the Atlantic Ocean in the early morning of Sunday October 31, 1999. Ezzat Mohamed Abdou, an Egyptian father of six and a resident of Alexandria, Virginia, in the Washington Metropolitan area of the United States was not a casualty of the plane crash because of his wife's intuition. Abdou had a confirmed ticket to travel to Cairo on Egypt Air Flight 990 on Saturday, October 30. He was to catch a flight out of Reagan National Airport to connect Flight 990 scheduled to depart Kennedy Airport in New York at 11.00 p.m. He gave up the trip at the last minute. As it turned out, the plane crashed into the Atlantic Ocean, killing all 217 people on board.

Holding up his unused Egypt Air Flight 990 ticket, Mr. Abdou explained to a reporter (Ann O'Hanlon) that he was not on the flight only because his wife had hidden his passport and had adamantly insisted that he should not travel. Mrs. Soad Abdou, his wife of 20 years, had told him, "I have a feeling that something is going to happen." They argued and quarreled, and he got quite angry but she never gave him his passport. Abdou had an import-export business out of Egypt, and for that reason he routinely travelled to Egypt by Egypt Air. According to him, this was the first time his wife would prevent him from making a trip. "I thought my mother was acting strange," said their 14-year old daughter.

Abdou said: "I was very angry. But I felt something, so I didn't fight her. I wanted to go, but I didn't want to go." As the time for him to leave for Reagan National Airport to catch a connecting flight to New York drew near, he yielded to his wife and cancelled the trip.

At 5:00 a.m. the following morning, the wife got up to take care of their 3-year old daughter. She turned on the television and heard the news that Egypt Air Flight 990 had crashed three hours earlier. She screamed. "She was crying and shouting. I thought there was fire in the house," Mr. Abdou said. "The flight is down. I told you I had a feeling something was going to happen", the wife announced.

This is a case of a wife's intuition saving the life of the husband. The husband also apparently had some intuitive sensing, but it was very weak. But for the wife, he would have embarked on the trip and would have perished in the crash. The incidence of tragedies as well as the number of casualties of tragedies would be considerably reduced if humans were as intuitive as they were meant to be. I will return to this topic in Chapter 17 on the problem of evil, where I explain the calamity that the distortion of the human brain has caused. Especially pertinent to the subject of this book is the fact that if we were as intuitive as we should be there would be no arguments regarding life after death and the existence of God; we would all know these as facts, even if we could not explain or offer proofs. But despite our generally distorted brains that have negatively affected our intuitive ability, there will always be many human beings who simply know that God exists! Those who speak of the 'end of faith' are in error; rather we should look forward to the 'reign of conviction' about God.

A person's intuitive knowledge comes from the innermost core — from the spirit! The spirit's perception is expressed as intuition. The clarified spirit receives ideas, which it impresses on the individual through the channels designed for communication between the spirit and its outermost cloak, that is, the physical body. The information or idea reaches the back brain (the cerebellum) as a picture and is transferred to the frontal brain (the cerebrum) which processes it for earthly understanding. Whether a particular idea is from true intuition or the product of intellectual reasoning, thinking, or imagination one learns from experience. In general, a piece of intuitive information immediately hits one as a picture without words, a 'flash', before it gets translated into other types of perception.

Related to intuition is the conscience, defined as the inner sense of what is right or wrong in one's conduct or motives and which seeks to guide one to do the right thing. In any situation in which one may find oneself, there are likely to be departed souls who had the same experience while on earth but took the wrong step and having recognised their error seek to help others still on earth to avoid the same mistake. Such departed souls may be permitted invisibly to approach specific persons with whom they are spiritually related in order unobtrusively to admonish them to take the correct actions; their admonishing becomes part of the inner voice of the person on earth. It is always the faults and weaknesses of the human being on earth, which determine the kind of helper he or she gets.

The spirit has a vastly wider range of perception than the physical body with its intellect, which resides in the frontal brain and which is limited to physical space and time. Therefore, the intellect, unaided by the spirit, cannot possibly bring about knowledge that lies beyond the worlds of matter. But the human spirit can probe beyond earthly conceptions of space and time, and can receive totally new knowledge and understanding, which the intellect may then adapt to the conditions on earth. It is an error to think that the intellect is the alpha and omega of knowledge and wisdom. True wisdom and spiritual knowledge are invariably 'received' and not 'thought out'. To think aright about God, we need to awaken our intuition, a gift which is inherent in all of us as human spirits.

5 Creation and Subsequent Creation

"I flew into space, but didn't see God." This is what the Russian Astronaut, Yuri Gagarin (1934-1968), was supposed to have said. On April 12, 1961, Yuri Gagarin became the first human to travel into space and the first to orbit the earth. It turns out that Nikita Khrushchev, the leader of the Soviet Union at the time, was the origin of the statement. In an address to members of the Central Committee of the Communist Party and the Young Communist organizations in which he sought to promote the Soviet Government's anti-religious policy and atheistic agenda, he asked: "Why are you clinging to God? Gagarin flew into space and didn't see God." Later, presumably with official encouragement, the statement was attributed to Yuri Gagarin. It is sadly true that many people imagine God to be some great long-bearded grandfatherly figure sitting on a throne out there in space and who might possibly be seen by a space traveller. It may well be that Nikita Khrushchev's conception of God was close to that.

This absurd idea arises in part from ignorance and misconception of God's Creation. God as the Creator is not to be found within Creation but outside all Creation, material and non-material. It is not possible to think aright about God if one does not know God's Creation, just as one cannot form valid opinions about an artist if one is unfamiliar with his or her art.

The First Cause and the Big Bang

Speaking of God as the Creator, I should remark on a common inconsistent position. The First Cause argument for the existence of God is an ancient one and it is that God is the First Cause and that Creation and everything that exists outside of God were caused by God. Some people consider the argument weak on account of the fact that it might be asked "what caused or created God?" Atheists, of course, delight in the question. Up until the 20th Century, most scientists assumed that the universe had no beginning; that it had always existed. However, scientists including atheists are now convinced that the universe came into existence according to the Big Bang theory some 13.7 billion years ago. Thus, they accept that there, indeed, was a moment of creation. The implication should be that the Act of Creation in various scriptures should, therefore, no longer be thought of as superstition, although the accounts should not be given literal interpretations.

A fundamental principle of classical science, its article of faith, is that for every effect there is a cause. The birth of the universe is surely one of the greatest conceivable effects on which all humans should be able to agree. Thus, the question of what caused the Big Bang arises just as it does for the matter of God in the First Cause argument. The Big Bang, obviously, must have had a cause. It follows that anyone who believes, rightly or wrongly, that the Big Bang had no cause should also be willing to accept that God had no cause, which is the point of the First Cause argument for the existence of God. But quite illogically, atheists and some scientists accept the Big Bang theory but reject the First Cause argument for the existence of God.

Joanne Baker, an Astrophysicist, responding to the question what caused the Big Bang, stated: "Because space-time was created in the Big Bang, this is not really a very meaningful question to ask – a bit like 'where does the earth begin?' or 'what is north of the North Pole?'"(*50 Ideas You really Need to Know: Universe*, p. 58). Richard Dawkins, one of the most well-known atheists of our time, refers to this line of reasoning in the following words: "Some scientists will tell you that time itself began in the Big Bang, and we should no more ask what happened before the Big Bang than we ask what is north of the North Pole. You don't understand that? Nor do I" (*The Magic of Reality*, p. 165). Dawkins claims that he does not understand the scientists' answer to the question. This is understandable, for if he accepts the answer wholeheartedly, he would be compelled to accept the First Cause argument, which would undermine the foundation of atheism. In general, atheists are inconsistent in this regard; they accept a First Cause argument for the Big Bang theory but not for the existence of God. At least now, most believe that the universe did have a beginning. That being so, one should ask what caused the beginning? It would seem to me that only some supernatural force outside of the universe and outside of time could have done that.

The Big Bang happened 13.7 billion years ago but our earth (age 4.54 billion years) did not form until more than 9 billion years later. This means that our material earth could not have been part of original creation, even going by science. Modern human beings are said to have existed on earth for no more than about 200,000 years (depending on how one defines anatomically modern human beings). Given the billions of years that separate the coming into existence of the earth and the arrival of human beings, one can conceive that there was more than ample time for the complex physical body to have evolved from unicellular organisms into an advanced form in which the spirit-germ then incarnated. Thus, science correctly asserts the fact of biological evolution but it is the physical, material body that was the product of evolution, not the spirit, which is what makes us human. It is correct to say that the human physical body, just like the bodies of lower animals, evolved according to modern evolutionary ideas. But it is wrong to believe that the human being, as human spirit, was subject to biological evolution. The endless debate between some religious believers and scientists on the truth of biological evolution results from ignorance on the part of both; it is pointless.

From One Galaxy to Billions of Them

Science has advanced in its knowledge of the Universe quite tremendously from the time it was presumed that the earth was the centre of everything. Then it became clear that the earth was only a mere planet of the sun, which in turn is only one of billions of stars in our galaxy. And for a long time it was thought that our Milky Way galaxy was the only galaxy in the Universe. On this point, a major debate took place between two great American astronomers in front of other distinguished astronomers and cosmologists on April 26, 1920 at the Smithsonian Museum of Natural History in Washington, DC. Harlow Shapley (1885-1972) from Mount Wilson Observatory in California and Heber D. Curtis (1872-1942), Director of the Allegheny Observatory in Pittsburgh, debated the issue. The debate was inconclusive! It was only in 1924 that Edwin Hubble (1889-1953) showed conclusively that Andromeda was definitely a separate galaxy from the Milky Way. Now we know that that there are billions of galaxies in the universe. Estimates based on data from the Hubble Space Telescope indicate a figure of 176 billion visible galaxies. Observations with radio telescopes, infrared cameras, and X-ray cameras can be expected to detect many more. One cosmologist speculates that the James Webb Space Telescope may detect as many as a trillion galaxies.

In addressing the extent and nature of God's Creation, let me continue with a further consideration of that part whose existence is not in doubt and in which we reside as earthmen – the earth and the physical universe. The earth appears to stand still; it seems motionless. The truth, of course, is that the earth is in a state of perpetual movement of various types. And that tells us that appearances and realities may be quite different. It also confirms the severe limitations of our physical sense organs, especially when unaided by scientific instruments. If appearances and realities are not always the same, and if our sense organs are quite limited, we all ought to be humble, to be willing at all times to learn, to examine objectively, and to listen to different points of view. The constant and varied motions of the earth give rise to many physical phenomena, some of which are apparent to our physical senses. These motions have already been mentioned in Chapter 2. But not all the consequences of the motions of the earth are physically observable or even knowable to the human intellect. Some of the consequences are of a spiritual nature and bring about conditions that have incisive impacts on the course of human development.

Because of the pull of the moon, the earth spins imperceptibly around its axis of rotation. This movement is called a precession, whose cycle is completed in about 25,920 years. This length of time is called the "Great Year" in astrology. "One month" of the Great Year (that is, one-twelfth of it) is called an Age and it is 2,160 years. While the rotation of the earth gives rise to day and night, and the revolution results in the succession of seasons, the precession or gyratory movement of the earth results in the change of Ages. Thus, there is an astronomical basis for the expression "New Age", regardless of the sense or senselessness of the doctrines associated with it.

The size of the known physical universe as well as the complex and great speeds of the motions of its members are simply mind-boggling; they are beyond human imagination, much less comprehension. Anyone who takes time to reflect on the subject should know a great measure of humility in the awareness that the earth and its inhabitants are no more than a tiny speck in the known universe. Abysmal ignorance is the only explanation for human arrogance and vanity. Unfortunately, only the relatively few who are truly inwardly alive and curious about creation make the time to reflect on such matters; and they become naturally humble. I should remark that a person may be intellectually brilliant and productive and yet be inwardly asleep and spiritually indolent. For such people, conceit about their specialized knowledge stands in the way of and hinders true humility.

And yet the known universe is itself only a part of the World of Gross Matter, which is situated at the outermost periphery of what we loosely call Creation. In fact the World of Matter is a *consequence* of the actual Creation; it was not created directly by God. For this reason, it is appropriately designated as a part of Subsequent Creation. The World of Matter constitutes only a very small part of what came into being as a consequence of the actual Creation by God.

The Beyond

In anticipation of the descriptions of the various sections of Creation, let us consider the expression "the Beyond". The so-called "Beyond" should be understood as those realms or worlds (not just one) that are inaccessible to man's five physical senses as well as to the technological devices and instruments that help those senses to do their work still more accurately and precisely and to extend their scope. Where is "the Beyond" in relation to the physical space all around us? The short answer is that they occupy the same physical space as we do. But they are of different consistencies and they vibrate at vastly different rates. It is in the same manner that radio transmissions, television transmissions, and cell phone transmissions occupy the same space as solid material objects. The whole of Creation is one united whole, without separation or gaps. In the words of Abd-ru-shin:

> There is no division between this world and the so-called beyond, but all is only one single immense existence. The whole mighty Creation, visible and invisible to man, gears together like an amazingly ingenious, never-failing mechanism; it does not function separately. *Uniform* Laws support the whole, penetrating everything like nerve-strands, holding it together and affecting each other in constant action and reaction!" (*In the Light of Truth, The Grail Message*, Lecture "Responsibility").

The expression "beyond time and space" requires clarification. There is a conception of time and space in the whole of Creation. But the conception always depends on the nature of the part of Creation concerned. Thus, the idea of space and of time exists in the so-called Beyond but they are of a different nature from the conceptions in our gross material world. And this is understandable on account of the differences in the rates of experiencing, which depend on the distance from the Source of all Power – God.

God and the Divine

A key revelation is that God is "Primordial Light", which cannot but radiate. Here we are not, of course, referring to the sorts of light known to us on earth and which are associated with the sun, other stars, and similar radiating objects. And the radiations of God, of Primordial Light, contain all that is necessary for Creation! Thus, the existence of God inevitably brings into being the Creations and all that exists outside of God has its origin only in the radiation of God.

Furthermore, *The Grail Message* states that what one can call the actual proximity to God is "a surging ocean of flames without the possibility to acquire form." Therefore, what we may loosely call the adjoining Realm or Sphere to God is much farther than the greatest distance which exists in human conception. This is the Divine Realm which came into existence as an inevitable consequence of the eternal and unceasing radiation of God. In other words, the Divine Realm has always existed and it is *not* a product of a willed act of creation; it is not part of Creation. It surpasses by far the magnitude of all the combined spheres of Creation that came into being with the fiat "Let There Be Light." Thus, the Divine Realm has many sections of different species formed by different direct radiations of God. The sections of the Divine Realm are so large that they can be thought of as worlds.

As landmarks in the Divine Realm, one should mention the four winged, knowing 'Animals' on "the steps of the throne of God" — the Ram, the Bull, the Lion, and the Eagle. It is better to think of these Animals as "Beings", since as Divine entities they have no relationship to the animals we know on earth. It is a deficiency in human languages that they are called Animals. One should always bear in mind the highly significant fact that the ultimate nature of reality transcends human languages. Otto von Gerlach in his Annotations of the New Testament published in Berlin in 1863, described the four Animals as a symbolical representation of the highest powers that rule in Creation and that they are living beings (cited by Herbert Vollmann in *A Gate Opens*, p. 192). All the radiations necessary for the formation and fashioning of the *Creations* are *accumulated* within these Animals.

The Divine Realm is also the abode of the Primordial Queen who bears the name Elisabeth as well as of Archangels and angels. There are very many angels in the Divine Realm as well as in the lower-lying Primordial Spiritual and Spiritual Realms.

The Archangels and the angels are also "beings" and like the four Animals or "Beings" have wings. Archangels and angels have no personal volition but swing completely in the Will of God, which they carry out and spread as messengers. Further downwards are the Eternal Gardens of all the Virtues of which the uppermost is the Garden of Purity, of the "Pure Lily". At the lowest end of the Divine Realm are "the Elders" who have always existed from eternity, as is everything in the Divine Realm. A Grail Castle terminates the Divine Realm. An annex to the Grail Castle arose before Creation could come into existence and it is thus, the Summit of Creation and the sole area of contact between Creation and that which has existed eternally. The Grail castle harbours a Sanctuary in which stands *the Holy Grail* from which Divine Power issues regularly to maintain Creation. Without the regular outpouring of Divine Power, Creation would gradually wither and cease to exist. The Grail Castle as the Summit of Creation hints at the significance of the Grail Message in the title of Abd-ru-shin's work.

I have already stated that the actual proximity of God is like an ocean of flames without the possibility to take form. It follows that to all creatures, God has no conceivable form and being without form, no picture or image of Him is conceivable. Indeed, human language has no appropriate expression for the notion. *The Grail Message* was written in German and the author had to introduce new expressions in the German language ("*Wesenhaft*" and "*Wesenlos*") to provide an earthly way of thinking about God in this respect. In English translation, these terms have been rendered as "*substantiate*" and "unsubstantiate". Everything apart from God is "substantiate", while God alone is "unsubstantiate". Thereby, we differentiate between the Divine and God; for the Divine is "substantiate" and formed but God is "unsubstantiate" and without form. For a better understanding of these expressions, the author asks that for "substantiate", one should imagine "*dependent*" and for "unsubstantiate" we should imagine *"independent"*. Thus, in earthly language, it is the case that God alone is independent and everything else is dependent on God and cannot exist without God.

Here we should draw a most important inference: God is not Divine, but God is *God*, because He is unsubstantiate (*independent)* whereas the Divine is substantiate (*dependent*). Since the Sphere or Realm that is correctly described as *spirit* is much further away from God than the Divine, it is clear that God is *not* spirit. That which is spirit is a part of Creation; the Creator cannot be part of His Creation. Therefore, the popular saying that "God is spirit" is wrong! The saying, indeed, appears in the *Gospel of John* (4:24) but this was only to stress the *non-physicality* of God as well as the manner in which we human beings should seek to worship Him. At that time, ordinary people could not conceive of anything higher than the spirit.

Since God is without a form conceivable to any creature, the idea of "the image of God", calls for explanation. To show Himself to the beings of the Divine Realm (which is not part of Creation, since it has existed from eternity), God must first clothe Himself in Divine essence. It is only when God is clothed in the Divine essence that those dwelling in the Divine Realm can to a limited degree see Him. The expression "image of God" refers to this Divinely-clothed form. And it is in the image of that form that the Primordial Spiritual Beings were created. But those dwelling in regions lower than the Divine Realm, such as those in Spiritual Creation, are not able to see God even in that Divinely-clothed form in which God shows Himself to those dwelling in the Divine. The special nature of the *spirit* stipulates the human form and when the *spirit* becomes conscious, the human form also comes into existence. Therefore, this form remains basically the same in whichever part of Creation the human spirit finds itself – on earth as well as back home in Paradise. The perfected human spirit in Paradise takes on the form that is in the likeness of the form of the Primordial Spiritual Beings, thus in the likeness of the image of God.

A Brief Overview of Creation

Let us now turn to an outline survey of God's Creation as revealed to humanity in the work *In the Light of Truth, The Grail Message*. Perhaps as a matter of common sense, we should accept that the Creator cannot be part of His own Creation. A sculptor does not carve his real self into his sculpture; an artist is not embedded in her art. The artist remains apart from her art, although it may be possible to discern something of the artist from her art. Therefore, we should expect God, the Creator, to be outside Creation.

With the fiat "Let There Be Light", an annex to the Grail Castle in the Divine Sphere was created as the highest point of contact between that which has existed eternally and that which is the product of the Act of Creation. Directly adjoining the Grail Castle is Primordial Spiritual Creation (the first and original creation) consisting of two sections. The first section comprises three principal steps or planes, while the second section of the Primordial Spiritual Realm contains four. Consequently there are *seven* basic steps in Primordial Creation, each of which has many sub-divisions. The first Primordial Spiritual Beings are conscious and perfect and are the ones who were made in the likeness of the image of God.

In descending order from Primordial Creation, we have Spiritual Creation. Like the Primordial Spiritual Realm, it also has two sections and seven steps. In the first section there came into immediate existence fully matured spirits that are called the Created Ones. These Created Ones were immediately conscious and fully mature and, therefore, did not need to descend into the worlds of matter. Those spirits that are in need of development are to be found in a lower second section of the Spiritual Realm. It is in the lowest step of the second section that human spirits have their origin as spirit-germs. And this place is the Paradise to which human spirits return at full maturity. Looking downwards from the Divine Realm, this human Paradise "lies at an immense depth, yet looking upwards from the earth it lies nevertheless at an indescribable height; for the planes of the Worlds of Matter, which are the spheres of development and fields of activity for the human spirits, are far flung!" (*In the Light of Truth, The Grail Message*, Vol. III, Lecture "The Primordial Spiritual Planes I").

Next to the Spiritual Realm is the Sphere, which the author of the Grail Message revealed for the first time and called in German "Wesenhaft". Early translations into English rendered the expression as "Animism" and "Animistic Substantiality"; more recent translations use the expressions "Substantiality" and "Substantiate", depending on the context. Therefore, I name the region next to the Spiritual Realm as the Ring of Substantiality. It is the Sphere which, in its activity serves primarily to promote movement and to form the material worlds, which it encloses, penetrating it, moving it, and thereby bringing heat and forming. The Ring of Substantiality forms the termination of Creation as well as the bridge to all that is below Creation, which is called Subsequent Creation or the World of Matter. The Ring of Substantiality has two sections: the Conscious and the Unconscious. The Conscious Substantiality is the home of Beings that take male and female forms according to the nature of their activity. They were known in olden times and misconceived as gods and goddesses by some, such as the Greeks, the Romans and many African and Asian populations.

Those Beings may be thought of as some of the many invisible servants of God. In connection with such invisible servants of God, Lao-Tse had this to say:

Not only among men does God have His servants, but the whole universe is filled with them. They live and work in every form. At one time all men could see them, when human beings were still less evil, and fulfilled the Will of God. Then these small and great beings were friends and helpers to them; yes, even teachers. This was a life rich in joy; for it is glorious to feel oneself surrounded everywhere by help and love. But men forgot about God, and in His place sought gods for themselves, whom they worshipped. Indeed they finally debased themselves to such an extent that they made demons born of their own fear into gods. (Cited in *Helping Words* compiled by Herbert Vollmann, p.13)

The Unconscious Substantiality is the sphere in which the souls of animals that we know on earth have their origin.

Subsequent Creation

The last sphere is the World of Matter (Subsequent Creation) made up of Ethereal Matter and Gross Matter, each of which has many divisions. The World of Matter is termed Subsequent Creation because, unlike the Primordial and Spiritual Realms, it came into existence through the volition of the Primordial Beings and is subject to the influence of human spirits, whose path of development leads through it. For this reason the World of Matter contains imperfections unlike the Primordial Spiritual and the Spiritual Realms. Moreover, the World of Matter is subject to evolution and dissolution, unlike the spiritual realms above it. Thus, the World of Matter and everything that is contained within it can suffer disintegration. Only the densest part of Gross Matter is visible to the physical eye, even with the instruments that enhance its functioning. To the World of Matter belongs the astral plane, which may be considered as a part of Medium Gross Matter.

Let me also mention that the World of Gross Matter consists not only of our universe but a total of seven universes. The distance between one universe and another is just as inconceivably large as the size of the universes themselves. Theoretical physicists have speculated about the possible existence of many universes; but they will never be able to prove the existence of other universes. The fact of the existence of seven universes is hinted at in the Biblical Book of Revelation where they are referred to as Churches and named after earthly communities in Asia (Revelation 1:4-20 and Chapters 2 and 3). By Church is meant universe and the earthly communities of Asia mentioned merely happened to have the same names as those of the universes that make up the World of Gross Matter. The Book of Revelation gives the names as follows: Ephesus, Smyrna, Pergamum, Thyatira, Sardis, Philadelphia, and Laodicea. Each Universe has an angel as Guardian. Our universe is Ephesus; therefore, in reading *Revelation*, one might wish to pay special attention to mentions of Ephesus.

Hell and Purgatory

It should be remarked that it is not clear what people are supposed to understand by "hell" as the concept is not usually explicated. Is "hell" supposed to be any place of torment or some particular location outside the physical world? Let's note that, even right here on earth, there are conditions and situations that can only be described as hell. Persons who share similar evil tendencies and fates flock together, in accordance with the Law of Like Attracts Like, which is one of the Laws of Creation discussed in Chapter 7. The automatic flocking together of the evil-minded and evil-fated becomes hell for those who have so gathered. *This is to say that hell is not the creation of God.* If men did no evil, none would be burdened with evil fate and there would be no gathering of the evil-minded; that is, there would be no hell! Moreover, evil is possible only in the World of Matter;

therefore, hell is confined to the World of Matter, to Subsequent Creation, which is not part of the direct Creation of God.

An idea related to hell is the so-called "everlasting fire" into which a human being who fails the Final or Last Judgment is supposed to be cast. It is possible that in the process of disintegration the human spirit may experience inconceivably intense and fatal heat. But the process is not everlasting. The spirit that suffers eternal damnation completely loses its consciousness and is returned to the state of a spirit germ.

In an attempt to answer the question regarding what happens to a person after physical death, one idea that some Christians, notably Catholics, came to accept was that of purgatory. Purgatory is supposed to be an intermediate state after death where the soul undergoes punishment as an opportunity for repentance and penance and from which it may proceed to heaven. Thus, the idea of purgatory assumes that there is a special judgment for each individual at death to decide whether he is to go straight to heaven or via the route of purgatory. Making the case for purgatory, Joseph Cardinal Ratzinger, later Pope Benedict XVI, stated that if there were no purgatory, we would have to invent it because no one would dare to say of himself that he was able to stand directly before God. In his opinion, purgatory makes it possible for God to "cleanse us in such a way that we are able to be with Him and can stand there in the fullness of life" (Joseph Cardinal Ratzinger *God and the World,* p. 129, and p. 131).

My first comment is that the reality is such that there is no question of human beings being able 'to be with God'; no creature can ever be with God! Human beings at their highest level of development and purity can only rise to the level of the Spiritual Realm, from where they originated. They cannot even be with the Primordial Beings in Primordial Creation, much less with the Divine Beings in Divine Creation. One might, however, take Cardinal Ratzinger's expression 'to be with God' as to be admitted into the Kingdom of God, the Spiritual Realm.

There is no place in the Beyond specially set aside for the purposes purgatory is intended to serve. The objectives that purgatory is supposed to achieve are possible in the Ethereal Matter and in Gross Matter (including right here on earth) through the Law of Reciprocal Action, the Law of Sowing and Reaping. If at death individuals are immediately judged and assigned to hell, purgatory or paradise, the question would arise as to the basis for judgment with respect to babies who die at birth. There is no judgment as such but rather the automatic working of the Laws of Creation, which manifest the Will of God and ensures that every human spirit goes to where it belongs. But the human spirit may return to the earth several times through the process of reincarnation, which provides opportunities for continuing development and maturing. We obtain clarity on this subject when we admit of the truth of the immutable Laws of Creation (discussed in Chapter 7) and the fact of reincarnation (see Stephen Lampe, *The Christian and Reincarnation*). I will revisit the subject in Chapter 12 on *The Love and Justice of God*.

6 Varieties of Unbelief and Belief

From the very beginning the unquenched longing for the recognition of God has been implanted in us human beings. Over the ages, various servants of God have helped to lead people to the right recognition according to the prevailing level of their capacity to understand. As people contemplated God, various groups of ideas have coalesced into shared opinions. Each group represents a form of unbelief or belief in God but within each group there are subtle or even major differences.

To facilitate discussion of ideas about God, we may identify three very broad groups. There is a notion of outright unbelief; for those who hold on to this notion, there is no God and there are no gods. Indeed, for them there is nothing beyond the material world. This is atheism and those who share the view are called atheists. Another group consists of persons who think that it is not possible to know whether or not God exists. But they concede that perhaps, at some indefinite future, evidence of God's existence may become available. For now, they assert that one must suspend judgment about God's existence. This is agnosticism and those who subscribe to that view are agnostics.

The third broad group includes all those who believe that there is God or there are gods. Such people may be called theists and their belief system is called theism. This third group has many divisions. Those discussed in this Chapter are: Polytheism, Pantheism, Panentheism, Deism, Monolatry, and Monotheism. I should immediately remark that within these subcategories, there are differences. For example, some monotheists (most

Christians) believe that there are three persons in the One God of their belief, whereas other monotheists (Jews and Muslims) believe that there is just One God, period. Indeed, some Christians (Unitarians) go along with Jews and Muslims in their conception of monotheism.

The fact of many varieties of belief and unbelief leads to an important point. It is one thing to say that one believes in God, how one conceives the God of one's belief is quite another matter. One can in fact assert that neither 'yes' nor 'no' is an adequate answer to the question "Do you believe in God?" Either answer is practically meaningless until you state in what sort of God you believe or do not believe. And, in practice, very few people can articulate the God or gods in whom they believe or disbelieve. Moreover, even what it means to believe also varies. The religion with which one associates does not necessarily determine one's *true* belief. How inwardly alive is the belief? To what extent has it gripped one's heart so that it influences one's instinctive actions and reactions, in private and in public? In this sense, people gathering under the same roof to worship may not really share the same belief. Let's bear these in mind in the discussions that follow.

Many books about God make strenuous efforts to argue for the existence of God. In the process, they review many ancient and more recent arguments by theologians and philosophers in support of the idea that God exists. I do not think that such arguments are particularly helpful. It is only the spirit, which is the innermost core of the human being that can sense the existence of God, not the intellect to which the arguments tend to be directed. Belief and the nature and strength of belief come to each individual through personal experiences and after a period of conscious genuine seeking. I am inclined to agree with the unknown author who wrote: "For those who believe, no explanation is necessary. For those who do not believe, no explanation is adequate."

Atheism

Atheism is the denial of the existence of God or of any deity. Atheists think that God is merely the fear-driven invention of human beings; that there is no such thing as the supernatural, and there is no life after death. Therefore, for atheists there are no invisible influences on humans and prayers and all forms of worship directed to the unseen are sheer superstitions and a waste of time. They believe that absolutely all phenomena can be explained or will eventually be explained by reason and science. Some atheists prefer the term 'secular humanism' to atheism and they call themselves secular humanists or scientific humanists. There are associations of such humanists in many countries. They and other atheists campaign against religions and religious beliefs and promote ideas they consider socially beneficial, such as freedom of speech. I should state in passing that atheists are unaware that the idea of freedom has always been so powerful only because of the spiritual nature of the human being, including its inherent Free Will, as discussed in Chapter 4.

Atheists are not a uniform lot. Some have adopted the methods and rhetorical style of religious fundamentalists and in the process have turned atheism into virtually a religion with science or intellectual knowledge as its god. Some have actually formalized it into a religion. In January 2013, some atheists did, indeed, form in London what they have called Atheist Sunday Assembly. The format of their 'non-worship' is patterned after the Sunday worship of the Church of England. The organizers plan to form satellite congregations worldwide. The Atheist Sunday Assembly gatherings are being called atheist churches!

One of the most prominent contemporary atheists is Richard Dawkins, a distinguished evolutionary biologist and a retired Oxford University Professor of the Public Understanding of Science. Central to his arguments is that the fact of biological evolution through the mechanism of natural selection necessarily means that there was no act of Creation and, therefore, no Creator. As a professor of the public understanding of science, he must know about the Big Bang Theory and ought to understand that it implies that there really was a moment of Creation! Dawkins capped his prolific writing about and energetic advocacy of atheism with his 2006 book entitled *The God Delusion*, which became an international best-seller. Like most atheists, Dawkins makes certain conclusions about God based on the evils done in the name of religion by some individuals and groups without conceding the possibility that they might be acting against the Will of God. He also ignores the much good that some organizations and individuals have accomplished in the world in the name of their religions. In my opinion, the many false conceptions of God and misunderstanding of His Will constitute one of the strongest cases for atheism. It is those misconceptions about God that this book seeks to expose and to correct.

Not all atheistic scientists are as extreme as Dawkins. Richard Lewontin, a Harvard Professor is a renowned evolutionary biologist like Richard Dawkins but, unlike Richard Dawkins, does not seem to share the atheistic implication of biological evolution. Lewontin even suggests that Dawkins misleads the public in his writings and television programs through misrepresentation of the mechanism of biological evolution. He wrote: "Dawkins's vulgarizations of Darwinism speak of nothing in evolution but an inexorable ascendancy of genes that are selectively superior, while the entire body of technical advance in experimental and theoretical evolutionary genetics of the last fifty years has moved in the direction of emphasizing non-selective forces in evolution."

And as regards the materialistic orientation of science, Lewontin wrote: "It is not that the methods and institutions of science somehow compel us to accept a material explanation of the phenomenal world, but, on the contrary, that we are forced by our *a priori* adherence to material causes to create an apparatus of investigation and a set of concepts that produce material explanations, no matter how counterintuitive, no matter how mystifying to the uninitiated. Moreover, that materialism is absolute, for we cannot allow a Divine Foot in the door" (Lewontin, "Billions and Billions of Demons").

The arguments of militant atheists, especially those of Richard Dawkins, have been adequately rebutted by persons of diverse backgrounds — philosophers, theologians, and scientists. Alister McGrath, who claimed to have once been an atheist, is a Professor of Theology at King's College, London and has a doctorate degree in molecular biophysics. He co-authored with his wife a book-length rebuttal entitled *The Dawkins Delusion?* The book got on the bestseller list.

Rupert Sheldrake has a doctorate degree in biochemistry from Cambridge University and is a prolific author of research papers in peer-reviewed scientific journals, including several in *Nature* (one of the world's most reputable journals for original science). Rupert Sheldrake, using established methods of science, has published diverse pieces of evidence in support of paranormal phenomena in humans and animals. In his 2013 book, *The Science Delusion*, he stated that while strongly believing in the importance of the scientific approach, he had become "increasingly convinced that the sciences have lost much of their vigour, vitality, and curiosity. Dogmatic ideology, fear-based conformity and institutional inertia are inhibiting scientific creativity.... I believe that the sciences will be more exciting and engaging when they move beyond the dogmas that restrict free enquiry and imprison imaginations."(p. 4).

Sheldrake describes his personal encounter with Richard Dawkins who interviewed him for a television series, which was broadcast in 2007 as *Enemies of Reason* (see *The Science*

Delusion, pp. 255-257). Dawkins had requested the interview through the television production company's representative to discuss Sheldrake's research on unexplained abilities of people and animals. Sheldrake agreed to be interviewed after receiving written assurance that the series would not be one-sided, that available evidence would be discussed, and that the material would be edited fairly. To facilitate discussion on evidence, Sheldrake sent to Dawkins some of his journal articles on the subject a week before the scheduled interview.

But when, on the day of the interview and while on camera, Sheldrake suggested that they discuss the evidence, Dawkins looked uneasy and stated explicitly that he did not want to discuss evidence. "Why not?" Sheldrake asked. Dawkins replied, "There isn't time. It's too complicated. And that's not what this program is about." At that point the camera stopped.

It would seem that Dawkins only sought to promote the cause of materialism and atheism and wanted the public to believe that the paranormal was non-existent and those who believed them were mere charlatans, not serious scientists. Therefore, he wished to hide from the public the contrary pieces of evidence collected by distinguished fellow scientists. Sheldrake concluded that Richard Dawkins wished to discredit at all cost anything that science cannot yet explain – and which might undermine atheistic arguments.

Another response to atheism comes from Dr. Francis S. Collins, one of the world's most accomplished geneticists and a long-time head of the Human Genome Project which deciphered the sequence of the DNA of the human species (the so-called code of life). Collins personally discovered some of the scientific evidence in support of biological evolution but unlike some evolutionary biologists, such as Richard Dawkins, he is convinced of the existence of God. In his 2006 book entitled *The Language of God* he tells the story of his own life from atheism to Christian faith and shows that modern science is in harmony with belief in God. But he acknowledges the dangers of literal interpretations of the Bible that leads to rejection of scientific truths by some Christians.

Terry Eagleton is an influential literary critic who has held professorships at Oxford University, University of Manchester and, as at the year 2013, was a Distinguished Professor of English Literature at Lancaster University. Professor Eagleton has become a vocal critic of the brand of militant atheism associated with Richard Dawkins. In October 2006, he published a review of *The God Delusion* in the *London Review of Books*. He concluded by suggesting that "Dawkins has not been attacking organized faith so much as a sort of rhetorical straw man." In April 2008 Eagleton delivered Yale University's prestigious Terry Lectures; his topic was "Faith and Fundamentalism: Is belief in Richard Dawkins necessary for salvation?" The Lectures were published in 2009 with the title *Reason, Faith, and Revolution: Reflections on the God Debate*. It is a continuation of the debunking of the arguments of Richard Dawkins, Christopher Hitchens, and other strident atheists.

Agnosticism

Agnosticism is the general claim that we do not know and cannot possibly know that there is God. Agnosticism does not claim that there is no God; rather, it asserts that we should suspend judgment on whether or not God exists. T. H. Huxley, a biologist and early promoter of Darwin's Theory of Evolution, coined the term in 1869 in connection with debates about the relationship between science and religion and whether or not the supernatural exists. According to Huxley, the core of agnosticism is to refuse to support religious doctrines for which there is no adequate evidence but to be open-minded about the possibility that adequate evidence might someday be obtained.

Siddhartha Buddha was Not an Atheist

Some versions of Buddhism deny the existence of an eternal, omnipotent God or Godhead and in that sense it is an atheistic teaching, and their adherents are atheists. But unlike most atheists, those versions of Buddhism accept the existence of non-material worlds. However, the non-material worlds of their conception are forever changing and are not permanent features of Creation, as is Paradise for example. Buddhists speak of Nirvana but the understanding of Nirvana varies according to Buddhist tradition. The popular understanding is that the greatest bliss is to be found in the dissolution of the human spirit that has attained to perfection. The notion that the successful outcome of spiritual development is dissolution of the spirit surely does not make sense, unless it is not meant in a literal sense. Dissolution of the spirit is the antithesis of the purpose of human existence, which is to develop into fully self-conscious personality able to exist eternally in the Spiritual Realm and take part in the further development of Creation.

A discussion of Buddhist philosophy is outside the scope of this book. What I do want to stress is the fact that Siddhartha Buddha believed firmly in the One Supreme God and he expressed his monotheistic conviction in the original elaboration of the Eightfold Path. Every Buddhist should, therefore, be a convinced monotheist. I discussed in Chapter 3 the *Forerunner Book Series* and their special significance. One of the books in the Series is *Buddha: Life and Work of the Forerunner in India*. It is a translation of the original German text which was first issued in the 1930s. In the following pages I present the account of the opening of the first school and the explanation of the Eightfold Path by Siddhartha Buddha as written on pages 86-89 of the book.

"On a radiantly beautiful morning, they all assembled in the great open square. Siddhartha prayed the Lord of the Worlds for

His blessing on the school, and laid down some laws that were to be binding:

"The Lord of the Worlds is the only God. School and settlement are dedicated to Him.

"No one may be compared with Him in any way, not even in thought.

"But all creatures of the Eternal One are equal. There are no distinctions in caste.

"All creatures, be they humans, animals or plants, are to be considered equal. No one may offend against them."

These laws were to apply to all adherents. For the school he laid down particularly:

"Take no intoxicating drinks. They dull your faculties, and tempt you to sin.

"Let your lives be chaste and disciplined. Bathe every day, and care for your body out of gratitude to Him Who gave it to you.

"Do not tell lies. That is contemptible, and degrades you as well as him to whom you lie. It is the duty of all to speak only the truth. Do not lie in your deeds either, by acting differently from your thoughts and intuitive perceptions.

"Let no man take from another what is his."

When Siddhartha had given these laws, he asked them all whether they would acknowledge them. A joyful avowal was the answer.

Buddha and the Eightfold Path

Actually it had been arranged that the pupils and their teachers should then go into one of the large school halls to hear what Siddhartha had to say to them. But because so many guests had come, and moreover all the other followers had begged to be allowed to be present also, they remained in the open square, especially as the sun was not yet too fierce. Siddhartha began to speak:

"My friends, pupils, guests, and also you animistic beings who are assembled with us, I greet you all!

"This is the first address that I give to you on the teaching of the Eternal One. Heed it well, and take it to heart! I hope that many another will yet follow, but this first one is particularly important.

"When we spoke about life, I told you that it is a chain of suffering even if it does not yet appear so to the younger ones among you. This suffering has been brought upon us by ourselves, mainly through wrong desires. Therefore we must overcome the desires, and then suffering will no longer be able to approach us to the same extent.

"Now comes the new, which I have not yet told you. Listen carefully!

"If we wish to conquer the desires, we must change. How can we do this, especially we older ones, we who already have the greater part of our lives behind us?

"I reflected upon this for a long time, and then help came to me from above. I found the way to the total transformation of man. It consists of eight stages, each of which must be experienced completely before we can then enter upon the next one. Nor can we omit any, for one arises from the other.

"If you wish to tread this path with me, you will first enter upon the stage above whose portal are inscribed the words:

"Right Belief.

"You must stress both words equally; for the belief is the main thing, but then it must also be the right one. Without belief you are helpless. But you must also believe what is right. You must cling unshakably to the belief that the Eternal One is the Lord of all Worlds. All others, like Shakra, Vishnu, Shiva and Lokapales are His servants, who can only help you if you serve the Eternal One with them. Maro is the evil one; turn away from him. If you believe all this in the right way, with your whole soul, you will come to the second stage, above whose portal is engraved the word:

"Resolution.

"The belief in the Lord of the Worlds must be so strong in you that you form the resolution to serve Him alone, to regard yourself as nothing, and to leave all former things behind. You must begin a new life, as most of you have already done. Away with the old! Away with all that would bind you to the past. Then you will move almost imperceptibly into the new stage, which is called:

"The Word.

"The Eternal One does not want loquacious servants. You should be sparing with words, but you should weigh every word you speak to see whether it is valid. This includes the commandment: Do not lie! Think about this. It is easy to sin with words, but to make amends for it again is hard. But out of the words arises:

"The Deed.

"This is the next stage. It is all the same in the end whether your words lead you or others into deed. If they were good words they will produce the good deed, but if you did not pay attention to your words, evil deeds will arise, bringing harm to you and others; so beware! Instead, strive with all your might to let no day pass without doing at least one good deed. Conquer yourselves. Force yourselves to do things that are hard for you. All the more easily will you master this stage.

"When I now announce the next stage, some among you will smile. It is called:

"*Life.*

"Indeed, you will think, we do all live! If that has to be mentioned at all, it should have come first. No, my friends, you do not yet live! To live does not mean merely satisfying the natural requirements, like animals or plants. It means bestirring oneself and moving, to show that one is alive. It means using every moment to the full, be it in work or in thought. Such a life carries us out of earthly life into true life in the beyond, when our time for it has come.

"Therefore the next stage is called:

"*Striving.*

"You should strive to live in such a way that you will find your starting point again. We have come from the beyond, and we must seek the beyond. You know that we cannot achieve this with *one* life. We must be born into this world many times.

"But I will explain to you: we come back as human beings, not as animals or plants. They are of a different species from ours. The two can never be intermingled. The Brahmans teach that an ill-tempered man becomes a tiger, a timid man becomes a mouse.

I ask you: what help is that to him? Can he make any progress by it? No!

"We come again, but as human beings. We shall continue to return until we are able to reach our starting-point. That comes about through working ourselves a little higher with each life. It means striving.

"But once we have succeeded in making our whole life a striving in the right way, then it becomes

"Gratitude

"to Him Who gave it. Gratitude should fill us; it will make us glad and happy. He who gives thanks has no time to complain; he who gives thanks, gives thanks in the right way, will let this gratitude become deed. He will help others as he has been helped.

"The last stage is open only to those who have faithfully passed through, lived through, all the others. It is called:

"Inner Absorption.

"When you have reached this point, you will be given the ability to listen within yourselves. Great things will be revealed to you there. Nothing that *you* think, but such things as the Eternal One allows to be proclaimed to you! He lets His servants speak to us in the stillness. He who can become absorbed, be it in contemplation or in prayer, will hear the voices, and will know that here he is already linked with the beyond.

"But with that he has become a new man. With that he has overcome all desires, all suffering!

"I would like to tell you one thing more: In the beginning I pointed out that you have to pass through one stage after the other. That you may not enter upon anyone stage until you have really fulfilled the foregoing one. But by this I do not mean that the old is then disposed of forever. You must not infer that from my words. On the contrary, what you have gained during one stage must have become so much your own that it goes with you into the ensuing stages as your inalienable property!"

They had all listened deeply moved. There was not one who failed to understand the Master's words, not one who would have departed without resolving to tread the eightfold path.

...

The above account is clear and simple and attests to the monotheistic teaching of Siddhartha Buddha. We note that he mentions some entities: Shakra, Vishnu, Shiva and Lokapales, which were worshipped by some people at that time. But Buddha implied that they should not be worshipped and should not be considered gods but servants of the "Eternal One", "the Lord of the Worlds." The original teachings of Buddha were definitely monotheistic.

Pantheism

Pantheism is the idea that God is identical with the universe and that nothing exists which is outside of God. It implies a rejection of the view that God is distinct from the universe; in effect it is the doctrine that 'God is everything and everything is God.'

Webster's Encyclopedic Unabridged Dictionary defines pantheism in two ways: first, as "the doctrine that God is the transcendent reality of which the material universe and human beings are only manifestations; it involves denial of God's personality and expresses a tendency to identify God with nature"; and second, as "any religious belief or philosophical doctrine that identifies

God with the universe." The Creator and His Creation cannot logically be identical; that would be like saying that an artist and her art are identical and inseparable. As discussed in Chapter 5 on Creation and Subsequent Creation, God is the Creator and He is necessarily outside Creation. Pantheism is, therefore, a wrong conception of God.

Panentheism

The *Stanford Encyclopedia of Philosophy* has a helpful essay on panentheism but it seems to me that the concept is inherently unclear and difficult to comprehend. The English word panentheism is derived from the German word *Allingottlehre*, that was coined by the German theologian Karl Friedrich Krause (1781-1832), although he was not the first to canvass the idea. The German word literally means "the doctrine that all is in God." Panentheism is defined by some as any view that portrays God and the world as essentially interdependent although God's essence is not contributed by the world. Thus, Alfred North Whitehead, the mathematician and philosopher and a 20th century promoter of panentheism said, "It is as true to say that God creates the world as that the world creates God." In this conception, God is not separate from Creation; as one proponent puts it, "God is not like a craftsman, supremely independent of his artifacts."

Panentheism as described by Marcus J. Borg is the idea that "God is not a supernatural being separate from the universe; rather God is a non-material layer or level or dimension of reality all around us. God is more than the universe, yet the universe is in God." According to Borg, in a spatial sense, God is not "somewhere else" but "right here." For panentheism, God is "right here," even as God is also more than "right here" (Marcus J. Borg, *The God we never knew*, p.12 and p. 26).

Borg differentiates Panentheism from Pantheism by stating that "Pantheism identifies the universe with God. God and the universe are co-extensive (literally "everything is God"). But in panentheism, God is not to be identified with the sum total of things. Rather, God is more than everything; even as God is present everywhere. God is all around us and within us, and we are within God" (p. 32). In the opinion of Marcus Borg, thinking of God as a supernatural being "out there" can make the reality of God seem doubtful, and can make God seem very far away. He states: "I have realized that one may be an atheist regarding the God of supernatural theism and yet be a believer in God conceptualized in another way, namely in the way offered by panentheism" (p. 29). Borg argues that "for the most part, modern skepticism and atheism are a rejection of supernatural theism, but if God is not thought of as a supernatural being separate from the universe, then the persuasive force of much of modern atheism vanishes." (p. 33).

It seems to me that panentheism is an illogical concession to atheism and materialistic thinking and fundamentally denies the concept of non-material Creation, implied by the existence of the Spiritual Realms, the Divine Realm, and God. The very last five pages of Marcus Borg's book-length explanation of panentheism are devoted to questions concerning the afterlife. Borg says that, on the basis of the evidence from near-death experiences, he thinks that "there is something beyond death rather than nothing. But I find it impossible to move beyond that very general affirmation to any detailed beliefs" (p. 172). In other words, life after death is not inherent in the doctrine of panentheism. How can one believe in God and not be sure that there is life after death? Borg says that he is an agnostic about the details of an afterlife. But he then states that "in the midst of the uncertainty, we can be confident of one thing: when we die, we do not die into nothingness but we die into God." What does it mean to "die into God"? It seems to me quite meaningless, in the same manner that the whole idea of panentheism lacks clarity. Panentheism is another of the false conceptions of God.

Polytheism

Polytheism is the belief in many gods. In the usual forms of polytheism, several or all of the gods are considered to deserve some form of worship. It should be noted that not every person who believes in the existence of a god necessarily worships that god. Sometimes above the many gods in which a polytheistic religion believes, there is a Supreme Deity who is the Creator of all things including the other gods and is the ultimate source of all power. This is essentially the case in traditional African religions, including that of the Yoruba people.

Although each of the four main denominations or sects of Hinduism claims to be monotheistic, they all also recognize many gods; for this reason, Hinduism is sometimes considered polytheistic. But Hinduism (based on the teachings of Krishna, born 3228 BC) spans many belief systems including monotheism, polytheism, panentheism, and pantheism among others. Its concept of God is complex and depends on the tradition and philosophy followed as well as upon each individual. In what is known as monolatrous polytheism (also called henotheism), belief in many gods goes hand in hand with exclusive worship of only one of them.

Deism

Deism emerged during the Age of Enlightenment and was an attempt to make sense of the idea of God in the light of new knowledge. Deism believes in a Supreme Creator, who established the laws that would govern Creation. The Creator then withdrew and left Creation to function automatically. Therefore, this Creator does not intervene in His Creation and in human affairs. Deism does not believe that anything can happen outside the laws of nature. The belief that God is uninvolved in the world worries some believers because it undermines the need for religious rituals and practices and denies belief in miracles, including those recorded in the Bible.

Thomas Paine (1737-1809) was one of the earliest promoters of deism especially through his book, *The Age of Reason*, which was published during 1794-1796. In it, he critiqued the Bible and criticized the Church. In contrast to the prevailing supernatural theism, he wrote: "But in deism our reason and our belief become happily united. The wonderful structure of the universe, and everything we behold in the system of the creation, prove to us, far better than books can do, the existence of a God, and at the same time proclaim His attributes."

There is a World Union of Deists, which promotes deism and its implications. The Union and some others claim that Albert Einstein believed in deism. But it is unclear whether or not he was a deist. Einstein did state that he did not believe in a personal God, that he was not an atheist, and that he saw a role for religion. In his book, *Einstein and Religion*, Max Jammer quotes Einstein as saying:

> I'm not an atheist, and I don't think I can call myself a pantheist. We are in the position of a little child entering a huge library filled with books in many languages. The child knows someone must have written those books. It does not know how. It does not understand the languages in which they are written. The child dimly suspects a mysterious order in the arrangement of the books but doesn't know what it is. That, it seems to me, is the attitude of even the most intelligent human being toward God. We see the universe marvellously arranged and obeying certain laws but only dimly understand these laws.

Einstein said he believed in Baruch Spinoza's God, "who reveals himself in the harmony of all that exists, not in a God who concerns himself with the fate and the doings of mankind." Baruch (also Bento or Benedictus – all three names mean "blessed") Spinoza (1632-1677) was born into the Portuguese-Jewish community of Amsterdam from which he was excommunicated on account of his beliefs just before he turned 24 ("Why Spinoza was excommunicated" by Steven Nadler). He believed that God is not involved in human affairs and to that extent his conception of God had an element of deism. But Spinoza's teaching about God was rather complex and has been described by many people as pantheism. That probably explains why Einstein would specifically state that he was not a pantheist.

Spinoza did not believe in miracles; he believed that everything happens only in accordance with natural laws. He thought that if anyone asserted that God acts in contravention to the laws of nature, such a person would be logically compelled to assert that God acted against His own nature. Deists share the same view. Miracles as they relate to the conception of God will be discussed in a later chapter (Chapter 16). Spinoza believed that everything is absolutely determined, which would mean that there is no such thing as chance. To the extent that Einstein shared Spinoza's conception of God, Einstein's reluctance to accept quantum theory (saying that God does not play dice) becomes understandable. In Spinoza's conception of God, the universe is governed by definitive laws, not probabilities. But we should note that we are obliged to depend on probabilities only because in many specific situations, we do not yet have a full understanding of the applicable natural laws. Moreover, the possibilities which are built into the mechanisms in Creation and which also take into account the unpredictable exercise of human Free Will are wide enough to accommodate what to the human intellect appear as probability or chance.

Errors of Deism

Deism is right in its emphasis on the Laws of Creation, which are immutable and by which God governs Creation. I will discuss this in the next Chapter. But deists are in error in believing that God has no continuing interest in Creation. Firstly, God was never in Creation; therefore, there was no question of withdrawing. Secondly, as part of the Act of Creation, a part of God, in a radiation process, was anchored at the Summit of Creation (the Grail Castle) and became the perpetual mediator between God and Creation. Therefore, one can say that God is ever mindful of Creation, always has an eye on Creation.

Thirdly, Creation can continue to exist only through regular infusion of spiritual power into it. If this regular renewal of power were to stop, Creation would gradually wither and disintegrate and only God with the Divine Realm, which is within His direct radiation, would remain just as it was before Creation. This most significant event of the outpouring of power into the entire Creation takes place on earth annually and was experienced in a dramatic fashion by the Disciples of Jesus on the occasion of Pentecost reported in the Bible.

Fourthly, I discussed in Chapter 3 how God sends His envoys and prophets at significant turning points to lead human beings to the necessary higher level of knowledge. In other words, God does intervene in Creation as necessary. The incarnation of Jesus on earth was such a case and was a prominent proof of God's continuing engagement with His Creation.

Finally, I should point out that there is room for prayers. True prayer is an attempt to be invisibly linked with the radiation originating from the Creator in gratitude or in petitioning. Whether or not one succeeds in being linked with the Creator and whether or not one's petitions are granted also depend on how one relates to the Laws that express the Will of God. How this works, we will discuss in the Chapter on "God and Prayer."

In the light of the above considerations, we are led to the conclusion that deism is a wrong conception of God.

Monolatry

The word monolatry is applied to the worship of only one God, without excluding belief in other gods. Monolatrous polytheism would correspond to the belief in many gods but exclusively worshipping only one, whereas in the usual forms of polytheism, several or all of the gods are considered to deserve some form of worship.

In practice, monolatry can seem like monotheism, since the exclusive focus on worshipping just one God means that all the other gods are ignored. There would be no temples built to honour them, they would be offered no sacrifices, and no prayers would be directed at those other gods – they might as well not exist. In such cases, monolatry might quickly become monotheism. For this reason, some scholars consider monolatry as an intermediate stage between polytheism and monotheism. Scholars claim that there is a mix of monolatry and monotheism in the ancient Jewish texts, with monotheism gradually taking over and replacing monolatry.   Monotheistic systems will explicitly deny the existence of other gods and reject non-monotheistic religions as false, whereas monolatrous systems will accept that the gods of other systems are indeed gods but advise against worshipping them.

Monotheism

Monotheism is the belief that there is but one God as opposed to polytheism which believes in many gods. The Abrahamic religions – Judaism, Christianity, and Islam – are the most prominent monotheists. Judaism, Christianity, and Islam all view God as the Creator and the singular source of all power. Judaism began in ancient Israel with the adoption of Yahweh as the only God to worship and the rejection of the gods of other tribes and nations; but they did not initially deny the existence of those other gods. Islam conceives Allah (God) as strictly and inherently one while Christianity holds that although God is One, He is in three persons. The idea of one God in three persons is the Holy Trinity which we discuss in Chapter 14. Judaism, like Islam, does not believe in the Trinity and there are Christians too who do not believe in the Trinity.

Thus, monotheism has many versions. Belief in the oneness of God is one thing, how that God is conceived is quite another. What, for example, are the attributes of the One God, what does He demand of His creatures, how does He relate to His Creation, etc.? These issues are covered in other Chapters.

Summing-Up

I have remarked that the longing for the recognition of God is implanted in the spirit, which is what makes us human. For this reason human beings from time immemorial have contemplated God and will continue to do so even as human beings become more intellectually and technologically sophisticated. There was never an era during which the majority denied the existence of God and those who have in the past imagined that most human beings would give up on the idea of God have been proved wrong. Those who imagine or hope for a future in which human beings will dispense with the idea of God will be disappointed. However, it is reasonable to expect that people will increasingly rid their minds of the false conceptions of God and seek greater clarity about God and how He relates to us creatures.

I have implied that atheists and agnostics are wrong and that God *does* exist. Since it is only the spirit that can truly recognize God, intellectual attempts to prove the existence of God are largely misguided.

Our outline of the broad structure of Creation and Subsequent Creation in Chapter 5 indicates that polytheism, pantheism, panentheism, and deism are wrong conceptions. We have noted that there are many confused conceptions among those who believe in the existence of God. Among them, those who believe that there is only One God and that He alone deserves worship (the monotheists) come closest to the right way to think about God. However, monotheists differ in the way they think about God and how God relates to us His creatures. We will elaborate on these in subsequent Chapters.

7 The Will of God

The Will of God is an expression frequently used by religious people especially in sayings such as "God's Will Be Done" and "Thy Will Be Done." Many use the expression almost exclusively when something has happened that they wished did not happen, such as bereavement. The tone usually carries the clear implication that the speaker would have changed "God's Will" if he had the power, even though the statement should suggest submissiveness to God. In such cases, it is not a matter of acceptance of God's Will, but mere resignation to it. Therefore, it is not always clear what people want when they say "God's Will Be Done". Do they really want God's Will or their own?

The prayer most commonly said by Christians is the Lord's Prayer (also called 'Our Father') but there is some misunderstanding about the Prayer. For example, when in the Prayer we say "Thy Will Be done on Earth as it is in Heaven", we are not pleading with God to do something for us. This is because it is the Will of God that brought Creation into being, supports and sustains it, and nothing can happen on earth except in accordance with His Will (rightly understood). God's Will rules the worlds. Therefore, no one needs specially to plead that the Will of God be done on earth. It is only human beings on earth who through the abuse of their Free Will act contrary to God's Will. A somewhat plausible interpretation of that statement might be that we are begging God to help us as we struggle to do His Will on earth. But the correct interpretation of that part of the Lord's Prayer is a vow on the part of the person praying to do the Will of God here on earth. Before making any petitions to God, one vows to think, speak, and act only in accordance with God's Will.

We recall that Jesus said that "Not everyone who says to me, 'Lord, Lord,' will enter the kingdom of heaven, but only the one who does the Will of my Father in heaven" (Matthew 7:21). And when he said, "No one comes to the Father except through me" (John 14:6), he meant that it is only by doing the Will of God contained in His teachings that one can get to the Kingdom of God, Paradise. He did not mean to exclude from Paradise non-Christians who may have learnt the true Will of God from other sources and who actually do It. But one can do the Will of God only if one knows and understands it. Yet the concept is unclear to many people. The meaning many people attach to it has to do with obeying the commandments, rules and regulations of their religions as well as accepting the doctrines and traditions dictated by their religion. Rightly understood, the Will of God is something universal, encompassing the entire Creation, visible and invisible. It does not depend on religion and it is the same for everybody.

The Will of God is expressed in eternal, immutable, and universal spiritual principles or laws. They are the system by which God relates to Creation and all creatures. Therefore, one cannot think aright about God without the right understanding of those laws and that is the subject of this Chapter. The laws have existed since eternity; indeed, Creation including human spirits came into and can remain in existence only through the operation of these laws. The various commandments, rules and regulations given through prophets are essentially explanations of what we should do in order to conform to the Laws that express the Will of God. They are like the manual of instructions, which we should study and follow strictly to ensure that the mechanisms that God put in Creation serve us and lead us towards the achievement of the purpose of our existence. Therefore, it is wrong to think that we do God a favour by obeying his Laws or commandments; just as we do not do a manufacturer any favour when we study and follow the operating manual of a piece of equipment.

The Laws are called by various names, including the Laws of Creation, the Divine Laws, the Eternal Laws, or the Laws of Life. They may also be thought of as the basic spiritual principles for life. In this book, I use the expressions interchangeably. The book, *In the Light of Truth, The Grail Message*, explains these Laws, in their greatness, simplicity, and sublimity and in a language that present-day human beings should be able to understand and appreciate. My discussions of these Laws of Creation in this and other chapters are based on my own understanding of *The Grail Message*. I believe that the prevailing strains and stresses in human affairs are a measure of the extent to which we have deviated from the paths indicated by the Laws of Creation and that solutions to all problems of life and existence can and will be found only through their conscious, correct, and consistent applications.

The Nature of the Laws of Creation
On account of God's perfection, His Will is also perfect and, therefore, the Laws manifesting this Will are perfect. They cannot be improved upon, and they remain absolutely unchangeable. Therefore, we simply must seek to understand and apply them and not imagine that we can come up with different principles that can work equally well. We human beings are only products of these Laws; therefore, there can be no question of our improving on them. Indeed, we can achieve lasting success only to the degree of our adjustment to the Laws of Creation. When individuals or groups deviate from these Laws, they invite chaos and confusion, as is the case today in much of the world. No one can subvert or overthrow the Divine Laws and they apply equally to all, regardless of personal circumstance or beliefs. The effects

of the Laws are the same on those who know them as well as on those who don't or choose to ignore them.

It should be noted that the laws of nature or the laws of science are simply the gross material, earthly *forms* of the Laws of Creation. In other words, any scientific law that is correct must necessarily conform to the Laws of Creation. If a scientific theory were to contradict a Law of Creation, such a scientific theory would eventually be found to be wrong! Thus, the best efforts of science can only discover fragments of the earthly manifestations of the Laws of Creation. Since science can successfully probe only what is material, it is forever precluded from a comprehensive knowledge of the Laws of Creation. And there is no question of its ever discovering the origin of these Laws.

It is necessary to stress that the same basic laws apply in all sections of Creation and the effects are uniform within each species of Creation. But the effects of the laws are influenced differently by different species of Creation. Thus, the manifestations of each of the Laws of Creation on earth will be different from their manifestations in the Spiritual Realm. We should even expect that the manifestations of the laws in the world of thoughts would differ somewhat from their manifestations in visible, tangible matter even though they are uniform in both worlds. From this fact, it can be surmised that as science, especially specialties like quantum physics, reaches into fine and finer Gross Matter, it may encounter changes in the *forms* in which the laws of nature express themselves. Indeed, it can be said that the indication that science is probing into a different subspecies of Gross Matter is the fact of a change in the *form* in which well-known natural laws manifest themselves.

For a deeper understanding of the nature of the Laws of Creation, let us contrast them with the laws that human beings make. Secular laws vary from society to society, whereas the

Laws that manifest the Will of God are the same everywhere. Secular laws may be changed at will; what was perfectly legal yesterday may be criminalized today. The Laws of Creation are immutable; they have always been and will ever remain the same. The immutability of these laws derives from the Perfection of God. God bears all the Laws within Him in the purest form and, therefore, will never act arbitrarily. All His actions can only be in complete harmony with the Laws of Creation in the forms applicable in each part of Creation.

Human laws are difficult to understand. Therefore, we depend, for their interpretation, on lawyers who have devoted years of study to secular laws and even the lawyers do not always agree on the interpretation of a given law. In contrast, the Laws of Creation that express the Will of God are simple, clear, and easy to understand. No schooling, in the ordinary sense of the word, is required to understand them. In fact, they are hinted at in the proverbs of many cultures. Human laws do not always promote justice. Indeed, quite often, they are exploited by lawyers to set free people who have actually committed crimes. In contrast, the Laws of Creation ensure that Justice and Love are simultaneously upheld.

Unlike the large number of laws that societies make for themselves, the Laws of Creation are rather few. For our purpose, they may be discussed as the following inter-related and complementary Laws: The Law of Movement; The Law of Reciprocal Action; The Law of Attraction of Homogeneous Species; The Law of Spiritual Gravity; and The Law of Balance. I will proceed to outline each of them.

The Law of Movement

All the Laws that manifest the Will of God in Creation operate within the framework of one basic Law — the Law of Movement. Motion is a fundamental principle throughout Creation. The lighter the plane of Creation, that is, the closer a plane is to the highest point of Creation, the more pronounced is the motion. And the further away it is, the more sluggish its motion. Progress, preservation, and restoration are achieved only through movement of the right kind. It should be noted that the earth, similar celestial bodies, and cosmic systems are not the only objects in perpetual movement. As with the largest bodies, so it is with the smallest atomic particles; everything is in constant and uninterrupted movement. Consider a solid rock. The stationary rock is composed of chemical compounds which are themselves made up of protons, neutrons, electrons, etc., all of which are in constant movement, quite apart from the fact that the rock is being carried along in all the motions of the earth.

Even the most casual observation on earth must indicate to us the utmost significance of motion. If a portion of a fresh, rapidly-flowing river is diverted to form a stagnant pool, the pool soon loses its freshness, and may begin to smell; thus, the river maintains its freshness through movement. The hands of a boxer get bigger and stronger on account of their use. A person who exercises stays healthier than one who does not. In general, any ability that is used improves; one that is not used atrophies. All these are effects of God's Law of Movement. The biological principle of adaptation is a consequence of the Law of Movement. There are birds which can no longer fly because their wings have deteriorated on account of failure to use them over thousands of years, and some fishes are obliged to stay at the bottom of the ocean because they have lost the ability to withstand the currents.

The human spirit is subject to this same Law of Adaptation. The spiritually receptive part of the brain, the cerebellum or back brain, has become stunted relative to the frontal brain, the cerebrum, because human beings have busied themselves almost exclusively with gross material activities. Thus, we have lost most of our spiritual abilities and find it difficult to think aright about God. This condition is responsible for many of the problems confronting the human race, and the dire problems which await many in the Beyond, after physical death. We will return to this matter of the distorted brain in Chapter 17 in which we discuss the problem of evil. The human being is subject to the Law of Movement in body, soul, and spirit. It is not sufficient to obey the Law only in so far as the body and earthly matters are concerned. We must also move spiritually.

The world of ideas, belief systems and religions are also subject to the Law of Movement, and consequently to the Law of Adaptation. Obedience of this Law requires that we continually and purposefully re-examine our religious and spiritual beliefs and have the courage to discard those that belong to an age and period of relative ignorance. And movement of the spirit calls for making spiritual pursuits our primary goals, with earthly goals being only secondary. In this connection, we may remind ourselves about the meaning of a spiritual goal. A spiritual goal always has furthering values; furthering in the sense of facilitating adjustment to the Will of God on earth. Such values are inherently noble, they promote love, justice, freedom and responsibility, and they eschew hatred and violence.

On account of the Law of Movement, one should expect that revelations from the Creator would be progressive. Therefore, one should expect new knowledge and new revelations which advance older teachings at critical periods in the development of Creation. This does not mean, however, that the new is necessarily a negation of the old. Without new revelations, there would be stagnation and retrogression and advancement to the next higher level of spirituality and consequently of civilization would be impossible. Without the periodic infusion of new spiritual knowledge the foundation of religious beliefs would gradually collapse. Many objective observers suspect that most religions are today in a situation of near collapse for lack of admission of new spiritual knowledge that would solidify their foundations and raise their followers to the next level of spirituality and vitality.

The Law of Movement implies that we cannot achieve anything of significance without effort. Thus, indolence of whatever description (physical, mental, spiritual) offends against the Law of Movement, and therefore against the Will of God. For this reason, no one should wish to be in a state of perpetual rest. And the different types of activities — spiritual, intellectual, and physical — must be kept in appropriate balance. Physical and intellectual efforts without spiritual activity are ultimately in vain. It should be stated that there is a rhythm to the movement in Creation. All our activities must be adjusted to this rhythm, so that we may swim with the currents of Creation; otherwise we harm ourselves. Motion without rhythm can easily become commotion. Workaholism (compulsive working without rest) and all frenzied activity go against the rhythm of Creation and are wrong.

In accordance with the Law of Movement, no individual or group should rest on past glories. When we have attained a particular level or position of honour, we must strive to maintain it or else we would fall. It is only the spiritual sluggishness of humankind that permits people to enjoy reputations or the privileges of a position long after their activities have ceased to qualify them for such. The Law commands us to live in the *present*, not in the past. Therefore, a person who is currently honourable should be treated as such, even if he had been a convicted criminal in the past. On the other hand, if a national hero becomes a criminal, he should be treated as a criminal. Persons who have been promoted to particular positions must continue to justify the higher appointments; they should be demoted to their new level of reduced competence should their performance decline.

The popular saying that "practice makes perfect", which associates improvement (though not necessarily perfection) with constant effort points to the Law of Movement. This Law, of course, applies in large as well as in small things. Some individuals, especially politically well-connected persons in some countries, have lost the ability and the discipline to do hard and honest work. This is because they have not done so for many years, having lived exclusively on political patronage and government largesse that were corruptly obtained. Society has a duty to create an environment in which such indolence and parasitism will become rare if not impossible. Culture and traditional practices are also subject to the Law of Movement; they must continually advance, guided by the Laws of Creation and adapt to changing times and circumstances.

The Law of Reciprocal Action

Another Law that manifests the Will of God is the the Law of Reciprocal Action, which is known by various other expressions, such as: the Law of Sowing and Reaping; the Law of Karma; and the Law of Retributive Justice. We know that if we sow corn, we can only reap corn, and if we want to harvest rice, we must sow rice. This Law ensures the maintenance of order and justice in Creation. Imagine what confusion and bewilderment would result if we could not be certain what the harvest would be whenever we planted any seed; if at one time, a planting of maize gave us wheat, at another time the same planting gave us mango, etc. Because of this Law, we know what harvest to expect with each planting, and what we must plant if we desire a particular harvest.

The Will of God does not depend on religion or religious opinions. Therefore, this and the other Laws are no respecter of religions. If a Christian sows corn, he will reap corn; so also will a Jew, a Muslim, a Buddhist, or an atheist. If an atheist sows goodness, he is bound to reap goodness; so will a Bishop, a Hindu monk, or a Muslim Imam. Indeed, the Creator in His perfect Justice cannot be expected to discriminate on any basis in the operation of His Laws. This fact should lead us to the realization that religions can only be a means to an end, and not ends in themselves. Any religion has value only to the extent that it aids in understanding the true Will of God and motivates one to do God's Will. But we would be wrong to imagine that membership of any religion, sect, or spiritual movement would guarantee salvation.

The Law of Reciprocal Action occurs in and is advocated by practically all scriptures, although it may not be rightly understood. For example, we find the following in the Bible: "Vengeance is mine and recompense" (Deuteronomy 32:35). It is through the operation of the Law of Sowing and Reaping that God metes out "vengeance" and "recompense" and not through personal intervention in the lives of individuals. While discussing deism in Chapter 6, we noted God's continual involvement in Creation on matters of Creation-wide significance. But God does not at all personally intervene to reward or punish individuals. His interventions are through the Laws of Creation and the activities of various elemental beings (servants of God's Will) that play roles in upholding the Laws. We have already discussed (in Chapter 4) Free Will as an inseparable part of the human spirit. The Free Will ensures that we are able to decide what we will sow in thought, word, or deed. Having taken the decision, the Law of Sowing and Reaping in cooperation with the other Laws takes over. *We are to leave vengeance to God's Law of Sowing and Reaping not out of kindness or consideration for those who may offend us but for our own sake.* In trying to retaliate, we might do something bad and thereby sow a bad seed that would result in more harm to us in future. Whenever we retaliate we open a new cycle of wrong-doing that may harm not only the original offender but ourselves as well, in accordance with the Law of Sowing and Reaping.

Let us learn a bit more about this Law, which holds the key to so many unsolved problems. First, we should understand that "sowing" is, of course, not limited to its ordinary agricultural sense. We "sow" through our thoughts, our words, our actions, as well as our volition. This implies that we are all constantly sowing, be it only in our thinking and in our general attitude to life. If our thoughts are always good, we reap harvests of blessings; if they are evil, we continually heap evil on ourselves. As we shift gear between good and evil, so do the harvests change. We know that quite often people's actions are different from their thinking and their volition. A man may be smiling at you and saying nice words to you while planning to harm you; his volition is in conflict with his words and gestures.

A man makes a donation to an organization even though he does not share the ideals and the objectives of the organization. He simply wants the publicity or seeks favour from members of the organization. In all such cases, the Law of Sowing and Reaping ensures that the harvests are weighed carefully to reflect not only the actions, but also the ulterior motives. Most human beings cannot read other people's thoughts nor fathom their real volitions. And so, they cannot be good judges in the sense of the Eternal Laws. Hence we must not make ourselves judges over other people, because most of us lack the ability to judge correctly. For even when we observe the action and hear the words, we may not know the motives.

Another aspect of the Law of Reciprocal Action, the Law of Sowing and Reaping, which we must note is that one planted seed yields at harvest many seeds. The harvest is of the same kind (quality or species) as what was sown but its quantity is much greater. Thus our actions, good or bad, return to us multiplied.

Interval between Sowing and Reaping. Yet another key aspect of the Law which should always be borne in mind is that the period between sowing and reaping depends on what is sown. Some grain crops are ready for harvest four months after planting, whereas some tree crops do not yield any harvests until after many years. Indeed, we plant some tree crops knowing full well that they will not be ready for harvesting in our lifetime. Even for the same crop, the period required for maturity may vary according to variety. For example, traditional varieties of cowpeas (black-eyed peas), a food legume that is highly relished in West Africa, northeast Brazil, and southern United States, mature in about 100 days. Some modern varieties of the same crop are ready for harvesting about 60 days after planting. Such differences in periods to maturity also apply to the actions, thoughts, words, prayers, and the volitions of people. Thus, we can understand why a person doing good or evil now will reap the consequences only in the future, near or distant.

The necessary interval between sowing and reaping is the key to the riddle of why good things may be happening to an apparently bad person and why bad things may be happening to an apparently good person. The good that may currently be falling on the laps of a seemingly bad person must be the good he did in the past. And the bad experiences of the person who is presently striving to do only what is good are the consequences of some wrong done in the past, which are only now ready for harvest. The perfect Justice of God does not permit any arbitrariness. One reaps only what one has personally sown, and nobody reaps what he or she has not sown. This will be further discussed in Chapter 12 on the Love and Justice of God.

In our vanity, often veiled, we are sure we deserve the good things that come our way but feel unfairly treated when bad things happen to us. There appear to be injustices in some cases only because of our own ignorance. A key aspect of this ignorance is lack of the knowledge of reincarnation or its deliberate rejection. The truth is that some "fruits" we now harvest, whether they are good or bad, were planted in some distant past, in previous earth-lives. On the other hand, some "seeds" we are now sowing may not be ready for harvest until a distant future, in the beyond, or in another earth-life. The Creator grants every human being the Free Will to decide what he may or may not sow; but once one has done the sowing, one is obliged irrevocably to "eat the harvest". It does not matter who the person is.

Love, Justice, and Forgiveness. Many persons, who have some knowledge of the Law of Reciprocal Action, readily and without any difficulty associate it with Divine Justice. But relatively few realize that in this Law also lies Divine Love. Consider a person who sows a good seed. The Law guarantees that at harvest he receives fruits of the same kind, and this can be perceived as Justice. But the effect of the Law is not only on quality or kind, but also on quantity. He, who sows, for example, one seed of maize, may reap two cobs of maize containing perhaps as many as a hundred seeds. Is it not Love, when for one seed, the Law of Reciprocal Action ensures a return of so many seeds? And from one seed of orange emerges an orange tree which yields perhaps hundreds of oranges year in, year out.

A reader might also wonder if forgiveness is possible given that we are obliged to reap the bad consequences of our wrongdoing. I discussed the subject in some detail in a whole chapter in my book, *The Christian and Reincarnation* (Legacy Edition, 2008), under the title "The Divine Laws and the Matter of Forgiveness." I will just state here that forgiveness is provided for within the framework of the Laws of Creation. The combined working of the Law of Reciprocal Action and the Law of Homogeneity (discussed below) grants or denies forgiveness for individuals. It will be revisited in Chapter 12 on The Love and Justice of God.

And let us not forget one of the petitions in the Lord's Prayer: "And forgive us our trespasses as we forgive them that trespass against us!" In other words, the forgiveness of our trespasses is the reciprocal effect of the forgiveness we grant others; we harvest forgiveness only after sowing forgiveness. This suggests one way by which a wrong-doing may be forgiven: the offended person (and nobody else) is able, through a genuine volition to forgive, free the offender from the consequences of that particular offence. By truly forgiving, the threads of fate woven by the offender are rendered ineffective. One may also obtain forgiveness through suffering the full consequences of a wrong-doing and resolving thereby never again to engage in such an act. Another process by which we earn forgiveness is through what may be called symbolic redemption. These processes are discussed in the Chapters on the Omniscience of God and The Love and Justice of God. Forgiveness is always possible, but it is never arbitrary.

Attitude to the Suffering. Let us, right away, raise and answer a question of great social importance that may well arise at this point in the minds of well-meaning people: does it follow that we do not have to worry about suffering people since they are themselves responsible for their suffering? That is, may we claim that they are only reaping what they sowed in this earth-life or in an earlier one and do not therefore deserve our help? The Law of Sowing and Reaping should suggest the *opposite* to us. The Law shows clearly the need to do good at all times – good defined in relation to the spiritual purpose of human existence. This is because whatever good we do and to whomever we do it, be it an evil or good person, we stand to reap the good fruits. In reality, any good we do, we do for ourselves; since the fruits return to us as multiples of the seeds we planted. Whenever we see somebody suffering, we should consider ourselves as having an opportunity to sow good seeds. And as we mature spiritually, this comes quite naturally in the form of genuine compassion at the sight of suffering and the thought of whether or not the sufferer deserves it does not cross our mind.

Moreover, we should know that, in the perfection of the Laws of the Creator, if a sufferer does not deserve help, nobody who is in a position to help will come into contact with him or her. And how do we know that our relationships in former earth-lives are not such that we owe the particular suffering person a debt that we must pay through offering help at that point? Let it be stressed, however, that true help is always only that which takes cognizance of and facilitates the recipient's spiritual advancement.

Mission Karma. Furthermore, we should know that not all suffering is a consequence of a past evil. One's suffering may be due to "mission karma". Mission Karma is a fate, a consequence, a sacrifice that a person voluntarily accepts in order to fulfil a particular mission. Suppose a house is burning and I enter it to save a child trapped in it. By undertaking the mission, I accept voluntarily the possibility, indeed the likelihood, of having some burns; any burns or harm I suffer are the karma associated with my mission of mercy.

We will revisit the topic of mission karma in Chapter 17 when we address the subject of God and the Problem of Evil. The idea of mission karma helps to deepen further our understanding of the working of the Law of Sowing and Reaping. Mission karma explains, for example, how it was possible for Jesus Christ to be murdered even though He obviously and definitely was sinless. That is, the murder was *not* the fruit of His sowing. Even before Jesus set out on His mission of salvation, it was appreciated that Darkness had descended heavily on earth, that men had become exceedingly evil and confused, that even their religious leaders sought only earthly power and influence and were no longer interested in the truth. It was, therefore, clear that earthmen could reject His teachings and might even kill Him. Because Jesus was, and is the personification of Love, He accepted the risk, in the manner that a man, who out of love, dashes into a burning house to save a trapped child accepts the risk of burns.

It should, of course, be easy to understand that the man who voluntarily, and out of genuine love, accepts a mission that is associated with dangers is at the same time sowing good seeds, seeds of pure love. The seeds will grow, mature and, in due course, yield a bountiful harvest. Such harvests arising from acts of selfless love are the treasures we store for ourselves in heaven; they form points of anchor for the invisible threads that pull us to Paradise.

The Law of Attraction of Homogeneous Species

"Like always attracts like" is a Law of Creation. This Law is known variously as the Law of Attraction of Homogeneous Species, the Law of Homogeneity, or the Law of Attraction of Similar Species. These terms are used in this book interchangeably. The proverb "Birds of a feather flock together" hints at this Law. So also does the saying "Show me your friends and I will tell you who you are." Just as birds of a feather flock together, so do fishes of the same kind swim together in large groups called schools. Such congregating has many advantages for them. For example, fishes in schools find food more readily and are less prone to attack by predators. Economists say that bad money drives out good money; this is like saying that unlike species repel, in accordance with the Law of Homogeneity. The Law manifests itself in the relationships among people, among animals, and even in the natural communities of plants. Those who have studied chemistry might see the effect of this Law quite clearly in the coming together of identical molecules to form compounds, as well as in many chemical reactions.

The Law of Attraction of Homogeneous Species ensures that if a particular species is split, the split parts will re-unite when given an opportunity. It is for this reason that opposite poles of a magnet attract. The fact that unlike poles of a magnet attract appears, at first, to be a contradiction of the Law of the Attraction of Similar Species. Let us, therefore, take some time to reflect on it. Consider a bar magnet. Suppose we hold this magnet in such a way that the left end is the south pole and the right end is the north pole of the magnet. Imagine that we then cut the bar magnet into two (the two parts need not be equal). We now have two bar magnets. Call the left piece "magnet A" and the right piece "magnet B". By convention, the right end of "magnet A" is a new north pole, while the left end of "magnet B" becomes a new south pole. But remember that the right end of "magnet A" (the new north pole) and the left end of "magnet B" (the new south pole) were one and the same spot before we cut the original bar magnet into two. Therefore, when the new north pole attracts the new south pole, we are merely witnessing the coming together of closely similar parts that were forcibly separated; adjacent molecules that were separated are given a chance to rejoin. And they do so, in accordance with the Creation Law of "Like Attracts Like". Whole species that are similar will attract. But so will the split parts of the same species seek to re-unite.

Thus, the Law of Attraction of Homogeneous Species is fundamental for everything that is striving for union in Creation. But what appears to be attraction can be differentiated into *genuine attraction*, which takes place between *whole* species that are similar, and the *desire for union of split parts* of the same definite species (as in the case of magnets). The human being is not a whole species but only a splitting which carries within itself the desire for union. And this (sexual instinct apart) explains the attraction between man and woman. However, the thoughts, deeds, and volitions of human beings are whole species that attract similar species. In general, a split species can give rise not only to split species but also to complete species.

In Creation and Subsequent Creation, there was no specific provision for hell. God did not create hell. Properly understood, hell is the flocking together of people who share similar weaknesses or evil. As evil people gather together, they inflict all sorts of evil on one another, thereby making life hell for themselves. Hell has different sections according to different wrong dispositions – the greedy, the quarrelsome, the murderous, etc. If nobody was evil, there would be no gatherings of the evil-minded and, therefore, there would be no hell. There are, of course, many gatherings of joy, peace, love, etc. formed under the pressure of the same Law of Homogeneity. The beautiful and the hellish sections of the Beyond arose out of the volition of human beings exercising their Free Will rightly or wrongly. We may also note that we encounter forms of hell right here on earth.

We have already stated that the effects of the Laws of Creation vary from species to species. With human beings on earth, the physical body influences the effect of the Law of Homogeneity in such a way that it is much less obvious than it is in the Beyond where the physical body has been discarded. Thus, it is possible for a criminal to infiltrate the ranks of noble people on earth, for a period. In the Beyond the effects of the Law of Attraction of Homogeneous Species are so pronounced that the boundaries between all shades of good and bad people are very sharply drawn. In the Beyond, a criminal can only change through the suffering inflicted by fellow criminals; he cannot possibly be in touch with a good man. On earth, however, a criminal has the advantage that he can be directly influenced by good men in addition to observing the punishments to which caught criminals are subjected.

A person with wrong spiritual convictions has many painless opportunities to realize his errors and, therefore, to change while on earth. However, in the Beyond he will find himself in the company of only those who hold similarly wrong ideas and it is only the perplexity and agony associated with their environment that may convince him of his errors. It is for these and other reasons that an earth-life is hugely important for spiritual advancement.

Spiritual Qualities Come First. Because we are spiritual creatures, spiritual characteristics should be for us the most important factors of homogeneity. On one occasion, Jesus Christ was told that His mother and His brothers were waiting to see Him. In response, he pointed to His disciples and said: "Here are my mother and my brothers! For whoever does the will of my Father in heaven is my brother and sister and mother" (Matthew 12:49-50). In this way, Jesus underscored the fact that spiritual relationships were more important than earthly kinship; in other words spiritual qualities come first.

It is to be expected that superficial people and those who do not have any understanding for the inner and finer qualities would be attracted most readily only by outward appearances, such as skin colour, physical look, fashion, religion, etc. The fact that race and ethnicity are for many people the key considerations in their relationships with others is clear evidence of the pervasive superficiality and inner immaturity of humanity today. With increasing spiritual knowledge, particularly the right knowledge of reincarnation and the Laws of Creation, the relative unimportance of a person's race and nationality become obvious. And one is then able to assess others on the basis of their worth as human beings, the values they uphold, their character, their personal abilities, etc.

Children and their Families. The Law of Homogeneity and the Law of Reciprocal Action determine the family, place, and other circumstances into which one is born. Every thought, word or act gives rise to a "form" that has a characteristic consistency. Each "form" can be perceived with the sense appropriate to it. Thus, for example, thoughts can be "picked." An act of conception sends a form into creation alerting the human spirits in the Beyond of an opportunity for an incarnation on earth. Of the many souls in the Beyond that might wish or be compelled to incarnate, the one that does incarnate is determined by the spiritual environment of the parents, particularly of the pregnant woman. Among possible specific factors would be the similarity between the volitions, strengths, weaknesses, propensities, etc. of the incoming soul and those of the prospective mother, father, or someone whom the mother allows to exert a strong influence on her around the time of incarnation. In addition to these, any threads of fate dating from past lives that link members of the family to the incoming soul, would also play a role.

Incarnation takes place about the middle of pregnancy at a particular stage in the development of the fetus. That is the time the incoming soul takes full possession of the growing body, which it will use for its new earth-life. To ensure that nobody draws a wrong conclusion from this fact, we should state right away that it must not be imagined that abortion may be committed at any time without spiritual repercussion. The act of procreation is like inviting the many anxious human spirits in the Beyond to get ready for a chance to experience an earth-life, with all the opportunities an earth-life offers for spiritual development. Termination of a pregnancy before incarnation thus, at least, amounts to frustrating and dashing the hopes of some aspiring souls. Such an act must have unpleasant consequences. It is, of course, clear that abortion after incarnation has already taken place is, from the standpoint of the Laws of Creation, like physical murder. The solution is to avoid conception. We should never delude ourselves into believing that an action is necessarily without sin just because earthly laws permit it. We must always allow ourselves to be guided by the Will of God as expressed in His Laws.

A noble spirit will, in general, incarnate in a family of noble people, by the Law of Homogeneity, and vice versa. Association with a not-so-honourable person by a pregnant woman may let down a bridge for the incarnation of a so-called black sheep. Nobility of spirit and indeed spiritual characteristics (such as faithfulness, truthfulness, modesty, courage, compassion, instinctive respect for justice, diligence, etc.) are not biologically inherited. When they occur among members of the same family it is through the operation of the Law of Attraction of Similar Species. Only physical, gross material characteristics are passed along through genetic processes. Nor are genetic processes by any means accidental. The Law of Reciprocal Action ensures that only those who have sown the necessary seeds are incarnated into families and places where they are bound to enjoy genetic advantage or suffer from hereditary handicap. For example, as a given disease is wiped out in a particular part of the world, those whose karma calls for that disease are precluded from incarnating in that part; they would be compelled to incarnate in a country where the disease has not been eliminated.

It follows that if we could rid the earth of all diseases and the causes of human suffering, any souls that need to experience suffering would be unable to incarnate on our earth. Similarly, if we would all strive to be noble in our thoughts, words, aspirations, deeds and intuitive perceptions, unworthy spirits would find it impossible to incarnate on earth. And thereby, the earth would gradually become like Paradise.

The Law of Spiritual Gravity
Another Law of Creation is the Law of Spiritual Gravity. This Law may be explained by reference to the physical law of gravity, which is the form in which this Eternal Law manifests on earth. Whatever is really light rises easily, whereas that which is heavy

tends to fall. The nature of the human being and of its inner cloaks was discussed in Chapter 4. A human being has not only the physical body but several other non-physical bodies. At death, the spirit drops its physical cloak; that is, it leaves its physical body behind. Where the spirit, with its non-physical cloaks (the soul) finds itself is then determined by the Law of Spiritual Gravity. Evil doing, bad thoughts, wrong aspirations and attitudes make the cloaks of the spirit heavy. Such heaviness causes the spirit to sink, to fall away in a direction opposite from that of its origin. That is, it retrogresses. How deep it sinks, depends on how much it has immersed itself in wrong-doing and, therefore, how heavy it has become.

Following its fall, it congregates with other spirits that have similar weaknesses; again, in accordance with the Law of Homogeneity. If, for example, greed is one of its major vices, it will get drawn to others who are as greedy and these will inflict greed on him continuously. The gathering of the greedy thereby forms a "greed section" of hell in which members constantly perpetrate greed on one another. Any member, who through the distasteful experience in this section, becomes disgusted with greed and no longer wishes to be a part of it, is automatically moved away — again according to both the Law of Gravity and the Law of Homogeneity. For, through his disapproval of the place, he would have become different from that environment, and the Law of Attraction of Similar Species ensures his separation.

Noble actions, thoughts, and attitudes keep the spirit light so that, once the spirit has shed the physical body it rises automatically toward its spiritual origin, its home. It rises along with similarly noble spirits from which it receives love, and to which it also gives love. Thomas Aquinas, recognized by the Roman Catholic Church as its foremost philosopher and theologian, in his *Summa Theologiae*, describes how departed souls reach their "places", their immediate destinations. Aquinas says that bodies have a tendency to sink as well as to rise whereby their places are determined. "The pull from the higher worlds makes itself felt through 'levitation', and the pull from the lower world is felt as 'gravity', according to the quality of the past earthly life. The soul then follows, as it were, the magnetic pull from that supersensible region to which it feels akin, either 'gravitating' or 'levitating' as the case may be." (*Summa Theologiae* Suppl. 69.2, cited by Rudolf Frieling in his *Christianity and Reincarnation*).

The description by Thomas Aquinas is remarkably consistent with the Law of Spiritual Gravity as outlined above. We should also note that the process described by Thomas Aquinas implies the working of the Law of Attraction of Similar Species. The Law of Gravity and the Law of Attraction of Homogeneous Species allow us to realize that God does not personally assign us to particular places after our physical death; rather, where we find ourselves depends on us – on our inner qualities at the time of departure. With His immutable laws, God ensures that each person judges himself. We place ourselves in the Regions of Darkness and Damnation or in the Regions of Light and Paradise.

The Law of Balance
The concept of balance is one with which we are all familiar. We normally sense that whatever is out of balance is unsatisfactory or wrong. There is a problem whenever accounts (financial and otherwise) cannot be balanced. We speak of "balanced diets", referring to the necessity to eat different kinds of food items in appropriate proportions to ensure good health. The stars, planets and other celestial bodies are maintained in their incessant motions along predictable paths through a "balance of forces". All these are manifestations of a Law of Creation — the Law of Equilibrium, the Law of Necessary Balance between Giving and Taking. This Law permeates everything and its strict observance in human affairs is a precondition for harmony and peace.

For a better understanding let us consider more manifestations of the Law of Balance. Actions are balanced by reactions. Food intake is balanced by waste elimination; we have constipation and feel sick when there is poor digestion and, therefore, no elimination of food wastes. Endless work without rest is harmful; complete retirement from work, that is, endless rest, is equally harmful. If after retirement from employment, a person does absolutely nothing, the person will soon fall ill and die. Therefore, to wish the soul of a departed person eternal rest is really to curse it! It is a sign of widespread ignorance of the Law of Balance and the Law of Movement that many people in many cultures wish dead persons "everlasting rest." Many wish the dead to "rest in perfect peace" also because they consider work as something of a curse and not the blessing that it is. We should engage ourselves in appropriate work until our very last day on earth, and we should wish the dead "joyful activity" in their continued existence in other realms, and not eternal rest. Just as a physical body in endless rest would soon die, so the soul in eternal repose would die – which, in this case, would amount to eternal damnation! Whereas happiness is associated with the active pursuit of worthwhile spiritual goals and earthly objectives that have a spiritual content, many human beings imagine that idleness makes for happiness. Base passions, indulgence, and indolence are detrimental and can only lead to unhappiness and ultimately to spiritual death.

In our breathing we observe the Law of Balance; exhaling is balanced with inhaling. Many people have recognized how important good breathing is for the maintenance of radiant health, and so there are people who teach the art of correct breathing. The simple key is to breathe out properly; with proper exhalation, proper inhalation automatically follows in accordance with the Law of Balance.

The balance, an instrument for weighing, is popularly used as a symbol of the judiciary and earthly justice. This symbolism is a good one; for it is correct to say that where there is no balance, there can be no justice. And we can sense that the Law of Balance between Giving and Taking reflects an attribute of God – Justice.

The Law of Balance is fundamental in all human relationships, whether interpersonal, between groups, or among nations. There must be balance in marriage, in the relationship between children and parents, between the employer and the employee, between the leader and the follower. In all these situations, harmony, peace, and progress are achieved only when giving and taking are appropriately balanced. The concepts of giving and taking as they apply in each situation must, of course, be correctly understood. Thus, the desire of a parent to have a child must be balanced with the duty to take care of the child. The protection which adults offer children must be balanced by the obligation of children to respect adults. And the child, as soon as it is physically able to do so, should be made to contribute something to the home to balance the parental care it receives. The contribution would take the form appropriate to the child's circumstance — it could be running errands around the house, helping with minor chores, etc.

Among other things, the above examples suggest that the Law of Balance does not necessarily imply quantitative equivalence; nor does it require that one should give back the same kind of thing that one received. In some circumstances, the requirements of balance are met when the receiver shows genuine and heartfelt gratitude or gives some good advice. Thus, everybody, rich or poor, is able to fulfil the demands of the Law of Balance. Most of us do not obey the Law only because of our individual weaknesses, such as selfishness, presumption, thoughtlessness, bad habit, and other manifestations of spiritual immaturity.

It also follows from the above that we really do not need to ponder what and how much we should give in return for whatever we receive. We should with a genuine intention simply give the best we can. And even the poorest can offer heartfelt prayers, gratitude and a kind and appreciative look to the giver. In this and in all matters, genuineness of one's intentions and the purity of one's heart are always the essential considerations from the standpoint of the Laws of Creation.

Giving is Better. In the Law of Balance between Giving and Taking, giving always ranks first. We can readily understand that this should be so on account of the Law of Sowing and Reaping. Without planting there can be no harvest; therefore, giving must naturally have precedence over taking. Each time we give, we are sowing. And we know that each seed we sow will, at the appropriate time, return to us multiples of the seeds of the same kind. On the other hand, the seed we take or receive is like a harvest; once we have eaten it, that is the end of it. A cycle is closed with each receiving, whereas we start a new cycle whenever we give. For these reasons, it is always better, more blessed, to give than to receive.

This is what Jesus Christ meant to teach when, as reported by Paul, He said: "It is more blessed to give than to receive" (Acts 20:35). And it is for the same reason that the Koran has so much to say about giving and how it should be done: "And be steadfast in prayer and regular in charity" (The Koran, Surah II:110). This passage and many more in the Koran are the basis of the prominence of alms-giving (Zakat) in Islam. Nobody is expected to indulge in one-sided taking, whereas everybody is urged to give. Hence whenever there is an opportunity to give, we should grab it joyfully. But we must always remember that we should give out of love, out of a genuine desire to help in the manner most beneficial, especially spiritually, to the recipient.

We should also note that what we get in return for what we give does not depend on the recipient – whether or not he deserves it, whether or not he is grateful or ungrateful, whether or not he is even aware of the help are all unimportant. What was said about the attitude toward the suffering in connection with the Law of Reciprocal Action also applies here exactly. We get the reward due to us and when it is due *only* in accordance with the Laws of Creation. And finally, we should bear in mind the fact that the principle is the same whether the giver or receiver is an individual, a group, or a nation.

Organizations and Doing the Will of God

From the foregoing discussion of the Laws of Creation, it is clear that to do the Will of God does not call for membership of any religion, sect, movement or cult. Rather, one should always strive to act, speak, and think in the sense of these Laws. In general, one ought to avoid the unconscious tendency to use organizations as crutches. Neither should one allow oneself to be excessively influenced by organizational rules, regulations, and traditions at the expense of one's personal convictions. This means that one must strive for conviction in everything one does and one must not relent in striving to deepen one's understanding of the Will of God as manifested in the Laws of Creation.

However, many individuals might find interactions with like-minded persons and participation in the activities of appropriately structured and managed organizations highly beneficial in deepening their understanding of the Will of God and in their striving to live accordingly. Such people should be thankful for and take advantage of such opportunities. But membership activities should not, of course, substitute for one's personal work on oneself. And it should be noted that the mark of appropriate organizations and relationships in spiritual matters is that, while providing opportunities for spiritual growth for their members, they encourage independence and the exercise of Free Will and do not seek to control their lives.

Unfortunately, there are increasing numbers of people who have a vested interest in making others believe that salvation depends on membership of particular organizations and who overtly and covertly encourage an attitude of sheepish followership. They discourage whoever comes within their sphere of influence from engaging in inflexible weighing and examining of traditional or customary religious practices, doctrines and beliefs. They also try hard to prevent them from studying sources of new knowledge or unfamiliar previous revelations. This is because such people wish to build expanding organizations, which in turn would increase their earthly wealth, power, and influence. They know that the truth not only sets human beings free from darkness and dark forces but also releases them from the unhealthy hold of earthly associations.

8 Beyond the Scriptural Portrayal of God

Some Scriptures present confusing and inconsistent ideas of the attributes and nature of God. Some passages say that no one can see God and live and another tells us that Moses spoke with God face to face as one speaks with a friend. God is described as love and yet He is alleged to have condoned series of genocides by ancient Israelites. He is even supposed to have demanded some of the atrocities. God is reported to have subjected those He loved, such as Abraham and Job, to inhuman tests of loyalty. And as for Divine Justice, one is left perplexed. He lets individuals reap whatever they sow, whether good or bad; and that is understandable justice. But He is also presumed to punish people for the sins of their parents and grandparents, which cannot be justice. By and large, God is portrayed in the Jewish Scripture as a superhuman magician whose primary concern was the weal and woes of Israel. Such confused portrayal provides ammunitions for atheists and unwittingly promotes blasphemy on the part of believers. This chapter addresses these issues. To think aright about God one must seek beyond traditional Scriptures.

Let me emphasize once again the fact that all past messages of God should be considered the common heritage of humanity. While each message was given to particular peoples according to their state of maturity and their most urgent needs for further development, it was never intended to be an exclusive possession. Moreover, as indicated in Chapter 3 on the progressive nature of the revelation of God, those messages did not define all truths for all time. They were meant to be integrated into new teachings as human beings matured spiritually and as the cycle of God's Creation advanced. Standstill is retrogression; and this also applies to matters of belief and faith. Therefore, no individual or group should feel obliged to take up arms in defence of past messages or in opposition to new teachings. The following words of Abd-ru-shin, the author of the work *"In the Light of Truth, The Grail Message"*, are instructive:

> For what comes from God, or what is carried out in purity at His behest, knows neither hate nor enmity, nor any contradictions.
>
> Take *this* truth as the touchstone for all things!
>
> *Wherever* you find intolerance and malice, or even enmity and stirring up strife against others who are not of the same faith, wherever men seek to harm those of different belief, either *the teaching is not from God* or it has been falsified! And such people serve only the Darkness, *never the Light!*
>
> The teaching that permits this *must* be distorted, whatever it is called; for a teaching that has not yet been distorted will also swing in purity in the Laws of God. It does not produce human beings who wish to harm their fellow-men!

Furthermore, we should read all Scriptures bearing in mind the world-views of their ancient authors and their immediate target audiences as well as the circumstances of the peoples of that period. The fundamentalist believer who argues that the particular Scripture he considers sacred is wholly true in a *literal* sense in the face of objective facts to the contrary does his religion a great disservice.

Not Like a Fellow Human

Consider this statement in the Bible (Genesis 2:2-3): "And on the seventh day God finished His work which He had done, and He rested on the seventh day from all His work which He had done. So God blessed the seventh day and hallowed it, because on it God rested from all His work which He had done in Creation." It is a classic case of thinking of God as if He were a human being. The writer implies that the Creator, God, got tired following six days of work and needed rest, just like a human being would get tired. It should be noted, however, that in the Book of Isaiah (40:28), it is stated: "Did you not know? Had you not heard? Yahweh is the everlasting God; He created the remotest parts of the earth. He does not grow tired or weary, His understanding is beyond fathoming" (The New Jerusalem Bible).

Here is another passage from the story of Adam and Eve in the Garden of Eden: "And they heard the sound of the Lord God walking in the garden in the cool of the day, and the man and his wife hid themselves from the presence of the Lord God among the trees of the garden. But the Lord God called to the man, and said to him, "Where are you?" (Genesis 3:8-9). The latter passage implies that God is just like a human being, taking a stroll in the garden (presumably preferring the cool of the day). Moreover, it was possible for Adam and Eve to hide from God. God did not know where they were; He had to ask, "Where are you?" This is, of course, a wrong way to think about God. Most Christians today do not conceive of God as one who can get tired, from whom we can hide, and who strolls in earthly gardens.

Unlike the above Genesis passages, Apostle Paul, in his letter to Timothy hints at the right way to think about God when he wrote:

> ... He (God) who is the blessed and only Sovereign, the King of kings and Lord of lords. It is he alone who has immortality and dwells in unapproachable light, whom no one has ever seen or can see; to him be honor and eternal dominion. Amen." (1Timothy 6:15-16, New Revised Standard Version)

> ...God, the King of kings and Lord of Lords. He alone can never die, and He lives in light so brilliant that no human can approach Him. No one has ever seen Him, nor ever will. To Him be honor and power forever. Amen." (1Timothy 6:15-16, New Living Translation Version)

A similarly lofty idea of God is found in the Koran:

> Allah! There is no God But He, — the Living, the Self-Subsisting, Eternal. No slumber can seize Him nor sleep. .... His throne doth extend over the heavens and the earth, and He feeleth no fatigue in guarding and preserving them. For He is the Most High, The Supreme (in glory) (The Koran, Sura II:255, Abdullah Yusuf Ali Translation)

A related idea is that God cannot dwell on earth, contrary to the impression created in Chapter 25 of the Biblical Book of Exodus. In the Chapter, it is reported that God told Moses to ask the people of Israel voluntarily to make offerings to Him and named the items which Moses should accept on His behalf. The items were to be used for a Temple, which God reportedly went on to specify in great detail. *"I want the people of Israel to build me a sacred residence where I can live among them"* (Exodus 25:8). In the Book of Deuteronomy, one of the regulations given to the people of Israel read:

The camp must be holy, for the LORD your God moves around in your camp to protect you and to defeat your enemies. He must not see any shameful thing among you, or he will turn away from you" (Deuteronomy 23:14, New Living Translation).

The question arises, 'Can God reside in a building among human beings and move around their camp?' The answer is emphatically, No! King Solomon sensed as much. The requested Temple was eventually completed by King Solomon. On the occasion of the solemn dedication of the Temple, Solomon recalled the original request and God's promise. But he then wondered:

But will God really live on earth among people? Why, even the highest heaven cannot contain you. How much less this Temple I have built! Listen to my prayer and my request, O Lord my God. Hear the cry and the prayer that your servant is making to you. May you watch over this Temple day and night, this place where you have said you would put your name. (2 Chronicles 6:18-20, New Living Translation).

A literal interpretation would be wrong. A spiritual interpretation might be that a much modified, highly transformed radiation of God would be anchored in the sanctuary.

Has Anyone Ever Seen God?

We have already cited the Letter to Timothy in which Paul stated clearly that no human being has seen, or is able to see, God. The Gospel of John makes a similar assertion: "No one has ever seen God. It is God the only Son, who is close to the Father's heart, who has made him known" (John 1:18) and "Not that anyone has seen the Father except the one who is from God; he has seen the Father" (John 6:46).

One would assume that both Paul and John were to some extent familiar with the Books of the Old Testament in which many cases of purported seeing of God are reported. Did they consider those stories false? Or did they believe that the seeing was not actual, but perhaps symbolic? Below are a few instances in which God is portrayed as visible to human beings.

Did Jacob Wrestle with God?

Jacob did not only allegedly see God but wrestled with him! There is a weird account of a physical wrestling encounter between Jacob and God; and God did not prevail! Yes, Jacob was reported to have wrestled with God for hours at night and as God was not winning, He struck Jacob on the hip socket putting his hip out of joint (Genesis 32:22-32). The wrestling continued until the day was breaking at which time God pleaded with Jacob to let Him go. This is the conversation that followed:

> But Jacob said, "I will not let you go, unless you bless me." So he said to him, "What is your name?" And he said, "Jacob." Then the man said, "You shall no longer be called Jacob, but Israel, for you have striven with God and with humans, and have prevailed." Then Jacob asked him, "Please tell me your name." But he said, "Why is it that you ask my name?" And there he blessed him. So Jacob called the place Peniel, saying, "For I have seen God face to face, and yet my life is preserved." The sun rose upon him as he passed Peniel, limping because of his hip. Therefore to this day the Israelites do not eat the thigh muscle that is on the hip socket, because he struck Jacob on the hip socket at the thigh muscle. (Genesis 32:26-32, New Revised Standard Version).

What should one make of this story? Can it be literally true? *The New Jerusalem Bible* (the 1985 Standard Edition) comments as follows: "This enigmatic story speaks of a physical struggle, a wrestling with God from which Jacob seems to emerge victor. Jacob recognizes the supernatural character of his adversary, and extorts a blessing from him. The text, however, avoids using the name of Yahweh and the unknown antagonist will not give his name."

In the story, a human being not only saw God, he engaged God in combat. Is it possible that there are people who actually believe that the story is literally true? Its admission into Scripture certainly contributes to the all too human and wrong conception of God that some people have and are bound to have if they believe that all the stories in the Bible are literally true. This implies a conception of God, which can only be described as ridiculous. It would be reasonable to suppose that either the encounter did not take place at all or that Jacob simply misidentified his adversary.

Did Moses and the Elders of Israel See the God of Israel?

At God's invitation, Moses and some Elders of Israel went to meet Him. "Then Moses and Aaron, Nadab, and Abihu, and seventy of the elders of Israel went up, *and they saw the God of Israel.* Under his feet there was something like a pavement of sapphire stone, like the very heaven for clearness. God did not lay his hand on the chief men of the people of Israel; also they beheld God, and they ate and drank." (Exodus 24:9-11, NRSV, italics added).

It is reported in Chapter 33 of Exodus that God routinely visited Moses in the tent which Moses had set up near the camp of the Israelites. In the process, God used to speak to Moses "face to face, as one speaks to a friend." Five of the pertinent verses (7-11) read as follows:

> Now Moses used to take the tent and pitch it outside the camp, far off from the camp; he called it the tent of meeting. And everyone who sought the LORD would go out to the tent of meeting, which was outside the camp. Whenever Moses went out to the tent, all the people would rise and stand, each of them, at the entrance of their tents and watch Moses until he had gone into the tent. When Moses entered the tent, the pillar of cloud would descend and stand at the entrance of the tent, and the LORD would speak with Moses. When all the people saw the pillar of cloud standing at the entrance of the tent, all the people would rise and bow down, all of them, at the entrance of their tent. *Thus the LORD used to speak to Moses face to face, as one speaks to a friend*. Then he would return to the camp; but his young assistant, Joshua son of Nun, would not leave the tent (NRSV, italics added).

But this story is contradicted in the same Chapter 33 of Exodus. It is reported at verses 20-23 that God told Moses that he could not see His face because no one could see His face and live. In other words, to see His face was to commit suicide! God said He would allow Moses to see only His back. This is the same Moses who, we are told, spoke with God face to face as one speaks to a friend (Exodus 33:11). The contradiction is reproduced below from both the New Revised Standard Version (NRSV) and the New Living Translation:

> "But", he (the Lord) said, "you cannot see my face; for no one shall see me and live." And the LORD continued, "See, there is a place by me where you shall stand on the rock;

and while my glory passes by I will put you in a cleft of the rock, and I will cover you with my hand until I have passed by; then I will take away my hand, and you shall see my back; but my face shall not be seen." (Exodus 33:20-23, NRSV).

But you may not look directly at my face, for no one may see me and live." The LORD continued, "Look, stand near me on this rock. As my glorious presence passes by, I will hide you in the crevice of the rock and cover you with my hand until I have passed by. Then I will remove my hand and let you see me from behind. But my face will not be seen. (Exodus 33:20-23, New Living Translation).

In addition to Moses reportedly speaking with the Lord face to face as one speaks with a friend, we are also told that Moses and a group of seventy elders of Israel had seen God on the Mountain. Moses and the elders did live! These inconsistencies leave one confused. Can we see God? The answer in the New Testament is *No*; only Jesus who came from Him can. In the Old Testament it is both *Yes* (Moses as well as the Elders did) and *No* (for whoever sees Him would die).

The truth is that God cannot possibly be on earth; therefore, there is no question of an earthman seeing Him. Even those who have existed in the Divine Realm since eternity can only see Him when He transforms Himself by wearing a cloak of the Divine essence. And as stated in an earlier Chapter, what might pass for the nearest vicinity of God is like an ocean of flames, which means that no one can get near Him except the ones who are part of the Godhead – Jesus, the Love of God and the Holy Spirit, the Executive Will of God as I will discuss in Chapter 14. But as human spirits, we do carry the endowment to recognize God in His works.

It should really be clear to us as it was to King Solomon that God cannot possibly dwell on earth and therefore cannot be seen. Were the authors of those stories simply writing fiction and was Moses lying? What could have been happening? I would assume that Moses was not making up the stories about his communications and visions of God. But it was certainly not God that he was in direct communication with and it was not God that he and others saw.

Mysterious Communications

Moses might have had regular contacts with a 'high being' permitted by God to help him in his calling to liberate the people of Israel from their Egyptian bondage and to set them on the path of spiritual development. Other invisible servants of God might have been assigned to help him at different times. In other words, the seeing was not of God and would not have been with the physical eyes, neither was the communication with the physical organs. The incidents described were most probably visions and were subject to misinterpretations with respect to the personalities involved.

To dismiss this interpretation of events as mere superstition would be narrow-minded. Consider the relatively recent development of the technology of GPS navigation systems that help vehicle drivers to get from point A to point B, some of them with features such as audible driving directions, spoken street names, and real-time traffic updates. It is conceivable that there are mechanisms in Creation that are analogous and which could have been applied in special circumstances like those of Moses and some other prophets. The idea of GPS navigation systems with their current capabilities would have been inconceivable a few decades ago. It should also be noted that in communicating with invisible beings, the matter of fidelity also comes into play.

The person on earth may not receive what is communicated accurately, may misunderstand or misinterpret it, and may not know the source.

I have heard the story of a man who in the mid-1960s had for a long time been prayerfully seeking the truths of life. He had examined various religious and spiritual teachings and was an active member of his church but these did not satisfy him; they did not give him conviction. One day while he was in London, he heard a clear voice which directed him to a bookshop where he was told he would find what he had been seeking. He got there and found a book that transformed his life, quenched his spiritual thirst, and gave him immeasurable conviction about the Will of God and the purpose of his own life. That book determined the course of his life until his physical death about 30 years later.

One famous Nigerian playwright, singer, and stage director and owner of a travelling theatre told me how he came about two of his most well-known plays. At the time he was advanced in years, had retired, and had nothing to prove to me or to anyone else. Moreover, he was well-known for his impeccable integrity. He said he had been working for a long time on one of his earliest plays, which subsequently brought him into the limelight. He was having difficulty with his intended theme song as well as the costumes. One day while staying at a hotel, he had gone late for breakfast and was alone at the dining room. All of a sudden he started hearing a song as if through earpieces and at the same time was seeing a stage with actors wearing costumes. It was quite brief but in that very short time, he had 'received' all he needed to complete the play that became a great hit.

He told me that, later in life, he had written another play responding to a particular socio-political crisis but was unable to come up with a good tune for the song he had written. While travelling in a car in the company of his wife, he suddenly could hear a song, again as if through earpieces. He requested that the car be stopped so he could write the tune he was hearing. Of course, neither the driver nor the wife heard anything or knew what was happening. But as the car stopped the wife, who was an actress and loved singing, started singing aloud one of her favourite songs. At that point, the song that the playwright was hearing was cut off. It was not until two months later while he was alone in another city that the same tune came back. And the song was another hit; so also was the play.

The playwright told me that he frankly did not understand how the phenomena came about; neither did he know the source. And the phenomena were certainly not something he could bring about at will; they just happened!

God Cannot Be an Accomplice in Deception and Lying

There is a story in the Bible (1 Kings Chapter 22, repeated almost verbatim in 2 Chronicles Chapter 18) which portrays God as one who could recruit members of his heavenly host to help trick a king to go to battle so that he might be killed (1 Kings 22: 1-38). One king of Israel wished to annex a place (Ramoth-Gilead) ruled by the king of Aram. When the king of Judah (Jehoshaphat) visited him, he requested Jehoshaphat to join him to wage war against the king of Aram. The king of Judah agreed provided God sanctioned the war. To ascertain God's wish in the matter, the king of Israel presented the case through his prophets. All the 400 prophets told him to go to war as God would grant him victory. To the question by the king of Judah if there was no other prophet, the king of Israel responded that there was Micaiah whom he hated because he always prophesied disaster, never anything favorable to him.

The king sent for Micaiah. The messenger informed Micaiah of what the other prophets had told the king. At first, Micaiah repeated what the other prophets had said but the king reminded him that he had made him to swear always to tell him nothing but the truth in the name of the Lord. Micaiah then told him that he saw Israel scattered and without a leader; in other words the king would die in battle. Micaiah explained how it came about that the other prophets were wrong in the following words (1 Kings 22:19-23; 2 Chronicles 18:18-22):

> Then Micaiah said, "Therefore hear the word of the LORD: I saw the LORD sitting on his throne, with all the host of heaven standing beside him to the right and to the left of him. And the LORD said, 'Who will entice Ahab, so that he may go up and fall at Ramoth-Gilead?' Then one said one thing, and another said another, until a spirit came forward and stood before the LORD, saying, 'I will entice him.' 'How?' the LORD asked him. He replied, 'I will go out and be a lying spirit in the mouth of all his prophets.' Then the LORD said, 'You are to entice him, and you shall succeed; go out and do it.' So you see, the LORD has put a lying spirit in the mouth of all these your prophets; the LORD has decreed disaster for you."

The king, of course, did not like the prophecy implied by Micaiah's vision. In anger he ordered that Micaiah be imprisoned and given reduced ration until he, the king, would return from the war. The war turned out as Micaiah had prophesied; the king was struck with an arrow and bled to death.

Let us note the significant points of the story: (1) Micaiah claimed to see God (presumably in a vision) sitting on his throne; (2) God sought volunteers among His host to entice King Ahab to wage war so that he might get killed; (3) the chosen volunteer said his strategy would be to act as a lying spirit in the mouth of all Ahab's prophets. God approved the strategy and assured the volunteer of success in enticing King Ahab to wage a war that would be fatal for him. Would God do such a thing? If God were to wish to get rid of a king, would He resort to a strategy of deception and lying? Would God have deceitful schemers among his servants? Does God personally intervene in human affairs in the manner implied in this story? No! This story is simply a case of Scripture presenting a false conception of God.

Reckless Murdering

An incident of reckless murdering, supposedly authorized by God and communicated by Moses, is reported in Exodus Chapter 32 as well as in Deuteronomy (9:6-29). Moses had gone up to the Mountain to receive the Ten Commandments and stayed there longer than the Israelites expected. They gave up on him and requested Aaron to give them a new leader in the form of a god. Aaron collected gold from them, melted the pieces and moulded the molten gold into an idol in the form of a calf for them to worship. God got to know and asked Moses to return to the camp immediately. God said He was angry and would destroy the Israelites and in their place make Moses and his descendants into a great nation. Moses pleaded with God who then changed His mind but said He would still send a plague upon them for making the gold idol.

When Moses arrived at the camp he found the Israelites dancing around the calf. He was so enraged that he threw down the two tablets of the Commandment at the foot of the Mountain and broke them. He melted the gold idol, ground it into fine powder and mixed it with water and made the people of Israel drink it! After asking Aaron for explanation, he concluded that the people had gotten out of control. The following passage (Exodus 32: 26-29) describes what followed:

So he stood at the entrance to the camp and shouted, "All of you who are on the LORD's side, come here and join me." And all the Levites gathered around him. Moses told them, "This is what the LORD, the God of Israel, says: Each of you, take your swords and go back and forth from one end of the camp to the other. Kill everyone – even your brothers, friends, and neighbors." The Levites obeyed Moses' command, and about 3,000 people died that day.

Then Moses told the Levites, "Today you have ordained yourselves for the service of the LORD, for you obeyed him even though it meant killing your own sons and brothers. Today you have earned a blessing."

Could the true God really have authorized the Levites' murderous rampage involving the deaths of 3,000 people and rewarded the murderers by consecrating them into His service? In today's world, those Levites would qualify as the most detestable religious terrorists and dangerous enemies of society. And anyone who would obey a command to engage in reckless murdering must be inwardly dead and should no longer be regarded as human. Such a person would not deserve appointment into public service, much less consecrated into the service of the true God.

It is hard to tell if such large-scale killings of brothers, friends, and neighbors actually took place. If the event actually happened, the god implicated would not be the true God. God would not authorize such heinous crime just to stop people from worshipping an idol. We should bear in mind the fact that one of the Commandments in the stone tablets that God had given to Moses was "Thou shalt not kill." Yet right on arrival from the Mountain, Moses commanded the Levites to go on a killing rampage.

At a later date, as the Israelites were about to cross the Jordan river, Moses recalled the incident of the golden calf, how it provoked the anger of God, and how he (Moses) had to fast for forty days and forty nights to beg God not to destroy the people of Israel. The recollection by Moses in Deuteronomy (9:8-21) did *not* mention the reckless murders by the Levites and gave a different account of what he did with the ground and powdered golden calf. Moses said that he "threw its dust into the stream that comes down from the mountain" (Deuteronomy 9:21); he did not make the Israelites drink it as reported in Exodus (32:20). Did the Levites murder 3,000 people? Did Moses fast for forty days and nights in order to appease God for the sin of the golden calf as he recalled in Deuteronomy but obviously did not in the account in Exodus? Did he compel the Israelites to drink the water contaminated with the golden calf that had been ground into powder or did he throw the powdered golden calf into the stream? These inconsistencies cast doubt on the alleged murderous rampage, which at any rate could not have been desired by the true God.

In Deuteronomy Chapter 9, Moses reminded the people of Israel of some of their past sins and stated that from the very day they left Egypt until they arrived at the Jordan, they had been rebels against God. He told them that they would take possession of the land of the Anakites (and the lands of other nations) that they were about to encounter not because of any right behaviour or uprightness on their part but because of the wickedness of those nations and also to keep the pact that God had made with Abraham, Isaac, and Jacob. "I will say it again: The Lord your God is not giving you this good land because you are righteous, for you are not – you are a stubborn people" (verse 6, New Living Translation). Why would God dispossess the lands of those nations because of their wickedness and give them to Israelites despite their serial sins? Would that not be inconsistent?

And this raises the issue of double standard and partiality. For example, Peter once declared: "Truly I perceive that God shows no partiality, but in every nation anyone who fears Him and does what is right is acceptable to Him (Acts 10: 34 - 35). The Apostle Paul made a similar point in several of his letters (see, for example, Romans 2: 9-11; Ephesians 6: 5-9; Colossians 3:25). He wrote: "There will be tribulation and distress for every human being who does evil, the Jew first and also the Greek, but glory and honor and peace for everyone who does good, the Jew first and also the Greek. For God shows no partiality" (Romans 2:9-11). God is indeed absolutely impartial. And God certainly does not kill people peremptorily because of a sin. He lets His perfect Laws take their course. He could not have ordered the Levites to go on a murderous rampage.

God and War Crimes in the Old Testament

The people of Israel were given rules of war outlining how they should prepare and those who should be excused from participation (Deuteronomy 20:1-18). It seemed rather easy for an individual to avoid military service. Excused were people who had built new houses but had not dedicated them; men who were engaged but not yet married; those who had planted vineyards but had not enjoyed the fruits; as well as "anyone afraid or disheartened." The priest was to assure them of victory "for it is the Lord your God who goes with you to fight for you against your enemies, to give you victory."

Before waging war, they were first to offer their adversaries terms of peace and if they accepted the terms, they should impose forced labour on them. But if the adversaries chose to fight and, if through the help of God, the enemies lost, all their males should be killed. They might, however, take the women, children, livestock and everything else as booty. "You may enjoy the spoil of your enemies, which the LORD your God has given you", stated the rules of war. Those actions applied to enemies living very far from them.

The reprisals were different for adversaries living in areas that God had promised them. "But in the cities of these peoples that the Lord your God gives you for an inheritance, you shall save alive nothing that breathes, but you shall utterly destroy them, the Hittites and the Amorites, the Canaanites and the Perizzites, the Hivites and the Jebusites, as the LORD your God has commanded; that they may not teach you to do according to all their abominable practices which they have done in the service of their gods, and so to sin against the LORD your God" (Deuteronomy 20:16-18, Revised Standard Version). This is a clear command to commit genocide. To think that God would command people to commit genocide is an absolutely false conception of God.

Defeat of King Sihon and King Og

Accounts of the defeat of King Sihon and King Og are narrated in Deuteronomy (2:24-35). At a point on their way to the Promised Land, the Lord told the people of Israel that he had handed over to them King Sihon and his land and that they should begin to take possession by engaging the King in battle. "This day, I will begin to put the dread and fear of you upon the peoples everywhere under heaven; when they hear report of you, they will tremble and be in anguish because of you" (verse 25). Thereafter, the Israelites, rather than threaten war, requested King Sihon to grant them safe passage, sell them food and water and let them pass through his land, promising not to stray from the road until they crossed the Jordan to the land that the Lord their God was giving them. But King Sihon was unwilling to let them pass through, "for the LORD your God had hardened his spirit and made his heart defiant in order to hand him over to you, as he has now done (verse 30.") King Sihon and his people engaged the Israelites in battle and the King was struck down, "along with his offspring and all his people. *"At that time we captured all his towns, and in each town we utterly destroyed men, women, and children.* We left not a single survivor. Only the livestock we kept as spoil for ourselves, as well as the plunder of the towns that we had captured" (verses 34-35, italics added).

This story alleges that God did not only authorize war crimes but prepared the way for it by hardening King Sihon's spirit and making him defiant. And the Israelites gleefully annihilated the men, women and children!

Another ancient kingdom suffered a fate similar to that of King Sihon and his people (Numbers 21:33-35; Deuteronomy 3:1-7). King Og of Bashan was geared to wage war against the Israelites when the Lord told Moses not to be afraid of him as He had handed the king with all his people and all his land to Moses. The Lord told Moses to deal with them as they had done with King Sihon. So the Israelites proceeded against King Og; the outcome is reported as follows:

> At that time we captured all his towns; there was no citadel that we did not take from them – sixty towns, the whole region of Argob, the kingdom of Og in Bashan. All these were fortress towns with high walls, double gates, and bars, besides a great many villages. *And we utterly destroyed them, as we had done to King Sihon of Heshbon, in each city utterly destroying men, women, and children.* But all the livestock and the plunder of the towns we kept as spoil for ourselves. (Deuteronomy 3:4-7, italics added).

The genocides committed against these two kings and their people came to be celebrated in liturgical hymns based on Psalms 135 and 136. "He struck down many nations and killed mighty kings - Sihon, king of the Amorites, and Og, king of Bashan, and all the kingdoms of Canaan —and gave their land as a heritage, a heritage to his people Israel" (Psalm 135:10-12). The whole of Psalm 136 recalls all what God had done for the people of Israel on account of God's steadfast love. One of the 'helps' is the genocide against the people of "famous kings" (verses 17-20).

Another case of genocide against the Amalekites and a subsequent brutal killing of their king Agag are narrated in the Book of Samuel (1 Samuel 15:1-33). The Lord sent Prophet Samuel to anoint Saul as king of the people of Israel and to let him know that He intended to punish the Amalekites for opposing the Israelites when they came out of Egypt. Saul was therefore to *"go and attack Amalek, and utterly destroy all that they have; do not spare them, but kill both man and woman, child and infant, ox and sheep, camel and donkey"* (verse 3, italics added). Saul amassed a large army and attacked the Amalekites and "utterly destroyed all the people." Prophet Samuel himself personally executed king Agag, who had been spared by Saul, and cut him into pieces.

There are numerous other instances of genocide committed by the Israelites supposedly in obedience to the instructions of God. Many were committed when Joshua was the leader. For example, the entire Chapter 10 of the Book of Joshua is the story of wars in which Prophet Joshua and his army committed war crimes, supposedly actively aided by God. It is an incredible account of multiple and most brutal war crimes. Fleeing enemies and their hiding kings were murdered. The recurrent statements in the chapter are "he utterly destroyed" and "he left no one remaining." Verse 40, for example, states: "So Joshua defeated the whole land, the hill country and the Negeb and the lowland and the slopes, and all their kings; he left no one remaining, but utterly destroyed all that breathed, as the LORD God of Israel commanded".

In one case, the battle between the Israelites and the Amorites was going well for Joshua and the army of the Amorites was crushed. The sun, however, began to set and the defeated Amorites would have the cover of darkness to escape genocide. Joshua took this concern to God, presumably in prayer. God appeared to answer Joshua's prayer; the sun stood still in the sky to allow Joshua more time to slaughter his enemies! This story cannot be wholly true. We know, for example, that God could not have made the sun to stand still against His own laws of nature, as stated in the account of the battle against the Amorites. It is simply impossible for the sun or any star to stand still; if it were to happen, the consequences would be unimaginable chaos and catastrophe, including the wholesale destruction of the earth with all its inhabitants.

All these cases of genocide, war crimes, and sheer brutality constitute blatant wrong portrayal of God and should be considered clear blasphemies of the true God. The correct conception of God must be sought beyond such Scripture.

God Misrepresented As Arbitrary

Some stories in the Bible misrepresent God as arbitrary in his actions. The story of Jacob and Esau is a case in point. Jacob and Esau were twin sons of Isaac and Rebecca and grandsons of the Patriarch Abraham. As told in the Old Testament, the story of Jacob and Esau is one of the bitterest of sibling rivalries, apparent favouritism, and injustice as well as despicable deception aided and abetted by a doting mother. The story raises many fundamental questions for those who wish to think aright about God. But first, let me summarize the story which is told in full in Genesis 25:19-34 and Genesis 27:1-45. Significant references are made to the story by the Prophet Malachi (1:2, 3) and by Apostle Paul (Romans 9:11, 14).

We are told that the struggle of the twins started from the womb and, perplexed by the struggle, the pregnant Rebecca 'took the matter to the Lord.' And the Lord reportedly said to her: "Two nations are in your womb, and two peoples, born of you, shall be divided; the one shall be stronger than the other, the elder shall serve the younger" (Genesis 25:23). Of the twins, Esau with red complexion and hairy body came first and Jacob with smooth body followed, holding Esau's heel. As they grew up, Esau turned out to be an outdoors person and a skilled hunter while Jacob "was a quiet man, dwelling in tents." Esau was beloved by the father "because he ate of his game; but Rebecca loved Jacob."

On one occasion, Esau was starving as he returned from the field. He requested Jacob to give him some of the pottage (thick soup) he was cooking. Jacob decided to take advantage of Esau's starvation and demanded that, in exchange for some pottage, Esau should surrender his birthright. The birthright, in practice, meant leadership of the family and a double share of the inheritance. Esau responded that the birthright was of no use to one dying from starvation as he was. Jacob asked Esau to swear to him that he agreed to give up his birthright and Esau did (Genesis 25: 29-34).

As Isaac got old and became blind, he sensed that the end of his days was near. He asked Esau to hunt game and use it to prepare his favorite meal so that he might enjoy it and bestow his last blessings on him. Rebecca, the mother, overheard the conversation and devised a scheme to ensure that Jacob, not Esau, got the father's last blessings. She asked Jacob to get two young goats from the flock so that she might prepare the food the father had requested from Esau. Jacob would then present the food to the father and would pretend that he was Esau. Jacob was at first reluctant fearing that the father might detect the deception as his skin was smooth whereas Esau was very hairy; in that event, Jacob feared that he would get a curse instead of blessing. Rebecca urged Jacob to do as she instructed and that any curse would be on her. She prepared the food, got Esau's best garments for Jacob to wear, and used the goat skins to cover Jacob's hands as well as the smooth part of his neck (Genesis 27:1-17).

Jacob presented the food to Isaac saying, "I am Esau your first-born. I have done as you told me; now sit up and eat of my game, that you may bless me." Isaac was suspicious as he did not expect Esau to find game and prepare the meal so soon. He asked: "How is it that you have found it so quickly, my son?" Jacob answered, "Because the Lord your God granted me success." Isaac asked him to come close so that he might feel him to know whether or not he was really Esau. Isaac felt Jacob's hands made hairy by the goat skin and said "The voice is Jacob's voice, but the hands are the hands of Esau." Isaac later also perceived the smell of the garments Jacob was wearing (which belonged to Esau) and was successfully deceived into thinking that Jacob was indeed Esau and so he blessed him. Soon after, the real Esau announced his arrival with the food. Isaac trembled violently and explained: "Your brother came with guile, and he has taken away your blessing" (Genesis 27:35). Esau remarked bitterly that Jacob had "supplanted" him two times: "He took away my birthright; and behold now he has taken away my blessing" (Genesis 27:36).

Many questions rush into the mind of a thoughtful reader of the story of Esau and Jacob. Is it a fable or a true story? Could it not be the case that the "two nations in Rebecca's womb" would live in peace and as equals cooperating with and helping each other instead of one serving the other? Was it the inevitable outcome of the characters of the two souls or the arbitrary decision of God? And why didn't Rebecca and Isaac pray for a better outcome? Why didn't Isaac simply bless both his twin sons, instead of inviting only one of them to receive his blessings? And why did he need to be cajoled with a special meal? What are we to make of Rebecca as a mother? What lessons are readers supposed to draw from this story?

In his reference to the story of Jacob and Esau, the Prophet Malachi wrote: "Is not Esau Jacob's brother?" says the Lord. "Yet I have loved Jacob but I have hated Esau; I have laid waste his hill country and left his heritage to jackals of the desert" Malachi (1:2-3). What did Esau do to deserve the hatred of God and how did the deceitful Jacob merit the Love of God? Is God, whose primary attribute is Love, capable of hating any person, especially one who has apparently done no wrong?

Rabbis at the beginning of the fifth century A.D. reflected on the story of Jacob and Esau. They were sure that God could not be unjust. Therefore, they thought that the only possible explanation for the different destinies of Jacob and Esau must be that Esau had sinned in the womb! According to Jacob Neusner (cited by Elizabeth Clare Prophet with Erin L. Prophet, *Reincarnation: The Missing Link in Christianity*, p.173) the Rabbis "conjectured that as Rebecca walked past 'houses of idolatry,' Esau indicated his preference by kicking, but 'when she went by synagogues and study-houses, Jacob would kick, trying to get out'." The Rabbis surmised that it was for those actions that God preferred Jacob over Esau and his descendants for generation after generation. The reasoning of the Rabbis seems rather fantastic and far-fetched. It is odd that anyone can believe that a fetus is capable of committing sin. But they were correct in their recognition that the true God is a God of Justice and that everyone is the architect of his/her fate. Belief in reincarnation would suggest that the different fates of Jacob and Esau would not be arbitrary assignments by God but the results of their actions in previous earth-lives (not actions in the womb).

The Apostle Paul puts the story of Jacob and Esau in a different context and raises a fundamental question about the nature of God. In his Letter to the Romans (9:10-21), he wrote:

> ... when Rebecca had conceived children by one man, our forefather Isaac, though they were not yet born and had done nothing either good or bad, in order that God's purpose of election might continue, not because of works but because of his call, she was told, "the elder will serve the younger." As it is written, "Jacob I loved, but Esau I hated."

> What shall we say then? Is there injustice on God's part? By no means! For he says to Moses, "I will have mercy on whom I have mercy, and I will have compassion on whom I have compassion." So it depends not upon man's will or exertion, but upon God's mercy. For the Scripture says to Pharaoh, "I have raised you up for the very purpose of showing my power in you, so that my name may be proclaimed in all the earth." So then He has mercy upon whomever He wills, and He hardens the heart of whomever He wills.

You will say to me then, "Why does He still find fault? For who can resist His will?" But who are you, a man, to answer back to God? Will what is moulded say to its moulder, "why have you made me thus?" Has the porter no right over the clay, to make out of the same lump one vessel for beauty and another for menial use?"

Paul says that there is no injustice on God's part. But rather than explain how justice is upheld in this story, he seems to be saying that in God's relations to His creatures, God acts as He pleases and without regard to human conceptions of fairness and justice. God deliberately makes Pharaoh wicked so that he enslaved the Israelis and subjected them to inhuman treatments, for God's own purpose (Exodus 9:15-16). The same God then turns around to punish Pharaoh and the Egyptians with plagues and deaths. Paul's comments also clearly make the case for the idea of predestination. He thinks that the Creator destines some human beings to be good and others to be bad. He predestines some people to be hard-hearted; yet He subjects such people to Judgment and condemns them to suffering, possibly to eternal death.

In these verses, Paul appears to believe that God is simply arbitrary in His actions. In his view, creatures are not entitled to question God and we should not ask for or expect justice from Him. This is a wrong portrayal of God. Paul's metaphor of the porter and the clay seems inappropriate. This is because clay is fundamentally quite different from human creatures that have consciousness and the ability to reason, to question and to make choices; God gave those abilities to us human creatures to be used for our spiritual and material development.

In his Second Letter to Timothy (2:20-21), Paul hints at a different explanation for the dissimilar fates of people. He wrote: "In a great house there are not only vessels of gold and silver but also of wood and earthenware, and some for noble use, some for ignoble. If anyone purifies himself from what is ignoble, then he will be a vessel for noble use, consecrated and useful to the master of the house, ready for any good work." Paul is here stating that whether or not one is made into a noble or ignoble vessel depends on one's own actions — whoever purifies himself can count on being made into a noble vessel and those who fail to purify themselves would be made into ignoble vessels. In other words, the vessel-maker is not arbitrary and is not unjust, contrary to what is implied in his Letter to the Romans (9:10-21).

The Koran in Sura III, verse 26 reproduced below makes a conceptually similar statement to that of Romans (9:10-21):

> "Say, O God, Owner of Sovereignty. You grant sovereignty to whom You will, and You strip sovereignty from whom you will. You honor whom you will, and You humiliate whom you will. In Your hand is all goodness. You are Capable of all things." (Translated into English by TALAL ITANI)

> "Say: O Allah! Lord of Power [And Rule], Thou givest power to whom Thou pleasest, and Thou strippest off power from whom Thou pleasest: Thou enduest with honour whom Thou pleasest, and Thou bringest low whom Thou pleasest: In Thy hand is all good. Verily, over all things Thou hast power." (Abdullah Yusuf Ali Translation)

This verse is often quoted as implying predestination. But it really should not be understood in the ordinary sense of predestination for that would imply that God acts arbitrarily. The right interpretation is in the sense that individuals and nations are the architects of their own fates (good or bad), in accordance with the Law of Sowing and Reaping. Part of verse 11 of Sura 13 affirms this interpretation: "Allah does not change a people's lot unless they change what is in their hearts." As a people change inwardly, their circumstances also change. God does not impose changes arbitrarily. One might note that predestination in Islamic doctrine is different from its popular conception. Thus, Afif A. Tabbarah states: "Through the doctrine of predestination, The Koran teaches believers that the universe has a well-planned system, providing laws harmonizing causes and effects and demonstrating that God's Creation is faultless and design-oriented" (*The Spirit of Islam: Doctrine and Teachings*, p. 100).

Let us return to Apostle Paul. I should remark that most Bible scholars do not believe that Paul is actually the author of the First and Second Letters to Timothy. Such scholars would, therefore, maintain that the statements of Second Timothy 2:20-21 do not represent Paul's position. However, Paul writing to the Galatians stated: "Do not be deceived; God is not mocked, for whatever a man sows, that he will also reap" (Galatians 6:7). This is a general principle which would have applied to both Jacob and Esau. Thus, contrary to what Paul says in Romans (9:10-21), their different fates would have been the fruits of their respective past sowings in previous existences.

Less than two centuries after Paul, Origen of Alexandria, acknowledged as the most learned as well as the most original thinker of the early Christian Fathers, commented on the story of Jacob and Esau. He argued that the only explanation for the different fates of Jacob and Esau was that they both had previous existences in which to earn God's "love" and "hatred". In his book, *On First Principles,* he wrote that we can believe that God is just only if we believe that Jacob was given preference in the womb as a result of his "merits in some previous life." Origen was convinced that this explanation applied to all cases of differences in the circumstances of birth. I should add that the teachings of Origen were condemned (anathematized) nearly 300 years after his death!

The biblical story of Jacob and Esau becomes clear and unproblematic if interpreted in the light of reincarnation. Both Jacob and Esau had lived before and during those earth-lives "sowed such different seeds" as would yield the different fruits they happened to harvest as twin sons of Isaac and Rebecca. Their acts of commission and omission in previous existences compelled their different fates. God did not favour Jacob arbitrarily, neither did He hate Esau; each of them was the architect of his own fate. Incidentally, reincarnation is one explanation for possible differences among twins, even physically identical twins.

Punishing Children for the Iniquity of Parents

Another biblical statement that portrays God as arbitrary is found in the first of the Ten Commandments given to mankind through Moses:

> ...For I the LORD your God am a jealous God, punishing children for the iniquity of parents, to the third and the fourth generation of those who reject me (Exodus 20:5, NRSV).

The same concept is to be found in the Book of Jeremiah (32:18): "You show steadfast love to the thousandth generation, but repay the guilt of parents into the laps of their children after them, O great and mighty God whose name is the LORD of hosts." I should first state that it is wrong to associate God with the human emotion of jealousy. And it is also the case that God does not *need* our worship; we worship Him only for our benefit. And obedience of God's commandments is solely for our benefit.

The idea that God would visit "the iniquity of the fathers upon the children to the third and the fourth generation" must have puzzled millions of thinking Christians. Why would a just God punish children, grandchildren, and great grandchildren for sins they did not commit but which were committed by their fathers, grandfathers, and great grandfathers? One hopes that no human being would seriously think that God is capable of such grotesque injustice. First, let us reassure ourselves that God has never punished, and will never punish a person for the sins of others, no matter how closely related such a person might be to the sinner; only the sinner may be punished for his or her own sin. In other books of the same Old Testament of the Bible, we find the following passages:

> The person who sins shall die. A child shall not suffer for the iniquity of a parent, nor a parent suffer for the iniquity of a child; the righteousness of the righteous shall be his own, and the wickedness of the wicked shall be his own" (Ezekiel 18:20).

> Parents shall not be put to death for their children, nor shall children be put to death for their parents; only for their own crimes may persons be put to death (Deuteronomy 24:16).

These last two passages are clear statements of the kind of justice with which we can identify God. And the two passages appear to be the exact opposite of the concept of "punishing children for the iniquity of parents, to the third and the fourth generation..." Surely, the Creator does not contradict Himself. As there are contradictions here, genuine seeking demands that one looks elsewhere for clarification. An understanding of the first of the Ten Commandments, which accords with the perfect Justice of God, takes into account the correct conception of reincarnation as explained in Stephen Lampe's *The Christian and Reincarnation*, pp. 135-142.

God and Slavery

Slavery is a moral evil that is naturally sensed and unequivocally condemned by civilized societies. To consider a human being as the personal property of another person is repugnant and abominable. But this is not the position one finds in the Bible. Some passages in the Old Testament acknowledge that to be a slave was not a good thing; hence the people of Israel were not permitted to hold fellow Israelites as slaves. But they were allowed to enslave others:

> The people of Israel are my servants, whom I brought out of the land of Egypt, so they must never be sold as slaves. Show your fear of God by not treating them harshly. However, you may purchase male and female slaves from among the nations around you. You may also purchase the children of temporary residents who live among you, including those who have been born in your land. You may treat them as your property, passing them on to your children as a permanent inheritance. You may treat them as slaves, but you must never treat your fellow Israelites this way (Leviticus, 25:42-46, New Living Translation).

There were, however, circumstances in which Israelites could be enslaved, as the following passage indicates: "A thief who is caught must pay in full for everything he stole. If he cannot pay, he must be sold as a slave to pay for his theft" (Exodus 22:3). Moreover, it was understood that a poor Israelite may sell himself and become a slave, even to a temporary foreign resident. There were specific regulations applicable to such cases. For example, there was this regulation: "If you buy a Hebrew slave, he may serve for no more than six years. Set him free in the seventh year, and he will owe you nothing for his freedom" (Exodus 21:2). It is fair to say that in the Old Testament, God was supposed to have given laws to promote kind treatment of slaves but the institution of slavery was accepted as a fact of life and there was no thought of abolishing it. The implication that God condones slavery is certainly a false conception.

The Apostle Paul stated his position on slavery in his Letters to the Ephesians (6:5-9), Colossians (3:22-25; 4:1), to Timothy (1 Timothy 2:1-3) and to Titus (2:9-10). His primary and consistent concern was that slaves should be completely obedient to their masters and serve them faithfully. He asked them to bear any suffering gallantly in the manner Jesus suffered for humankind. But they were never told to nurture any aspiration for freedom. Paul's Letters to the Ephesians and to Timothy are representative of his position.

> Slaves, obey your earthly masters with deep respect and fear. Serve them sincerely as you would serve Christ. Try to please them all the time, not just when they are watching you. As slaves of Christ, do the will of God with all your heart. Work with enthusiasm, as though you were working for the Lord rather than for people. Remember that the Lord will reward each one of us for the good we do, whether we are slaves or free.

> Masters, treat your slaves in the same way. Don't threaten them; remember, you both have the same Master in heaven, and he has no favourites. (Ephesians 6:5-9).

> All slaves should show full respect for their masters so they will not bring shame on the name of God and his teaching. If the masters are believers, that is no excuse for being disrespectful. Those slaves should work all the harder because their efforts are helping other believers who are well loved." (1 Timothy 6:1-2).

In other words, believers among slaves were to be satisfied with and embrace their slave status in order to please God. In none of his letters did Paul hint at the inherent evil of slavery, neither did he inform believing slave-owners that slavery did not accord with the teachings of Jesus, the personification of love. Thus, Paul did not suggest to slave-owners, even those among them who were supposed to believe in Jesus, that they ought to free their slaves.

Apostle Peter's position is practically identical with that of Paul. He wrote:

> You who are slaves must accept the authority of your masters with all respect. Do what they tell you — not only if they are kind and reasonable, but even if they are cruel. For God is pleased with you when you do what you know is right and patiently endure unfair treatment. Of course, you get no credit for being patient if you are beaten for doing wrong. But if you suffer for doing good and endure it patiently, God is pleased with you. For God called you to do good, even if it means suffering, just as Christ suffered for you. He is your example, and you must follow in his steps (1 Peter 2:18-21).

Thus, we find that the New Testament, like the Old, portrays God as if He does not consider slavery an evil that should be roundly condemned and abolished. Paul and Peter in their writings often addressed believers as 'brothers and sisters' and they were supposed to love one another as such. Yet it did not occur to these Apostles that it was particularly odious to hold fellow brothers and sisters as slaves. It is no wonder that people of the 'Bible Belt' of the United States were the most unrepentant slave owners and opponents of civil rights. Indeed, people are brothers and sisters on account of their common spiritual origin. As human spirits, they should never be treated as chattels without a will of their own. Given that God endows human beings with Free Will, which they should constantly exercise, slavery is unnatural. And no one should encourage others to be loyal slaves as Paul and Peter did; it is a case of wrong portrayal of the Will of God.

Abraham Commanded to Slaughter His Son

In the Old Testament Bible as well as in the Koran, Abraham is reported to have been subjected to an extreme test of faith by God. God asked him (presumably in a vision) to go and offer his son as a burnt offering on a mountain in Moriah. Abraham loyally took his son to the mountain, built an altar, bound the son and was about to slaughter him as sacrifice when an angel suddenly appeared and stopped him. At that point Abraham sighted a ram whose horns were caught in a thicket; he substituted the ram for his son as burnt offering. Abraham had passed the test and as a reward, God blessed him and promised as follows: "I will make your offspring as numerous as the stars of heaven and as the sand that is on the seashore. And your offspring shall possess the gate of their enemies, and by your offspring shall all the nations of the earth gain blessing for themselves, because you have obeyed my voice."

The Biblical account (Genesis 22:1-18) names the son as Isaac who is described by God as Abraham's only son whom he loved. The account in the Koran (37:99-112) does not give the name of the son but Muslims believe it was Ishmael not Isaac. Ishmael was indeed the first son, born by Hagar who was Sarah's servant. As Sarah, Abraham's wife, could not bear any children, she encouraged the husband to have one through her maid Hagar. Hagar gave birth to Ishmael and thirteen years later Sarah was able to give birth to Isaac. Subsequently, Sarah could no longer stand Hagar and urged Abraham to send her and her child away. Abraham agreed and banished both Hagar and Ishmael into the desert, where they might have died had they not received unexpected help. The Muslim position regarding who the intended "sacrificial son" was is understandable; Ishmael is considered the forefather of the Arabs. The story of the testing of Abraham's loyalty and submission to God's Will is commemorated annually at Eid al-Adha or Festival (Feast) of Sacrifice by Muslims.

Let's reflect on this story as it relates to portrayal of God. Would the true God need to test a man's faith? Wouldn't He know whether or not a person was faithful through his or her everyday thoughts, words, and actions? It seems to me that it would take the most insecure dictator to subject a person to such an extreme and unnatural test of loyalty. Why would God, who commands us not to kill, demand human sacrifice? Some might say that it was only later that God gave the commandments through Moses, implying that the commandment against killing was not valid at the time of Abraham. But that would not be true. The commandments of God and the Will of God do not change; they have been the same since the beginning of Creation.

Even though Abraham did not go through with the murder, we should note that his son, who had been bound and readied for slaughter, must have been thoroughly traumatized. The Koran, however, indicates that Abraham discussed his vision with his son and the son agreed to be sacrificed! Let it be said that God absolutely does not need burnt offerings, whether human or animal. Indeed, God is fully independent and complete; He needs absolutely nothing. What He expects of us are simply what will help *us* to achieve our goal of spiritual development and ascent to our original home in the spiritual part of Creation. And in general, God's commandments are not about His needs (for he has none) but about our own well-being!

It seems to me that the story of Abraham's attempted sacrifice of his son originated from the primitive culture of animal and human sacrifices of ancient times. The incontrovertible truth is that we should never commit a crime in a deluded attempt to be pleasing to God; the end never justifies the means. God does not need anybody's fanatical expression of faith and would not demand proof of such faith.

It is a pity that the idea that God would demand that a father kill his son to demonstrate faith is believed by so many religious people. But in a sense this is not surprising. A key tenet of the Christian faith is the idea that God sent His son Jesus to the world so that he would be killed by men, as sacrificial lamb, in order that the same God might agree to wipe away the sins of men. This is despite the fact that one of God's standing commandments is that men must not kill. The belief amounts to God saying: "Human beings on earth have wronged me and I will not forgive them. But I will send my son to them so that they may kill him and thereby shed his blood. The shedding of my son's blood will please me and I will then wipe away their sins." Of course, that does not make sense either in consideration of love or of justice or of ordinary fatherly responsibility. Jesus came to the world to bring the *knowledge* about the true Will of God, which brings salvation and the forgiveness of all sins to those who *understand and do* the Will. Because the doctrine of sacrificial death is patently nonsensical, people speak of divine mystery. But it is not mystery; it is simply a wrong and bad doctrine.

Living in accordance with the true Will of God as taught by Jesus and other prophets is the only path to salvation. If Christ were to renounce or denounce His own teachings, His life might have been spared. That He did not do so is confirmation of the utmost importance of His teachings, a demonstration of His love for humanity and proof of the Divine Love that He personified. But much of His teachings were misunderstood and/or distorted. Hence He spoke of the coming of the Spirit of Truth.

Dr. Walter R. Matthews (1881-1973) was a highly influential British theologian and philosopher, who was Chaplain to the King, Dean of King's College, London, Canon Theologian of Liverpool, and Preacher to the Honourable Society of Gray's Inn. In his 1930 book, *God in Christian Thought and Experience*, he wrote: "It is my own opinion that the present period of intellectual development will rank in history as one of the most important and that it will be found that even the confusions of the mind of the age contained the germs of a great advance in insight. *In any case, the Christian idea of God is scarcely likely to be the creed of the future if its defenders feel obliged to ignore or minimize every acquisition of new knowledge*" (pp. 111-112, italics added).

We do ourselves and others a great disservice and we unwittingly commit blasphemy if we allow ourselves to be stuck in the contradictory and unclear ancient conceptions of God encountered in the Scriptures.

9 God is Unlike Human Beings

A common misconception about God is the tendency to think about Him as if He were a human being who happens to be the most perfect, most ideal, and loftiest of the human type. For a person who truly understands that God is the Creator and that we humans are mere creatures, it should be easy to appreciate that such a conception cannot be correct. Consider a creative artist and her work. Even though, a close study of her work may permit one to say something about the artist, we know that the artist is quite different and distinct from her art. If the art is destroyed for one reason or the other, the artist is not thereby demeaned, since she probably has other pieces and, moreover, she can create new pieces. It is also self-evident that a piece of art cannot describe its own creator.

The creative artist and his work faintly reflect the relation of God to Creation. If we think of Creation as a work of art of God, human beings would be only a minuscule element of that art. And that puts us in the position to which we belong in relation to God. This is not generally made quite clear in the Scriptures, obviously because an overview of the structure of Creation was not known. On the contrary, God is frequently portrayed in the Scriptures as if He were a fellow human being.

Old Testament scholars have identified in the Book of Isaiah the work of at least three different authors. One of them wrote Chapters 1-39 in the eighth century BC, another wrote Chapters 40-55 in the late sixth century and the third wrote

Chapters 56-66 in the late fifth century BC. Whoever was the actual author of Isaiah Chapter 55 sensed correctly that God was unlike human beings, for he wrote:

> For my thoughts are not your thoughts, nor are your ways my ways, says the LORD. For as the heavens are higher than the earth, so are my ways higher than your ways and my thoughts than your thoughts. (Isaiah 55: 8-9).

God is Not a Spirit

In outlining the structure of Creation (Chapter 5), I indicated that God, as the Creator, is outside Creation and, therefore, utterly alien to the human species. Any suggestion that human beings have anything of the nature of God is wrong. This is the reason why human language and human intellectual faculties are so inadequate when we think and speak about Him. To all His creatures, which include human beings, He is without form and thus defies description. It is presumably in this understanding that the Bible and the Koran tell us not to make pictures or "carven images" of the Creator. Such pictures or images would quite simply be wrong and would certainly demean the true conception of the Creator.

We noted that human beings on earth originated from the spiritual part of Creation that came into being subsequent to the Creation of the Primordial Spiritual Realm. Thus, human beings are properly called spirits because they have their origin in the Spiritual Realm, below the Primordial Spiritual Realm. Since God is *not* in Creation but outside of it, it follows that God is *not* spirit.

A statement which appears to contradict the fact that God is not a spirit occurs in the account of a conversation between Jesus and a Samaritan woman at Jacob's well (John 4:1-42, especially verses 19-26). The disciples had gone away to buy food and

Jesus was alone at the well when the Samaritan woman came to fetch water. Thus, the disciples were not eyewitnesses to the conversation. Jesus asked the woman to give him water to drink but the woman wondered why a Jew would make such a request to a Samaritan given the taboos in the traditional relationship between Jews and Samaritans. Jesus responded that if she knew who He was, she would plead with Him for the living water which quenches thirst for eternity. At that point, the woman sensed that Jesus was a prophet and wanted to be enlightened about the worship of God. She raised the issue of the Samaritan belief that the worship of God should be at Mount Gerizim while Jews believed that it should be done in Jerusalem. The response of Jesus was that the time would come and, indeed, had come when the place of worship would no longer be an issue. True worshippers would have to worship God in "spirit and truth" as God desired:

> But the hour is coming, and is now here, when the true worshipers will worship the Father in spirit and truth, for the Father seeks such as these to worship him. God is spirit, and those who worship him must worship in spirit and truth (John:23-24, New Revised Standard Version).

> But the time is coming and is already here, when by the power of God's Spirit people will worship the Father as he really is, offering him the true worship that he wants. God is Spirit, and only by the power of his Spirit can people worship him as he really is (verses 23-24, Good News Translation).

In the discussion of the progressive revelation of God (Chapter 3), I mentioned the *Forerunner Book Series* as invaluable new sources of information on the lives and teachings of past Truth Bringers. One of the Books in the Series is *Past Eras Awaken* Volume III, which is in two parts. The first chapter of Part Two (pages 191-269) is entitled "Unknown Events from the Life of Jesus, The Son of God." One of the events included is the encounter of Jesus with the Samaritan woman at Jacob's well, near Shechem (pp. 226-229). It is much more detailed than the account in the Gospel of John. On meeting Jesus, she enquired if the men (the disciples) she met going towards Shechem were His companions. Jesus confirmed that they were. She observed that they must be Jews and remarked that Jesus did not look like a Jew. It turned out that she hesitated to give Jesus water to drink only out of concern for Jesus not to violate Jewish regulations unwittingly, with respect to dealings with Samaritans; she did not want to be responsible for somebody else's wrongdoing.

Jesus told her pleasantly: "If you knew who I am, you would ask *me* for water. And I would give you of the eternally-sparkling Fount of Life, so that you would never again thirst." For a moment the woman wondered what the stranger was talking about. Then, "suddenly she discerned a clear light surrounding the whole figure of Jesus and rays, which emanating from His eyes, seemed to penetrate her soul. Now she knew that Jesus had not spoken of earthly water. In tremulous tones she begged, 'Sire, give me of the Water, that the never-ending thirst of my soul may at last be quenched!'" Jesus responded by asking her to go and bring her husband. The Samaritan woman confessed that she had had five husbands and the man she was living with presently was not her husband but one she was taking care of out of love because he was critically ill. Jesus, calmly and without condemnation or rebuke, told her: "You have spoken the truth. I knew it." The woman for the first time started narrating all the oppressive guilt of her life, disclosing everything that had tormented and preoccupied her for as long as she could remember.

Concluding, she said: "Sire, I know that you are a Prophet of the Most High. Help me! Where can I find God? I seek Him, but I do not find Him. You Jews declare that He must be worshipped in Jerusalem in the Temple; it is there that He reveals Himself. Our forefathers taught us to seek Him on this mountain. Nowhere have I found Him. Sire, good sire, help me!"

Jesus was deeply moved as never before had He encountered such genuine seeking on the part of a human being. As the woman gazed at Jesus with beseeching eyes, aglow with expectation, Jesus turned to her and said:

> God is not visible to human eyes. He who would worship Him must seek Him beyond this World of Matter. He must search in his own soul, for only in spirit is he able to reach upward for a faint perception of God. That, you must first learn again, you human beings. (*Past Eras Awaken*, Vol. III, p. 228)

This is the statement of Jesus that is recast in John 4:24. Apparently, Jesus did *not* say that God is Spirit. By the expression, "God is Spirit", John in that passage of his Gospel pointed to the fact that God is non-physical, and, therefore, human beings who wish to worship Him must do so with the non-physical element in them (the spirit). At that time, the structure of Creation had not yet been revealed – that knowledge would be one of the tasks of the Spirit of Truth (a personality). "Spirit" was thus the loftiest term that human beings could conceive; it was, therefore, understandable that it would be applied to God. On the Spirit of Truth, the same John reported Jesus as saying (John 16: 12-15):

> I still have many things to say to you, but you cannot bear them now. When the Spirit of truth comes, he will guide you into all the truth; for he will not speak on his own, but will speak whatever he hears, and he will declare to you the things that are to come. He will glorify me, because

he will take what is mine and declare it to you. All that the Father has is mine. For this reason I said that he will take what is mine and declare it to you. (New Revised Standard Version)

I still have many things to say to you, but they would be too much for you to bear now. However, when the Spirit of truth comes he will lead you to the complete truth, since he will not be speaking of his own accord, but will say only what he has been told; and he will reveal to you the things to come. He will glorify me, since all he reveals to you will be taken from what is mine. Everything the Father has is mine; that is why I said: all he reveals to you will be taken from what is mine. (The New Jerusalem Bible)

Jesus later told his disciples about the encounter with the Samaritan woman. And subsequently, crowds of people from Shechem came to see Jesus whom the woman recognized as the Messiah. Jesus remarked that the people came to Him neither out of curiosity nor the desire to witness miracles. They were prompted by the desire for the salvation of their souls. At the request of the Samaritans, Jesus remained in their midst for two days. He said to his disciples: "Behold, now will salvation be taken from the Jews and made available to all people. Henceforth all who seek me shall be allowed to come to me. Later on, you will reap more abundantly among the Gentiles where you have not sown, than among the Jews where all the sowing was in vain." (*Past Eras Awaken* Volume III, p. 229).

The Protestant Mystic
The book *Modern Mystics* was written in 1935 by Sir Francis Younghusband, a British army officer, explorer, guru, and mystic whose travels mainly in northern India and Tibet made

major contributions to geographical research. *Modern Mystics* describes in separate chapters the lives and mystical experiences of people of diverse backgrounds: Hindu mystics; Muslim mystics; a Roman Catholic mystic; a Protestant Mystic; and of Mass mysticism in Wales.

Of particular interest to me is Chapter 4 which narrates the mystical experience of a self-effacing English lady who grew up in an ordinary Protestant family. She suffered intensely partly because of the absence of her husband during the First World War. She prayed to God incessantly and fervently. Finally, she began to have overpowering spiritual experiences, which she eventually published anonymously. Over a period of years she had visions of the Beyond, which she described as 'celestial living.' In this celestial living are:

> "happenings which cannot be communicated, or even indicated to others, because they reach beyond words, beyond all other experiences, beyond all particularization, beyond any possible previous imagination..."

She said that as a little girl, she believed in God with complete faith and when she shut her eyes she thought she saw God very plainly: "He was a white figure in white robes, on a white throne amongst the clouds."

When in her vision, she experienced God, she found that God was no Figure at all, no concrete Object, no Form. She wrote: "It cannot possibly be said that in ecstasy we see God; it is a question of 'knowing' Him through the higher part of the soul in lesser or in deeper degrees." She emphasized that she did not see God but experienced Him.

Asked if God does not feel like a fire, she said:

> Yes, and no, for we feel we shall be consumed, and yet it is not a burning which is experienced, but a blissful energy of the most inexpressible and unbearable intensity, which seems to disintegrate or disperse the flesh. So long as this is given with certain limits the experience is blissful to heart and mind. Beyond that limit is a bliss-agony. Beyond that again, it would soon be death to the body – a very terrible feeling, which does not bear remembering or thinking about (pp. 204- 205).

She commented that the value to him to whom the experience is granted is that "it raises him above faith into certitude." She remarked on the difficulty of communicating her experiences of the Beyond with an illustration. Suppose you put a blade of grass and a leaf of a tree in the hand of a man born blind and you say to him 'This is grass, and this is a leaf, and both are green.' "And what," the blind man asks, "is green?" If your life depended on it, you could not make him know what it is. She concluded that God, who can neither be seen, nor heard, nor touched, cannot be made known to another. "God must be experienced to be known." This implies that to *prove* the existence of God is pointless and fruitless.

Limitations of Human Language

We should also note that human languages are too limited to transmit even relatively simple revelations about the Creator. For example, we commonly refer to the Creator, God, using the masculine pronoun. This is simply because our languages do not permit us readily to think in terms of a genderless condition and so there is no word in common usage for any genderless being. It would be erroneous to imagine that the Creator has the form of a human male. We have already explained in the Chapter on

"Creation and Subsequent Creation" (Chapter 5) that God has no form that can be conceived by human beings or any creature. To show Himself to the beings of the Divine Realm, God must first clothe Himself in Divine essence. It is only when God is clothed in the Divine essence that those dwelling in the Divine Realm can to a limited degree see Him. The expression "image of God" refers to this Divinely-clothed form. And it is in the image of that form that the Primordial Spiritual Beings were created. But those dwelling in regions lower than the Divine Realm, such as those in Spiritual Creation, are not able to see Him even in that Divinely-clothed form in which He shows Himself to those dwelling in the Divine. And being formless, one cannot think of God in gender terms. It follows that the attribution of human features or qualities to the Creator (anthropomorphism) is erroneous but somewhat inevitable.

I stated in Chapter 5 that the fact that God is higher than the Divine means that to say that God is Divine is wrong. The Divine is substantiate (dependent); God is *unsubstantiate* (independent). Therefore, God is not Divine; God is God! Let me expatiate. It is, indeed, correct to *associate* "Divine" and "Divinity" with God. However, it is *wrong* to say that God is Divine, as I will proceed to show. "Divine" and "Divinity" are best described with reference to the great basic structure of the whole of existence, which may be envisaged as consisting of two parts: the first, which is the origin of everything, is God and the second part is everything else. God alone is Primordial Light and everything else is a direct or indirect consequence of the radiation of God. Before Creation came into existence, the natural radiation of God resulted in the sphere of existence known as the Divine Sphere. Thus, the Divine Sphere is the sphere of the immediate radiation of God and it surpasses by far the magnitudes of all the combined parts of Creation. The Divine Sphere has, like God, always existed and will always exist, because of the inevitable and unceasing radiation of God.

To further differentiate between God and the Divine, I should state that whereas God is without a form conceivable to us and to any creature, the Divine Sphere and its inhabitants can all be conceived as having forms. Whereas God is wholly autonomous and independent, the Divine Sphere and its inhabitants (that is everything which is Divine) depend completely on God. When we leave out God and all that is Divine, we are left with the rest of existence that can be properly called products of Creation because they came into being only at a particular point in time, with the fiat "Let there be Light!" We may, therefore, extend our two-part description of existence to three parts, namely: God; the Divine Sphere; and Creation/ Subsequent Creation. It follows from these explanations, that God is not Divine, for only what exists within the Divine Sphere can be described as Divine.

It is a fact that, even today, we are compelled to use what might be called 'verbal images' when we communicate about God. But we should understand that really and truly, God is 'wholly other', as theologians would put it; He is completely different from us and from anything we know. We are compelled to use verbal images only because we must speak about God and within the limitations of our human languages. We should always, however, advise ourselves that God does not have human nature and that human beings do not have the attributes of God.

Some people have suggested that the misconception that human beings have something in common with God arose from the Biblical passage in the first of the two accounts of the story of Creation, "Let us make man in our image, after our likeness..." (Genesis 1:26). The truth is that the Genesis story of Creation is not to be taken literally and does not refer to our physical world. Therefore, we should not be guided by a literal interpretation of that verse. To underscore this fact, let us note that there are two different accounts of the story of Creation in Genesis. In the first account, God created man "male and female" as the last of the creatures (Genesis 1:27), whereas in the second account, "the Lord God formed man of dust from the ground and breathed into his nostrils the breath of life…" (Genesis 2:7). In the second account man (male) was created as the first of the creatures but the female was not created along with the man. The female was only formed later from the rib taken from the man while he was in deep sleep (Genesis 2:21-22). Which is which? Were male and female simultaneously created or was the female later formed from the rib of the male? The real Act of Creation did not take place on earth but at the highest heights at the summit of Creation, mentioned in Chapter 5.

Because of our own nature as creatures and the limitations of human languages, we are not able to describe the nature of God; He is wholly unlike anything we know or can know. However, this does not mean that we cannot experience the reality of God. Our preoccupation should be to continually enhance our understanding of His Will and how it relates to particular situations. And we should strive to think, speak, and act in accordance with God's Will. In practice that is all we need do to accomplish the purpose of our existence.

A Benedictine monk, Dom Hubert van Zeller (1905-1984) in his book, *Prayer and the Will of God*, cautioned against thinking about God in terms that are too human. Specifically, he wrote that we should not think of Him as a stern parent who is likely to get angry, who has to be kept in a good mood, whose children have to walk on tiptoe and sit up straight. Neither should we think of God as touchy, given to misunderstandings and liable to hold against us the fact that we made mistakes in the past (p. 28). The idea of a wrathful God, quick to anger, is totally wrong. Unlike earthly fathers, God, the Father, loves us all the time and always want the best possible for us. He is Love and can never change. When we reap the harsh and bitter harvests of our bad actions, it is only love; for thereby we are taught to desist from doing that which is bad and which impedes the attainment of the purpose of our existence on earth. In such situations, we see at work, the Law of Sowing and Reaping – the Law by which we can bring abundant joy into our lives if we simply act in accordance with God's Will. I will return to this subject in Chapter 12 on the 'Love and Justice of God.'

It seems to me that the wrong conception of God as merely a superhuman being is an inevitable consequence of ignorance about the structure of Creation and the mechanisms at work in Creation. These we have discussed in Chapter 5 on "Creation and Subsequent Creation" and Chapter 7 on the Laws that express the Will of God. It is because of this wrong conception that some people imagine that the Creator Himself speaks to them directly. Indeed, it is possible for human beings on earth under certain conditions to receive direct communication from sources outside the physical world. The sources and processes are very varied and may include contact by way of dreams or visions with departed human beings residing in the immediate Beyond. The communication may come from noble beings in the Beyond or mischievous departed individuals inhabiting the low regions of the Beyond. They may be the result of delusion or hallucination and there may also be cases of deliberate lying. Thus, the value and reliability of purported communications from the Beyond depend on the source, which cannot generally be ascertained, as well as the character of the receiver. Therefore, such communications may be true or false and deliberately misleading. What is certain, however, is that human beings cannot engage in direct conversation with God.

In conclusion, we should think of God as completely unlike human beings, as infinitely lofty and inconceivably sublime. In acknowledgment of this sublimity, some religious people speak of the mystery of God, using 'mystery' to mean not a puzzle that can be solved, but a reality that surpasses human understanding. They are right but the new revelations make Him much less mysterious. Moreover, there is no mystery in the manner in which God relates to us human spirits; it is through His immutable Laws, which arose out of God's Perfection. Since these Laws cannot be changed and cannot be improved upon, they form a basis for telling infallibly what is possible and what is not.

10 The Perfection and Omnipotence of God

Perfection and Omnipotence are fundamental concepts about God. Both are related because God exercises His Omnipotence only in the light of His Perfection. By ignoring this inseparable relationship, many believers accept and promote wrong conceptions of God's Omnipotence. In this Chapter, I explain the Perfection of God and its implications for how we should understand God's Omnipotence. I indicate the errors that most people, including many philosophers, theologians, and religious leaders, make when they think about these concepts.

The Laws through which God operates in Creation and Subsequent Creation are perfect and immutable. Since God relates to us only through His Perfect Will as expressed in those Laws, the exercise of His Omnipotence is subject to the dictates of His perfect laws. God, as the Creator, is the sole and ultimate source of all power on which, in myriad transformations, everything in Creation and Subsequent Creation depends. Whatever God wills for Creation always prevails ultimately, and the effects of all contrary volitions are ephemeral. This is the sense in which His Omnipotence should be understood. It is a mistake to think that with God everything is possible.

As regards Perfection, the difficulty is not so much with its literal meaning. The problem is that its logical implications often tend to be denied even by religious authorities, and one finds that some basic doctrines are in direct contradiction of the fact of God's Perfection. What is perfect cannot be changed without rendering it imperfect; perfection implies unchangeableness.

The perfection of God, therefore, means that God does not change; neither does His Will.

God has always existed, while Creation came into being at some particular point in time. As mentioned in earlier Chapters, Creation is the consequence of an extension of the reach of God's direct radiation and it was exclusively for the benefits of the creatures which emerged. It is, therefore, easy to understand that God must be fully complete in Himself, absolutely independent, and needing nothing for His eternal existence; hence His attribute of Perfection.

In contrast, everything in Creation and Subsequent Creation depends on God's power. In human terms, one may say that God is Perfection personified. The absolute independence of God has implications that some may find startling. God does not need Creation! If Creation were to cease to exist, God would continue to exist together with the Divine Realm, which necessarily exists as a consequence of the inevitable reach of the direct radiation of God. Thus, all teachings that suggest that God *needs* human beings for one reason or the other are in gross error. The reluctance to accept the self-sufficiency of God and thereby to acknowledge that God can do without us is due in part to our self-conceit and vanity.

Some Christian theologians have argued against the idea that God can do without human beings by pointing out that if God so loved human beings that He was willing to sacrifice His own son to ensure their salvation, it must mean that He needs them. Part of the argument is that the presence of sins in the world somehow makes God incomplete, sad, and unfulfilled. One must first understand that the mission of the Son of God was to show and explain the path that human beings should and must follow in order to achieve the purpose of their existence. As Jesus is the personification of the Love of God, that mission logically fell to him. Jesus was *not* sent as a sacrificial lamb of atonement for the sins of the world.

As mentioned in Chapter 4 regarding the origin of human beings, at our own request we, as unconscious spirit-germs were permitted to descend into the world of matter to acquire self-consciousness and to mature spiritually. God's act of creation built in the possibility and the process for achieving such a purpose. And the process involves doing the Will of God. The mission of Jesus was a reflection of God's eternal attribute of Love. That Love sought to explain the Will of God to human beings, who had failed to comply with the messages of earlier prophets. By His teachings, Jesus was to help human beings mature sufficiently and in time to return to their origin in the Spiritual Realm. The mission was about the needs of human beings and a demonstration of the Love of God; it had nothing to do with the imagined need of an absolutely self-sufficient God.

It has also been remarked that the Bible (specifically the Gospel according to Luke) indicates that there is joy in heaven over one sinner that repents and this is taken to indicate that such rejoicing means that God has a need for a sinner to repent. In other words, they think that the presence of sinners in the world somehow diminishes God's Perfection.

Luke in Chapter 15 of his Gospel reports three parables narrated by Jesus all of which have the one theme of a sinner repenting. The parables were in response to the grumbling of the Pharisees and the Scribes who accused Jesus of welcoming and eating with sinners. In the Parable of the Lost Sheep, Jesus pointed out how it was natural to look out for and fuss over one lost sheep out of one hundred; he concluded "Just so, I tell you, there will be more joy in heaven over one sinner who repents than over ninety-nine righteous persons who need no repentance." In the second Parable, the Parable of the Lost Coin, the female owner of ten silver coins lost one of them and took a great deal of trouble to find it. On finding it, she invited friends and neighbors to rejoice with her. Jesus again remarked: "Just so, I tell you, there is joy in the presence of the angels of God over one sinner who repents." Sinners were like lost sheep in that they had strayed from the path leading to the Spiritual Realm and, therefore, required attentive effort to set them on the right course.

As in the Parables, there would be rejoicing by residents of the Spiritual Realm if and when the former lost ones find their way there. Those residents would include human spirits who did not need to descend to the World of Matter because they were mature and self-conscious from the beginning. They would also include angels and other servants of God's Will. It is clear that in these parables, Jesus was declaring His real mission. The owners of the one hundred sheep and the ten silver coins, respectively, acted as a matter of due diligence and concern, not necessarily because they could not do without the missing ones. Jesus was acting out of Love and not because of a personal need. It is in this light that the concern about sinners and the joy over their repentance should be seen.

The third Parable is about a young man who demanded his inheritance from his father, journeyed to a distant country, squandered the inheritance and thereafter had many unpleasant experiences. He came to his senses and decided to return home to seek forgiveness and to plead for his father's acceptance. The father received him warmly and with great celebration. Even if taken superficially, this Parable of the Prodigal Son (Luke 15:11-32) with the rejoicing and celebration of his return is about the Love, not the need, of a father. In reality, with this parable, Jesus hints at the journey into the World of Matter (distant country) of the human spirit-germ, immature and unwise like the prodigal son, and his eventual return to the Spiritual Realm having become more mature and wiser as a result of experiences in the World of

Matter. But I have to stress that the father in the Parable is not God, and the place of departure and return of the Prodigal Son is the Spiritual Realm (Paradise) and not the Abode of God, which as indicated in Chapter 5 (Creation and Subsequent Creation) is unapproachable by human spirits even at the highest point of their development.

Jealousy Does Not Apply to God

An inadequate understanding of the first of the Ten Commandments, which forbids having, worshipping, and serving any other gods or making idols of any type may lead to the presumption that God needs human beings. This is especially because it is written "for I, the Lord your God, am a jealous God." The *New Living Translation* of the Bible puts the statement even more starkly: "for I, the Lord your God, am a jealous God who will not share your affection with any other god!" The idea that God can be jealous arose from an anthropomorphic misconception; from the error of thinking of God as if He were like human beings. But as I stated in Chapter 9 and as shown in the structure of Creation outlined in Chapter 5 God is outside Creation and is completely unlike human beings; thus the human emotions of jealousy and envy do not apply to Him.

The intent of this First commandment is to ensure that we are so exclusively focussed on God and His Will that we would have no strong attachment to anything earthly. Such exclusive focus on God becomes something of a binding of our spirit to the Spiritual Realm in such a manner that it is as if we are at all times holding tight to the invisible lifebelt stretched down to us from above so that we would continually ascend and never be lost in the Material World. On the other hand, other gods and idols would keep us earth-bound after physical death and make ascent to our spiritual home impossible. The other gods and idols should be understood as including whatever becomes a propensity for us and whatever distracts our attention from God and His Will. These may include wrong attitudes to earthly power, fame, affluence, and influence, the so-called good life, obsessive love of a woman or man, etc.

The Second of the Ten Commandments says "You shall not take the name of the Lord your God in vain" (Exodus 20:17; Deuteronomy 5:11). This commandment, which is unfortunately, all too frequently flouted, even in the course of what people imagine is praying has as its objective only the spiritual well-being of human beings. The word in every language, which expresses the most sublime and loftiest conception of the Creator, should be used sparingly and with the utmost reverence. This is because if it is misused as if it were just any other word, it loses its significance for the human spirit, which would then have nothing special to hold in times of real and urgent need. The concept of God loses its significance for all those who overuse the word and for them it is as if God does not really exist, contrary to what they imagine. Such people, not God, are the losers!

The Creator's commandments, including the Ten Commandments, have but one aim: to enable human beings preserve and maintain for themselves all the possibilities of spiritual progress and development that the Will of God offers on earth and throughout Creation and Subsequent Creation. By observing them, we align ourselves with the Laws of Creation outlined in Chapter 7 and thereby we co-operate in the further sound development of the World of Matter in addition to ensuring the achievement of the spiritual purpose of our own existence. The commandments are to help and support human beings, not to meet any needs of God (since God has none).

I have addressed the arguments of Christian theologians and other thoughtful Christians who are genuinely and objectively interested in the question of the absolute independence and self-sufficiency of God. Unfortunately, there are some religious leaders who have a vested interest in believing that God needs them and needs members of their congregations, especially their money. The false doctrine enhances their importance and earthly influence and facilitates collection of tithes and assorted donations that are promoted as collections for God! It is such practices which keep commercialized religion going and support the lavish life-styles of some religious leaders.

We ought to stop imagining that we can do anything for God Himself. The services people render (in whatever capacity) to their churches, temples, and mosques are at best in aid of fellow human beings. If our religious activities are such as to mislead human beings (even though we might mean well), we should know that there will be unpleasant repercussions. In the light of the true nature of God, our understanding of "service to God" should change. For example, since God does not need anything, it follows that He certainly does not need our tithes and donations. Whether or not we derive spiritual benefits from donations depends on our personal motives and the use to which the donations are put. If they truly benefit fellow human beings, we can expect reciprocal benefits to come our way; but if they simply serve to enrich a few scheming individuals or merely promote the egos and earthly influence of some people, we would be participating in wrong-doing for which the consequences would be unpleasant.

As religion has become increasingly commercialized, small sects and denominations have mushroomed. In many cases their founders' primary, if not sole, motivation is to collect donations and tithes from gullible members. In societies where insecurity, superstitions, and suffering abound founders often successfully and rapidly recruit large numbers of members using various unscrupulous methods, such as staging fake miracles and making false claims of abilities to solve all sorts of problems.

The founders give themselves lofty-sounding titles. One of the many self-appointed bishops wrote about tithes in a March 2014 Sunday newspaper. Among the false, outrageous, and self-serving statements he made in his pompously titled column, *Divine Message*, were the following:

> Your tithes open the windows of heaven so that God can give you insight, concepts and ideas that will result in your greatness...Your tithes give God an opportunity to prove Himself in your life as a God who is faithful to his covenant... When you are faithful in tithing, God pours out so much blessing upon you from heaven; you would not have enough room to contain it... If I were you, I would never play games with my tithes anymore. I would be faithful and consistent in giving it to God, allowing Him to prove Himself in my life...God places a lot of premium on correct tithing.... The purpose of the tithes is to provide food for the house of God. The tithes are to pay the wages of the workers on God's altar, to make sure they are well fed and catered for. The tithes are not for building project. God has a different plan for that. The tithes are not for crusades and missions. That is a different matter. The tithes are to be brought to the house of God, so that there may be 'meat in mine house'.

The bishop declares blatantly that God needs to be bribed. In one breath, he says the tithes are for God and in another breath, he says that the tithes are exclusively for the use of the church workers (in practice the founders, their family members, and close associates). In any case, don't ask him to give account of the tithes! Moreover, he gives advance notice that, in addition to their tithes, members of his congregation should be ready to pay levies for other projects. This is a clear case of crass commercialization of religion. It must take a depressing level of spiritual indolence to follow religious leaders of that ilk.

The simple truth is that God does not need to be bribed and He does not need anybody's money or material donations. It does not matter what any prophet, ancient or modern, may say. In compliance with the Law of Balance (discussed in Chapter 7), one should contribute voluntarily and in the amount one considers appropriate to one's church, mosque, synagogue, movement, etc. so that the activities and projects which one personally values can be developed and sustained. To think that such contributions are for God is delusional and blasphemous. Spiritual salvation and earthly blessings are not granted because of financial contributions to one's religious organization. To gain salvation, the first step is to keep the hearth of our thoughts pure and to pay close attention to the Laws of Creation!

Not Everything is Possible

Major errors can arise when people think about how God exercises His Power. The errors are generally the result of a tendency to think of God as if He were merely super-human, the highest conceivable of earthly rulers, merely the King of earthly kings. But we have in earlier Chapters discussed the errors of that conception. God exercises His Power quite differently from the erratic manner in which human beings exercise earthly power. We know of absolute monarchies of times past as well as political leaders in some countries who exercise their powers arbitrarily, without legal or moral constraint. There are, unfortunately, people who measure how powerful they are by how much they 'can do and undo' and in a completely reckless and unrestrained manner. To a given action they may react one way today and respond exactly the opposite way tomorrow. They may reward Mr. A for a given action and punish Mr. B for the same action. A government may cause one person to be jailed for stealing something worth less than a hundred dollars and refuse to charge another person who stole a million dollars. In other words, human idea of power often presumes a licence to be arbitrary. Given such human misconceptions of power, it is not surprising that so many people think of the Omnipotence of God as the power to do *absolutely* anything and in any manner. They think that they are venerating God by believing that there is *absolutely nothing* that God cannot do.

God's Creation is a law-governed system. Out of the Perfection of God arose the Laws through which Creation and Subsequent Creation came into being and by which everything is maintained. The Laws, arising directly from God's Perfection, are necessarily perfect. And perfection implies unchangeableness. This is because any change to what is perfect renders it imperfect. It follows that the Laws of Creation are unchangeable, immutable! The Laws of Nature and the valid laws of science are gross material manifestations of the Laws of Creation. Nothing can happen that does not also precisely conform to the logical development in the firmly established Laws of Creation; nothing can happen outside the dictates of these Laws. And it is only through these Laws that God maintains Creation and not through personal interventions. The sending of Envoys to the earth and the fulfilment of the earthly missions of such envoys must also follow the course determined by these Laws. Thus, for example, the entry on earth of any envoy is subject to the biological laws governing birth (including physical procreation), growth, development, physical death, etc. No exceptions are possible. The processes are a necessity of the Perfection of God; to argue for exceptions is to deny the Perfection of God.

Obviously, the Omnipotence of God cannot mean that God is able to do anything that we can possibly imagine. One must at least concede that God cannot do the many evils and irrational things that human beings can easily imagine, for such would be clearly against His nature. God who is characterized by Love and Purity cannot be expected to promote hatred and evil. The Perfection of God and of His Will mean that He does not and cannot act arbitrarily. It is in this understanding that we should think about

God's attribute of Omnipotence. His Omnipotence can only be exercised in absolute harmony with His perfection. It follows that there are, indeed, things that God cannot do.

However, it should be noted that on this issue there are contradictions in the Bible. There are several often-quoted passages to the effect that with God nothing is impossible or that all things are possible for God. We can confidently say that such Biblical passages cannot mean that God is capable of illogicality, injustice, and arbitrariness. If it was literally the case that nothing is impossible with God, He would have made every person on earth a true and righteous believer! Then He would not have needed to send prophets to preach to earthmen. The mission of Jesus with the attendant exposure to earthly hardships and death on the cross would have been completely unnecessary.

Moreover, there are Biblical passages, not as well-known, indicating that *not* everything is possible with God. For example, in his Epistle to Titus (1:2), Paul states: "...in hope of eternal life which God, *who cannot lie*, promised before time began (italics added)." Speaking of Christ, Paul also wrote that if we are faithless, He remains faithful, "He cannot deny Himself" (2 Timothy 2:13). Some versions of the Bible render the expression differently: "he cannot be false to himself" or "he cannot disown his own self." We may infer that God too cannot deny Himself, that is, He cannot contradict Himself. One might, therefore, say that in the understanding of Apostle Paul, it is not literally the case that God can do anything. For one thing, He cannot do anything that is morally reprehensible. He is incapable of telling lies and cannot commit any sin. And to the extent that God 'cannot deny Himself', He must be faithful to His own Will. Thus, He cannot override His own Laws of Creation!

The Power of God which streams through all Creation is neutral and, therefore, may be applied for good or evil by creatures that have Free Will. I discussed Free Will in Chapter 4 and will revisit it in Chapter 17 dealing with the problem of evil in the world. But misapplication by God of His own Power is out of the question; therefore, it is impossible for God to do evil. To generalize, we may say that God *cannot* act against His own nature of Love, Justice, and Purity.

"With God nothing is impossible" is an especially strong article of faith among those religious sects that are pre-occupied with miracles. But the notion that "with God nothing is impossible" can quite easily be shown to be a wrong conception of God's Omnipotence. One may infer from what I have already stated that God cannot commit sin or abet the commission of sin; He cannot be unjust or aid the perpetration of injustice. Thus, He cannot punish Mrs. Doe for the sins of Mr. Doe, since that would be unjust. The Omnipotence of God must work in such a way that Mr. Doe bears responsibility for his own sins, while Mrs. Doe accounts only for her own sins. God cannot cause a planting of rice to yield a harvest of wheat, against His own Law of Sowing and Reaping.

In philosophical discussions of the concept of the Omnipotence of God, a classic question sometimes raised is the following: *"Can God create a rock so massive that even God cannot move it?"* The reader should stop and think about this question for a moment. If you are a literal believer in the idea that "with God nothing is impossible" you are likely immediately to answer, "Yes, God can make such a rock". In that case, how would you explain God's *inability* to move such a rock? This question carries the seed of absurdity. The question, whether or not God is able to kill God, is similarly absurd since by definition God is eternal. Whether you answer "yes" or "no' to those questions, you wind up admitting that there may be things that God cannot do. God cannot be the architect of absurdity; God *cannot* do the absurd.

Furthermore, Omnipotence does not mean that God can change *the past*. For example, He cannot now prevent the crucifixion of Jesus. That's an absurdity, for that sad and abhorrent event is already indelibly recorded in world events.

From this line of reasoning, we may draw some conclusions of general applicability. There are logical and temporal limitations to Omnipotence. God cannot take actions that amount to a contradiction or an absurdity. Therefore, God's Omnipotence must be understood as the ability to carry out such actions that involve neither a contradiction nor an absurdity. Another conclusion is that the Omnipotence of God is exercised in a manner that never leads to inconsistencies. This is assured through the strictest adherence to God's Primordial Laws. God is completely unlike earthly rulers and leaders who put themselves above the laws they make; God abides by His own Laws! This is because those Laws arose out of His Perfection; therefore, to go against them would be to do something imperfect. God's Omnipotence is inseparable from His Perfection.

We may, therefore, assert that the mundane human idea of Omnipotence is inapplicable to God. God wields His Power in a manner that is *ever* consistent and *never* arbitrary. Only what complies with God's perfect Laws of Creation can flourish and be sustained in Creation. Attempts at carrying out activities inconsistent with the Laws must eventually come to grief and are guaranteed to fail. That is why what is good (defined as that which accords with God's Will) is forever assured ultimate victory over what is evil.

We human beings, even at our highest level of development, are unable to overlook the *whole* of God's activity. And this inability to overlook the whole leads some, in all goodwill and respect, to expect arbitrary acts from God. But this impossibility of arbitrary actions on the part of God, because of His flawless Perfection, is in no way a disadvantage from the standpoint of one who can overlook the entire Creation, who knows the purposes of all world events, and the final goal to which everything *must* lead – a goal determined only by God! The flawless Perfection *necessarily* ensures ultimate attainment of God's design for Creation; it dictates that victory ultimately belongs to God.

W.R. Matthews (1881-1973), who was Dean of King's College, London and Chaplain to the King, in his 1930 book, *God in Christian Thought and Experience* (p. 243), suggests an analogy that may be helpful in thinking of God's assured ultimate victory. It is that of the master chess-player in competition with an unskilled player. The master chess-player cannot foretell the moves of his unskilled opponent, and the latter's unorthodox moves may often astonish the chess master. But the professional's vastly superior skills give him unshaken confidence that whatever the moves of the unskilled player may be he can meet them and turn them to the advantage of his game plan. In like manner, we can assert that, whatever the inactions, actions and the machinations of creatures (including humans) may be, God's plan for Creation will surely eventually prevail. And that is true Omnipotence.

11 The Omniscience of God

When people ordinarily use the word omniscience, they have in mind complete and exhaustive knowledge. Such knowledge would include actual facts, events, and possibilities relating to the past and the present as well as pertaining to the future. It is this popular meaning that most people have in mind when they think about the Omniscience of God, except that they presume that such all-knowing would be developed in God to the highest level imaginable. They attribute and project to God such meaning of Omniscience because they picture God as "the *crowning point* of what is *human*". They think of God as though He were merely the highest superhuman conceivable. To put God at the peak and pinnacle of human possibilities is to belittle Him. God is God; there is nothing like Him! Thus, popular ideas of God's Omniscience are wrong. But first, what are these wrong ideas?

God is presumed to know what each of the billions of individuals on earth and in other realms is thinking, saying, and doing at all times. On account of His Omniscience, God is supposed to know the minutest details of the conditions of all living and non-living things at all points in time since the beginning of Creation. Illustrative of this misconception are the first five verses of Psalm 139:

> O LORD, you have searched me and known me. You know when I sit down and when I rise up; you discern my thoughts from far away. You search out my path and my lying down, and are acquainted with all my ways. Even before a word

is on my tongue, O LORD, you know it completely. You hem me in, behind and before, and lay your hand upon me (New Revised Standard Version).

It is thought that God *personally* maintains, and has eternally maintained, a 24-hour watch every day of every year over all His creatures. Thus, He is supposed to be aware that you are reading this book right now. Indeed, many believe that God is able to tell the number of hairs on the heads of all the billions of people on earth today and presumably to be updating the count every second as people around the world visit their barbers or shave in the morning or at night. In this erroneous conception, God is expected to be able to tell, for example, how many hairs any 70 year-old man had at the time he celebrated his 30th birthday!

When the Scriptures of some religions extol the Omniscience of God, it is the knowledge of these sorts of petty pieces of information that they often cite; knowledge that would in many cases be quite pointless. What would be the value of the literal knowledge of the constantly changing number of hairs on an individual's head? Knowledge in the sense of accumulations of immense mountains of data of doubtful value is *not* wisdom. The human conception of God's Omniscience, which calls for a petty and earthly all-knowing, is completely wrong. The assumption that Omniscience entails acquiring unlimited amounts of information on the activities, thinking, and speaking of every individual on earth amounts to a belittling of God's Omniscience.

We come close to the correct conception if we think of Omniscience in relation to God as meaning all-*wise* rather than all-knowing. In other words, we should speak of *wisdom* not of knowledge or learning when we think of the Omniscience of God. For omniscience, the German language uses the word *Allweisheit*, which literally means All-wisdom; this expression points directly to the correct conception of Omniscience as it relates to God.

I suppose most people can appreciate the fact that a person may be highly knowledgeable and yet be quite unwise. Historically, many earthly leaders with access to huge amounts of data and the cleverest resource persons were proved by events to be unwise. Some major companies with very knowledgeable and clever individuals on their governing and management boards have collapsed quite calamitously for lack of wisdom. Some were crushed by their own fraudulent practices because they lacked the wisdom that comes from the understanding of the immutable Laws of Creation, especially the Law of Reciprocal Action, which applies to corporate entities just as it does to individuals.

I have on many occasions come away from conversations with non-literate peasant farmers with the conviction that they were much wiser than many university professors known to me, despite the vast amounts of knowledge possessed by those professors. Knowledge of the meanings and etymologies of all the words in the multi-volume *Oxford English Dictionary* would be a major feat but would not confer the status of a literary giant on the person. Greatness does not arise from sheer acquisition of facts. In the 1980s, I knew one ten-year old child who knew by heart practically everything in the *Guinness Book of Records*. That accumulation of knowledge made him a source of reference for his peers and even his parents. But I doubt that it made him wiser than other children of his age.

To illustrate further the difference between knowledge and wisdom, let's consider a hypothetical owner of a large business enterprise. The businessman develops a clear vision of what he wishes to accomplish with the enterprise, defines the mission, formulates the strategies by which to accomplish the mission, identifies the major functions which must be performed, hires the right people in key positions, assigns each of them broad responsibilities, and provides resources with which to work. The key persons hire other staff at different levels and together with these other employees go about their work of implementing the owner's broad strategies to achieve his mission. The owner sets up a system to monitor performance and leaves the day-to-day work and decision-making to his key employees, relying on the monitoring system to indicate when and what interventions are necessary.

The owner of the enterprise does not attempt to cram the names of all the 10,000 or more employees, the educational institutions they attended, the sizes of their families etc. He does not seek to know who came late on a given day, who needs a new computer, who is rude to a customer, who has no sense of humour, who routinely works long hours, etc. A business owner who attempted to acquire such knowledge of small and diverse details would certainly not be considered wise; he would be regarded as strange, meddlesome and petty and a danger to the long-term health of the business. Similarly, rational heads of government do not busy themselves trying personally to know how every individual is faring and who is breaking the law. A wise head of government does not personally get involved with the functioning of every individual business in the economy or every institution in the educational system, etc. He ensures that the right policies as well as the implementation and enforcement mechanisms are put in place. Possession of huge amounts of detailed knowledge is not a mark of wisdom; wisdom takes a different path.

The Omniscience of God has to do with infinite wisdom; it is not about earthly all-knowing. Technological advances in recent years, especially in computer and information technologies as well as remote control systems, make it much easier for human beings today to picture the working of God's Omniscience than it was for past generations. Human beings are now able to develop systems that work automatically and that have built-in self-correcting features. Therefore, they can conceive of an infinitely more sophisticated system devised by God. In His Omniscience or infinite wisdom, God established from the very beginning of Creation mechanisms that ensure that His vision for Creation is fully accomplished. The mechanisms take into account all conceivable and even humanly inconceivable possibilities and include self-acting monitoring devices which restore order whenever disturbances are extraneously introduced.

These mechanisms are the immutable Laws of Creation with the invisible entities that ensure their scrupulous enforcement. The invisible entities may be described as servants of God's Will. It is through the working of the Laws of Creation that God's Omniscience, which is united with His Justice and Love, manifests itself.

The right conception of Omniscience is indicated in the following translated words of the author of The Grail Message:

> Therefore do not think that God's Omniscience should know your thoughts and how you are faring on earth. The working of God is entirely different, greater and more comprehensive. With His Will God spans everything, maintains everything, and furthers everything from out of the Living Law which brings to each individual *that* which he deserves, i.e., that which he wove for himself!

> Not one can thereby escape the consequences of his deeds, be they evil or good! *It is in this* that God's Omniscience, which is united with Justice and Love, manifests itself! In the working of this Creation *everything* for man has been wisely provided! Also that he *must* judge himself!

> That which comes in the Judgment of God is the *release* of the sentences which men had to pass upon themselves in wise Providence according to the Law of God! (Volume III, Lecture "Omniscience")

In His Omniscience, God has always offered to human beings new revelations at each Cosmic Turning-Point. We are presently living at the period of the Great Cosmic Turning-Point and in the work, *In the Light of Truth, The Grail Message*, we are again granted an extension of the knowledge which human beings need urgently.

Omniscience at Work: Symbolic Redemption

The Omniscience of God works in a comprehensive yet unobtrusive and subtle manner. An illustration of such working may be appreciated in symbolic redemption — a mechanism by which we can atone for any wrongdoing symbolically. And the same mechanism ensures that we do not reap the good fruits which we do not deserve. A man who is firmly resolved to give purity to his every thought, word, and deed radiates good forms. These forms attract their own kinds and thereby constitute a strong layer or cover of goodness around the person. Any evil forms, arising from his past thoughts, words or actions that may approach him are deflected and repulsed by the layer of good forms now surrounding him, since unlike forms must repel. Thus, he is able to avoid unfavourable experiences resulting from his earlier wrongdoing.

The power of the invisible protective layer of good forms depends on the strength of the person's genuine determination to live aright. It can happen that the protective layer is not strong enough to block completely the incoming evil forms; but even then the force of the incoming evil forms would be weakened and the impact reduced. As an illustration, a guilt which would otherwise have imposed years of suffering on a man could be redeemed through his simple act of lovingly helping a child or an elderly person to cross a busy street. The help so rendered, purely out of love, becomes the act that redeems his past grievous guilt. He has earned symbolic redemption. The circumstances of another person may be such that instead of years of imprisonment, he is found guilty of a minor crime, which calls for only a modest fine. For such reduced karmic repercussion, the Yoruba people of Nigeria have an apt saying: that one should be grateful in that what could have cut one's head, has merely removed one's cap!

As a further aid to our understanding, we may liken the process of this kind of forgiveness or redemption to tuning a radio. If, at 2300 Hours GMT, one tuned to 5975 Kilo Hertz, one would in some parts of the world, hear "World News" from a particular broadcasting service. But if one shifted to another wavelength, say 6000, one would no longer receive the World News. The wavelength can be thought of as one's spiritual condition, and the incoming message the returning consequence of one's previous thoughts, words, or deeds. When a man has changed from evil to good, or vice versa, it is as if he has tuned to a different wavelength. The message he would have received on the old wavelength would still arrive but he would not be aware of it, instead he would hear a different programme from a different station.

In a somewhat similar manner, the Omniscience of God stipulates that by becoming good, a person may redeem symbolically his previous sins; he earns forgiveness. Conversely, one might not harvest the joys one had sown in the past, if one has become evil at the time the good fruits are due for harvest. Moreover, the positive help sent to us in answer to a prayer may hover around us but may be unable to reach us because of a layer of evil that surrounds us. And, in the Omniscience of God, this happens through the same mechanism that leads to symbolic redemption. Thus, we see in all simplicity that we are, indeed, the architects of our own fates, and that forgiveness depends on us and is always within our reach. That is Omniscience at work!

Omniscience at Work: A Mirror into Our Inner Being

We note that the Law of Homogeneity, the Law which ensures that like attracts like, is prominent in the mechanism of symbolic redemption. Through this same Law, the Omniscience of God has ensured that every human being is forced to carry openly for others to see a mirror in which his true self is quite clearly recognisable to the dispassionate and discerning observer. It is really not difficult to peep through the inner life of people around us because what they think of other people they draw out of themselves, out of their own nature. A really *good* human being will always only find the *good* in others and give expression to it. He will first consider everything according to *his* own nature, which is *good*. It is not a deliberate, willed process but an automatic one. The good person's inner goodness automatically attracts goodness in the person she comes across. Therefore, she instinctively sees and assumes goodness in the other person; unless, of course, there is no goodness to attract and to see.

But an *evil* person is able to assume only *evil intentions* in other people, especially when it concerns matters which elude his understanding or are somewhat unclear to most people. His evil disposition radiates evil and automatically seeks out evil. An evil human being will interpret everything he does not yet understand as coming from the evil volition of another, because in accordance with his own nature, he simply does not expect anything else. As Abd-ru-shin puts it:

> An evil man can never believe in a good volition; he cannot believe that certain actions could spring from it, because he himself is incapable of it. He will dismiss selfless action as a myth, or even as a lie, because it is alien and incomprehensible to him. Only the *good man* can believe in it, because he himself is capable of acting likewise. Thus a person's opinion of his fellow-men is always simply the

reflection of his own inner state, which he clearly expresses in this way. Those who speak evil of their fellow-men, and spread it abroad, *must be evil in themselves,* or they would not do such things! (Lecture "Distrust").

The fact that there is so much distrust and cynicism all around is proof of the abundance of evil human beings in the world. Those who regularly engage in and enjoy vile gossips often consider themselves better than those they gossip about. But the truth is that such people thereby unintentionally announce and publicize their own evil inner nature. 'By their works you shall know them.' Our works include what and how we speak! Dispassionate but uncomplimentary comments can, of course, be made. But these can be easily recognized as they are usually sensitively expressed and invariably carry hints of understanding and love, whereas with gossips there is usually an undertone of superiority and arrogance. It is often the case that the most vociferous critics of public office holders do not necessarily perform better or even well when appointed to the positions of those they criticised. Their nature may be simply such that they are able to see only what is actually wrong or what they merely imagine to be wrong. By their criticisms they carry a mirror showing their own true nature.

Omniscience at Work: The Speck in Our Neighbour's Eye

Jesus Christ alluded to a closely similar principle that expresses the Omniscience of God in the following admonition reported in the Gospel According to Matthew (Matthew 7: 1-5):

> Do not judge, so that you may not be judged. For with the judgment you make you will be judged, and the measure you give will be the measure you get. Why do you see the speck in your neighbour's eye, but do not notice the log in

your own eye? Or how can you say to your neighbour 'Let me take the speck out of your eye,' while the log is in your own eye? You hypocrite, first take the log out of your own eye, and then you will see clearly to take the speck out of your neighbour's eye (New Revised Standard Version).

The word 'brother' is used in place of 'neighbour' in some versions of the Bible. The first two sentences are specifically about judging others. The correct judgment of individuals in any situation usually involves many factors that human beings are incapable of knowing and, therefore, cannot take into account. For example, the volition, motive, and the thought underlying any speech or action ought to be taken into account to make a fair judgment but invariably a third party cannot ascertain these. And, of course, our own nature and prejudices come into place in our assessments of even the factors that are observable. Thus, to avoid errors and sin, we should desist from judging.

The remaining verses, rightly understood, deal primarily with how we can infallibly know *our own* faults! Those verses are generally interpreted superficially as meaning that we should be lenient in considering the faults of other people. It is a good thing to be gracious and lenient when considering other people's faults but that is not the primary lesson of the cited admonition of Jesus. In previous paragraphs, we stated that through what we instinctively say about and associate with other people we each hold a mirror into our own inner state. We noted that an evil person sees evil in others, even where such evil does not exist, whereas a good man readily sees what is good in another person, unless and until he is shocked into realization of the other person's evil nature. Thus, we must have faults if we routinely and quickly see the faults of other people. Apart from leniency towards the faults of others, this should immediately suggest to us that we need to work hard on *ourselves*, if we care about self-improvement and wish to do the Will of God.

The primary objective of Jesus Christ with the admonition cited above is to make individuals mature spiritually by recognizing *their own* faults and striving to deal with those faults. Each individual is to use the faults of others that really disturb him as a measure of his own faults. Let us consider how we go about it. If a person studies himself *objectively* he will soon realize that the faults which most disturb him in other people are very strongly rooted in himself and a cause of annoyance to his neighbours! Some people would simply shrug their shoulders or indicate only a mild and calm reaction when they notice a fault in another person, whereas some individuals would get agitated and visibly angry. The truth is that the agitated and angry persons are characterized by the observed fault to a much greater extent than the person in whom the fault was observed.

The expression of great annoyance and anger at the fault of another does not indicate moral high ground but rather the unintended announcement of the same but greater fault on the part of the disturbed person! When a person resorts to outbursts of rage because he has been lied to, do not be deceived into thinking that he is a truthful person. On the contrary, habitual liars are the ones most likely to react in that manner and they are also the ones who, even when dealing with obviously truthful persons, usually presume that those other people are lying.

To become convinced of the truth and reality of this process, it is best to start by closely observing other persons rather than oneself. Everyone can find persons in his circle of acquaintances who are highly critical or even indignant about one fault or the other in other persons. One should take one of such persons under close scrutiny. Before long, one would discover that it is just those faults which the particular person so strongly deplores in others that are present in him to a far greater degree! He would eventually find that this is invariably always the case and would come to the conclusion that a person who gets excited about this or that fault in another person is sure to have those same faults within himself to a far greater extent! One would then be compelled to accept that the same applies to oneself. Thereby, one finds a sure path to the discovery of one's own faults and the path to a fulfilled life, provided that one addresses seriously every fault so discovered. One would then be preoccupied with overcoming one's own faults rather than with finding and condemning faults in others. This is a process that would lead to salvation, as desired by Jesus as well as by all the past true prophets of God.

Such was the value of the enlightenment that Jesus offered with the statement, "You see the speck in your neighbour's eye, but do not notice the log in your own eye"; or, as might be more familiar to readers belonging to the older generations, "Thou beholdest the mote that is in thy brother's eye and considerest not the beam that is in thine own eye!" This is Omniscience at work.

The Matter of Foreknowledge

An issue that often comes up with respect to the Omniscience of God is the extent to which God knows or can know future events. This matter of foreknowledge is one with which philosophers and theologians have occupied themselves for centuries. Some argue that God knows absolutely everything about the future. Such people imagine, for example, that on account of His Omniscience, God knows all those who will end up in hell and will suffer eternal damnation from the moment of their birth on earth. Similarly, God is supposed to know those who are destined to be saved and who would enjoy eternal life. Others think that God's knowledge of the future cannot be absolute because He would not be able to determine in advance what human beings will do given that they are endowed with Free Will. Related to the matter of knowledge of the future is the question of whether or not God can be surprised.

As we have already discussed, the Omniscience of God does not imply knowledge of specific actual events, past, present or future. It is not about earthly all-knowing but rather it is "All-Wisdom." The above discussions of symbolic redemption and of the unintended exposure of our own inner state as well as of our own faults illustrate how this Wisdom works. Therefore, the matter of foreknowledge is not as significant as theologians, philosophers as well as the masses of thinking people have assumed.

To understand the matter of foreknowledge in relation to God's Omniscience it is necessary to be clear about Free Will. Let us, therefore, briefly recall what we said about it in Chapter 4. Free Will is an inherent attribute of human beings, as human spirits. All that is spiritual exercises the power of attraction in a manner analogous to magnets. The human spirit would attract indiscriminately if it did not have Free Will. Think of a hypothetical magnet that could attract indiscriminately — paper, iron, wood, soil particles, etc.; such a magnet would be useless for most practical purposes. Similarly, the human spirit's ability to attract would overwhelm and incapacitate it, if it could not put a check on what it draws to itself. Therefore, as a counterpoise to the ability of the spirit to attract, it is given the ability to decide what to attract and what to leave alone. This is also a demonstration of a principle that rests in Creation: the principle of balance. The inherent ability of the spirit to attract is balanced with the ability to choose what to attract.

The human spirit, by exercising its Free Will and by being subjected to the consequences, acquires knowledge of good and bad through experience, and thus matures. As it matures, it is increasingly able to make the right decisions. And at full maturity, it can make only the right decisions — the decisions that accord with the Will of the Creator. Thus, on account of their Free Will, human beings are free to decide what to think or not think, to speak evil or good, act uprightly or criminally, etc.

It follows that God cannot know in detail what human beings will do in future because Free Will would be meaningless if God could decide in advance how it would be exercised. However, God's Omniscience, exercised through the immutable Laws in Creation, ensures definite consequences for every volition, thought, word, or deed. For this reason, all the possible consequences for all the possible ways in which a person may exercise his Free Will can be foretold and arrangements for appropriate responses to each eventuality can be made. For example, the Omniscience of God knows that it is possible for human beings to commit murder as the result of wrong applications of their Free Will. In response to such possibilities, the Laws of Creation, including the Law of Reciprocal Action, already exist to respond appropriately to acts of murder as well as to account for the circumstances of potential victims. But the murderer cannot be prevented from exercising his Free Will. In general, it is only after an individual has actually taken decisions that the future resulting from those decisions can be known. To avoid possibly distracting digression, I cannot go into the mechanisms that guide us to use our Free Will aright. I should, however, mention that the Omniscience and Love of God are such that there are helpers in the Beyond which acting through the inner voice, the conscience, of each individual always seek to make inputs into our decision-making; thus, for example, to warn a murderer to desist.

A person's present state (representing the full effects of his present volition, past and current thoughts, words, and deeds) indicates the direction in which the person is headed at that moment. If the person thinks, speaks, and acts consistently, the consequences lead him in a predictable direction either towards or away from the Light and he attracts appropriate experiences, guidance, and help along the chosen path. His future can be predicted on the assumption that he will continue on the same path. If he changes, for better or for worse, perhaps as a result of some significant experiences, and exercises his Free Will in a manner different from the way he did in the past, the predicted direction and the experiences associated with that path will necessarily change.

This process explains, at least in part, why the predictions of even genuine astrologers or seers with respect to particular individuals may not come to pass. A true seer's prediction can only be based on the direction a person's volition and threads of fate are leading him at a particular point in time. If a person changes substantially, his path changes and his threads of fate are automatically modified; therefore, the former predictions or prophecies would no longer be valid. In other words, such a person has changed his fate; we are all the architects of our fates. Therefore, we should never allow ourselves to become dependent on seers, soothsayers, and self-styled prophets. It also follows that God does *not* arbitrarily determine from birth who would be saved and who would suffer eternal damnation. We are equipped as spirit-germs with all the abilities we need to accomplish the spiritual purpose of our existence and are given appropriate guidance on our journey through the World of Matter. How we fare depends on the extent to which we develop our inherent abilities and how we respond to the guidance provided through the Omniscience of God.

As with individual human beings so it is with nations and, indeed, the entire humanity. It is possible to perceive from the highest heights the direction in which particular groups of people and even the entire humanity are moving at particular points in time. Whenever the direction is the wrong one, appropriate help is sent by the Light in the form of prophets or Envoys (as in the case of Jesus). The teachings of the prophets or Messages of the Envoys are intended to help human beings realize that they are taking the wrong path, see the necessity for change, and understand how to make the required changes. However, human beings cannot be compelled to change because of their Free Will. But what has a beginning in the World of Matter must have an end, in accordance with the Law of the Cycle. Therefore, those who continue on the wrong path must eventually wind up in the funnel of disintegration at the closing of the cycle of the World of Matter.

The Law of the Cycle. Let me comment briefly on the Law of the Cycle. This Law, also called the Law of Revolution, ensures that, in the World of Matter, whatever has a beginning must have an end and that the end must always flow back into the beginning. Nature provides many examples. When, for example, we plant the seed of maize, it germinates and the seedling grows rapidly at first. Then the growth rate slows down as the maize plant matures. The plant bears flowers, followed by the cobs with its seeds. Finally, growth ceases, the cobs ripen, and the plant dies. The dry seeds from the cobs may be planted again, and the cycle is repeated.

Consider also the seasons. In Spring, there is an awakening in nature with fresh growth. This is followed by development and maturing in Summer and then a ripening and harvest in Autumn. A period of rest and recuperation follows in Winter, after which another cycle begins. This cycle of coming into existence and passing away is without end. However, every phase of the cycle, every happening during the cycle does have an end.

Our earth and the entire World of Matter (which includes the Ethereal World) had a beginning and will come to an end, in obedience to this Law of the Cycle. The end is a disintegration, which is not a shattering, but takes the form of infinite compression rather like the manner in which 'black holes' are formed, according to cosmologists. The end of a particular phase of the World of Matter puts an end to the possibility of human existence and further incarnations in that part. Any human spirits that have not matured sufficiently to have left the disintegrating part of the World of Matter would experience spiritual death, suffer eternal damnation.

Consider: any animal that does not get away from a burning bush because it is indolent, inattentive, or fails to find an escape route gets burnt with the bush. So it is with the human spirit in the material parts of Creation. Human beings who, for whatever reasons, have not left the World of Matter by the time the part of the world in which they inhabit must come to an end will suffer disintegration, spiritual death. In His Omniscience and Love, God affords human beings various helps, which rightly used would ensure that we do not suffer the fate of spiritual death but rather return to the Spiritual Realm as fully self-conscious mature human spirits able to participate in the further development of Creation.

Can God be surprised?

In connection with the matter of foreknowledge, the question of whether God can be surprised is sometimes asked. The question arises from the presumption that the Omniscience of God is such that He should know everything and, therefore, nothing can happen that should surprise Him. Since it has already been emphasized that God's Omniscience is not about earthly all-knowing, the question of surprise also loses some of its significance.

The specific future actions of human beings cannot be assuredly predicted, because they have Free Will. For the same reason, it is not difficult to envisage that human beings *may* make wrong choices and that perhaps some of the choices and actions may be outrageous. But whatever choices human beings may make would not be baffling to God and however outrageous some of their actions turn out to be would not surprise God. This is because, in line with the immutable Laws of Creation, the *possibility* of each of such choices and actions could be foretold and contingency plans put in place to address them. The hope, of course, is that certain possibilities would never become realities.

However, I suppose that the servants of God's Will might sometimes be disappointed and disgusted when human beings on earth behave outrageously and atrociously. This is so because of the inherent spiritual endowments of human beings, the many sacrifices made to keep them on the right path, and the careful guidance given to them over millennia at various stages of their development in the World of Matter.

12 The Love and Justice of God

To reflect the fact that the Love of God and the Justice of God are inseparable, it is appropriate to discuss them in the same Chapter. To use a rather crude analogy, they are like two sides of the same coin. The inseparable nature of the Love of God and the Justice of God helps to dispel some wrong human conceptions. It follows, for example that, in the process of showering His Love on humanity, God cannot and will not commit an injustice, either to other creatures or to Himself. Any sacrifices made out of love cannot take the form of an obvious injustice. And God's Justice is always accompanied with Love.

Both the Love of God and the Justice of God rest in the Laws of Creation, which have existed since the very beginning of Creation. This fact implies that those two attributes of God are never dispensed in an arbitrary manner and they do not depend on the opinions of human beings. Moreover, there can be no contradictions in their expression and their manifestations on earth. Thus, in dispensing His Justice, His Love cannot be and is never compromised.

Let me illustrate. Many persons, who have some knowledge of the Law of Reciprocal Action, the Law which ensures that we reap whatever we sow in thought, word, or deed, readily and without any difficulty, associate it with Justice. But relatively few realize that in this Law also lies Love. Consider a person who sows a good seed. The Law guarantees that the harvest is of the same kind, and this can be perceived as Justice. But the effect of the Law is not only on quality or kind, but also on quantity. He, who sows, for example, one seed of maize, may reap two cobs of maize containing perhaps as many as a hundred seeds. It is surely Love, when for one seed, the Law of Reciprocal Action ensures a return of so many seeds. And from one seed of orange emerges an orange tree which yields perhaps hundreds of oranges year in, year out.

The Love of God and the Justice of God were also inseparable with respect to the mission of Jesus on earth. The mission, as is well known, was one of immeasurable love. Human beings were following paths that could only lead to catastrophic failure to achieve the goal of their existence, as discussed in Chapter 4. The Love of God manifested in Jesus who was then sent into Creation and incarnated on earth so that He might help redirect humanity onto the right path. This He did through His mere presence on earth (through His radiation as one whose innermost core was a Part of God) as well as through His teachings and exemplary life. His mission of love could not have been *intentionally* tainted with any injustice. Thus, He, being absolutely sinless, could not have been sent to be killed in order to carry away the sins of others, which would be an obvious and grave injustice. This is a quite straight-forward matter that calls for no mystery.

Jesus was confronted with trumped up charges orchestrated by the religious authorities of those days who were intent on protecting their own earthly influence and power. Jesus might have recanted His teachings but that would have been unthinkable given His origin and it would have meant a complete failure of His mission. His steadfastness and defiance of crucifixion put a seal on His teachings and fortified the faith of His contemporary and future followers. And so the Jewish leaders murdered Him. He demonstrated the personification of Love that He was, and is, when He said on the cross, "Father, Forgive them for they know not what they do." But at the same time, Jesus thereby declared that they were simply committing a heinous crime, doing something contrary to the Will of God and contrary to God's plan. The crucifixion, a plain injustice, was not a planned part of the mission of Jesus. The predominant doctrine of sacrificial death amounts to waving joyfully a flag of injustice in the name of 'the mystery of Divine Love'. And that is wrong.

It can be rightly said that Jesus suffered and died on the cross because of the sins of humanity as a whole as well as the specific sins of those responsible for His crucifixion. If mankind had not sinned and were not following the wrong paths, Jesus would not have needed to embark on His mission and could have been spared His path of suffering and His crucifixion. But in accordance with the Justice of God, sinners must still redeem their own sins. However, such redemption has been made easier because Jesus has shown the way in His teachings. Anyone who strives to understand His true message and to live accordingly, regardless of the person's professed religion, would be on the path that leads to Paradise, in line with what Jesus wished to accomplish with His mission.

I should here again mention the concept of 'mission karma'. Mission Karma is a fate or a consequence that a person *voluntarily* accepts in order to fulfill a particular mission. Mission karma explains, for example, how it was possible for Jesus Christ to have been a victim of murder even though He obviously and definitely had not sown any evil seed that could have ripened in the form of crucifixion. Out of love, Jesus incarnated on earth to teach humankind how they should think, speak, and act in order to be admitted into the Kingdom of God, which for us human beings means Paradise. He undertook the mission even though He was aware of the dangers, including the possibility of murder, since He knew that darkness had taken hold of the religious leaders of that time.

The Goal of God's Love is Spiritual Benefit

God's Love is purposeful. It considers only what is of spiritual benefit to us. The Love of God takes a comprehensive overview and considers a person's whole existence and what would ultimately be most spiritually beneficial to the person. And what carries spiritual benefits may sometimes be quite uncomfortable or painful to the beneficiaries. Whenever we taste the bitter fruits of the bad seeds we sowed, we are being reminded of the fact that, at some point in the past, we strayed from the way ordained by the Creator; such experiences are not intended as punishment but as potentially beneficial help on our path of spiritual development.

Any adversity, pain or suffering should be seen as cues, hints of the need to reexamine our understanding of the Laws of the Creator and how we stand in relation to them. Such reexaminations, if done with integrity and genuine humility and then acted upon, are bound to help us to grow spiritually and also to achieve happiness here on earth. As we learn the right lessons and make necessary adjustments so that we sow only good seeds, the Law of Sowing and Reaping assures us of bountiful good harvests at the appropriate times. And this, surely, is Love. Therefore, we see that the Law of Reciprocal Action is the mechanism by which God shows His Love while at the same time ensuring His Justice. Thus, we see demonstrated again the fact that God's Justice and God's Love cannot be separated; they are one!

God Does Not Punish

The human concept of punishment is unknown to the Justice of God. God does not punish! Neither does God threaten and tempt. The Ten Commandments, which were given through Moses, are only a guide to show how man can attain to a life of bliss. God does not inflict suffering and tragedy on people. People bring them about purely by themselves, and by a process through which they could also ensure abundance, happiness and bliss for themselves. Out of love, human beings are warned when they make wrong decisions and take wrong paths which must lead to definite unfavourable ends. When they refuse to heed such warnings, which take many forms, including individual consciences, admonitions of wise individuals, etc., they must eventually come to the unfavourable ends. Such ends are not brought about by God as wanton punishment but only by the choices that human beings made. We are collectively and individually the architects of our fates. It is sacrilege to blame God for our fates.

Whenever tragedies occur, whether they are natural or man-made, questions are asked about the Love and Justice of God. In particular, many people imagine that tragedies and catastrophes hit and pick their victims randomly and this assumption makes them fearful for themselves, for members of their families as well as for their friends. Indeed, we would be justified to be fearful if tragedies picked their victims randomly. It would mean that we could not act individually to protect ourselves in the face of an increasingly tragedy-prone world. The truth is that we need not be afraid. Because of His Perfection, God is incapable of acting, and does not act, arbitrarily. Rather, He maintains His Creation by means of immutable Laws to which all creatures, including all human beings, are subject. And built into God's Laws are Love and Justice, which ensure that we experience only that which we need and deserve. Indeed, the final effects of all the Laws in Creation contain only mercy and love.

Reincarnation and the Justice of God

Reincarnation holds the key to the explanation of the many apparent injustices and seemingly undeserved misfortunes that befall people in what appears to be a haphazard, random and inexplicable manner. These circumstances lead many to ask if there is justice in the world. A common answer is that God's ways are mysterious. But those who say so thereby leave room for doubt in the Justice of God. Reincarnation is the fact that a human spirit, *in one continuous existence,* is given the opportunity to come to the earth more than once. The human spirit takes on a different human body on each occasion and the circumstances of each birth are determined by the Laws of Creation. This process is repeated until the human spirit attains that degree of maturity and of inner purity, which ensure that the earth no longer can hold it back from its ascent towards its spiritual home that is popularly called Paradise. My book, *The Christian and Reincarnation*, is a comprehensive treatment of the subject. Any benefits or disadvantages conferred on children by the circumstances of their birth are consequences of the Law of Sowing and Reaping and the Law of Homogeneity and they take into account the activities and predispositions of their past incarnations.

Cardinal Joseph Ratzinger (later Pope Benedict XVI), responding to the question of the diverse circumstances of birth of human beings, acknowledged that there are extreme cases of people who are seriously disadvantaged and, therefore, cannot find any way to realize their potential. He stated that it was, yet again, the problem of why there is so much suffering in the world and that we should not suppose that we can ever find an answer to it (*God and the World: Believing and Living in Our Time*, pp. 117-118). His argument against reincarnation is that "it would empty human existence of its once-for-all character and undermine human responsibility." He said we don't know if each individual is responsible for his own state; in other words, the future Pope was not sure that individuals were and are the architects of their own fates. "We can only say one thing: God has made a very varied world, even in the pre-human realm, and humans too offer a spectacle of great variety. That is not necessarily a bad thing." (Joseph Cardinal Ratzinger, *God and the World*, p. 117).

Contrary to Cardinal Ratzinger's argument, human responsibility is very much strengthened with the recognition that our words, thoughts, and deeds determine our state of existence now and in the future through the mechanisms of the Laws of Creation and of reincarnation. In my view, to believe that God designed a world of gross inequities, with grand opulence sprinkled in the midst of appalling deprivations and suffering, is to deny the fact that God is Justice and that He is Love. Divine Justice ensures that a human spirit, in its *continuous existence*, reaps only what it sows in every earth-life as well as in the intervals spent in the immediate Beyond. There is no arbitrariness in God's Creation. And God certainly did not introduce handicaps and adversities to ensure variety in the world. I revisit aspects of these ideas in Chapter 17 on 'God and the Problem of Evil'.

The Grace of God

In contemplating the Love and Justice of God, the question of the Grace of God comes up. The word "Grace" tends to conjure in popular imagination the idea of something that is not earned, which is given free of charge, and without the expectation of any duty or obligation. God and the Divine Realm have existed from eternity and will continue to exist with or without Creation. The act of creation was an act of God's Love and Grace. The creative act made it possible for entities that could not come into conscious existence in the Divine Realm to do so successively at greater distances from Him. And this Grace was a response to such entities' earnest desire and pleading for conscious existence.

Moreover, the act of Grace continues in the processes through which Creation and Subsequent Creation as well as the creatures therein are kept in existence. On earth, for example, we have the air we breathe, solar radiation, and water without which neither the righteous nor the unrighteous would live! Thus, God's Grace provides all that is essential for human existence on earth in order to develop their spiritual potentials.

But the same mechanism that granted the Grace also laid down the conditions for our sustained, joyful and purposeful existence as human spirits – the Laws of Creation, which are the immutable expression of God's Will. Therefore, to continue to enjoy the Grace of God, creatures are obliged to adhere to the Laws of Creation. We are obliged, for example, to act in ways that would ensure that the air and water that we are graciously and freely given are not polluted. As a Grace of God, the earth enjoys protection from certain harmful radiations from the sun through the way the earth's atmosphere is constituted. To continue to enjoy the protection, we have the duty to ensure that the ozone layer is not destroyed through thoughtless and careless human activities. The question of whether or not God's Grace carries obligations is thereby answered. It does!

And this is in line, in particular, with the Law of Balance between giving and taking. The Law implies that human beings must give something as balance for God's Grace. In short, to enjoy God's Grace, we must strive strenuously to know and understand the Laws of Creation and then to act, think, and speak according to their dictates at all times. Then, we would continually obtain Grace automatically and without further ado!

Justice and Forgiveness
The Grace of forgiveness of sins must also comply with the requirements of the Justice of God. In the prayer Jesus gave to humankind, we find this statement: "And forgive us our trespasses, as we forgive those that trespass against us." And on another occasion, Jesus Christ told His disciples: "And whenever you stand praying, forgive, if you have anything against anyone; so that your Father also who is in heaven may forgive you your trespasses. But if you do not forgive, neither will your Father who is in heaven forgive your trespasses" (Mark 11: 25-26). These are clear declarations that there are preconditions for forgiveness. If

we want forgiveness, we must work for it. It is also a statement of the Law of Sowing and Reaping – to obtain forgiveness, one must sow forgiveness.

We discussed symbolic redemption as an illustration of the Omniscience of God (Chapter 11) and we need not revisit it here. Symbolic redemption, which amounts to pre-redemption of bad karma, is an example of the Grace of God. This happens only to those who have genuinely changed and become truly good. The reduction or elimination of a particular bad karma that results from the mechanism of symbolic reduction is an instance of love. And the same mechanism can lead to a reduction or cancellation of the beneficial results of past good deeds by those who have become impure or evil and so no longer deserve such benefits; that would be a case of Justice. This again underscores the inseparability of Love and Justice.

The Justice of God is Not Ambiguous

In Chapter 8, I referred to Exodus 20:5 as portraying the Justice of God as arbitrary and ambiguous. I will here elaborate on the verse, which states:

> "...For I the LORD your God am a jealous God, punishing children for the iniquity of parents, to the third and the fourth generation of those who reject me" (Exodus 20:5).

The same wrong idea that God punishes children for the sins of their parents is to be found in the Book of Jeremiah (32:18):

> You show steadfast love to the thousandth generation, but repay the guilt of parents into the laps of their children after them, O great and mighty God whose name is the LORD of hosts.

Why would a just God punish children, grandchildren, and great grandchildren for sins they did not commit but which were committed by their fathers, grandfathers, and great grandfathers? Such an action would be the exact antithesis of the Justice of God. One hopes that nobody seriously thinks that God is capable of such grotesque injustice. Let me state right away that God has never punished, and will never punish a person for the sins of others, no matter how closely related such a person might be to the sinner; only the sinner may be punished for his or her own sin. Any suggestions to the contrary are misconceptions and misrepresentations of the Justice of God.

In other books of the same Old Testament, we find the following passages:

> The person who sins shall die. A child shall not suffer for the iniquity of a parent, nor shall a parent suffer for the iniquity of a child; the righteousness of the righteous shall be his own, and the wickedness of the wicked shall be his own. (Ezekiel 18:20).

> Parents shall not be put to death for their children, nor shall children be put to death for their parents; only for their own crimes may persons be put to death. (Deuteronomy 24:16).

These last two passages are clear statements of the kind of justice with which we can identify God, the Creator. They appear to be the exact opposite of "visiting the iniquity of the fathers upon the children." Surely, God does not contradict Himself. We are left with two possibilities: either the statement is wrong or our understanding of it is faulty. A literal interpretation of the passage and similar statements is certainly wrong. Therefore, we should endeavor to achieve a greater depth of understanding. So what might "visiting the iniquity of the fathers upon the children" mean?

In an age of science, some might imagine that the visiting refers to heredity. That's not the point of the passage. There is no such thing as spiritual heredity; heredity applies only to the physical body. It is true that the wrong habits of parents, the abuses they commit against their own bodies may affect their children adversely. The children of drug addicts, for example, may suffer physical defects, and the children may, therefore, be thought to be suffering from the sins of their addicted parents. A baby born to a mother who has the dreaded AIDS (Acquired Immune Deficiency Syndrome) may have AIDS. This is not what is meant by "visiting the iniquity of the fathers upon the children."

Both the Law of Homogeneity and the Law of Sowing and Reaping govern what child is born to what family. A child born with physical defects caused by the addiction of the mother is not an innocent victim considered from the spiritual standpoint, which is the only valid standpoint in this case. The attraction to the family might be the result of a major weakness that the child shares with the mother; a weakness which, in the mother's case, has manifested in drug addiction. The physical defects acquired by the child might also be the appropriate fruits for seeds which the child sowed in an earlier earth-life. The Justice of God is such that nobody is ever a victim of chance, and nobody suffers for the iniquities of others. It should be stated, however, that while it is true that children are not the innocent victims of the physical defects arising from the bad habits of or drug abuse by their parents, such parents do not go scot-free. The parents have thereby sown bad seeds that will yield multiple bitter fruits for them to reap sooner or later; unless they change and thereby enjoy symbolic redemption.

Consider a case that is sadly not uncommon among those who consider themselves 'enlightened'. A father instills into his children the false idea that with death everything is ended. The children accept this viewpoint and adjust their lives accordingly.

They also pass this falsehood to their own children, and a series of far-reaching adverse effects is set in motion. The various parents, not God, are responsible for the adverse effects of such a wrong belief. While these effects last, the originator of the wrong idea (who may have died physically) cannot make any progress in the Beyond. In the Beyond, he recognizes his error and its sad consequences on the earth-lives of his children, grandchildren, great grandchildren etc. These consequences cause him great agony. His own spiritual progress is halted until in one generation of his descendants, the right conception of life after death arises. It is only then that the originator is able gradually to redeem himself from his guilt. The point is that in every case the parent suffers for his own iniquity.

How about the children who have suffered from their parents' wrong instructions? Everybody has the responsibility and duty to reexamine and weigh carefully what he learnt from his parents and teachers during his years of childhood. An adult who continues to retain without question any ideas and concepts fed to him while he was a child and adjusts his adult life according to those childhood teachings fully deserves any unpleasant consequences. What one retains in adult life should only be those that one has carefully examined and considered valid. Nobody needs to inherit the ideas, religion, preferences or prejudices of his parents. Similarly, we should carefully and seriously examine the traditions and cultures of the societies into which we are born and accept only those that we are convinced are right and reasonable.

To interpret aright the statement "visiting the iniquity of the fathers upon the children unto the third and fourth generation" and to resolve any apparent contradictions with other Bible passages, we require the knowledge of reincarnation. Armed with the knowledge that the same human spirits come repeatedly to the earth in other bodies, we can recognize a new conceptual relationship between "fathers" and "children". It is a relationship in which "father" and "child" are one and the same human spirit. That is, we might speak of Smith who is a reincarnation of Jones as the "child", and Jones as the "father". We may even consider earlier periods when Jones had lived as Stone and Wood, respectively. Wood, Stone, Jones and Smith are the same human spirit. They may have changed nationality, race, religion, and even gender, but they are all simply cloaks worn by the same single human spirit in one continuous existence. Thus, it is justice when the iniquities of Wood are visited upon Stone, Jones or Smith. Therefore, in the sense of reincarnation, we can conceptualize situations in which the sins of the "fathers" are visited upon the "children." We, ourselves, reap the fruits of the iniquities we committed in one earth-life in subsequent earth-lives, as long as we refuse to change.

We may also say that the unpleasant experiences we now go through are the fruits of iniquities that we ourselves committed earlier on, in this earth-life or in previous ones. And, conversely, the fortunes that fall on our laps are in fact the fruits of works performed at an earlier period in this earth-life or in previous incarnations. "Visiting the iniquity of the fathers upon the children" is thus seen, through the knowledge of reincarnation, to be in line with our concept of an absolutely just God. The statement expresses the Law of Sowing and Reaping, of Cause and Effect, in the same manner as this Old Testament passage: "As I have seen, those who plough iniquity and sow trouble, reap the same (Job 4:8)."

Justice, Generations, and the Law of Homogeneity
Although implied in what has already been stated, it is necessary to indicate clearly how the Law of Homogeneity, the Law of Like Attracts Like, may give the appearance that, in a purely earthly sense, the "iniquity of the fathers is visited upon the children

to the third and fourth generation." Take, for example, the case of Mr. Thorn, known to be a really wicked man. In accordance with the Law of Homogeneity, he may attract as children souls from the Beyond that are, like him, wicked. In other words, his children are wicked souls, and are born wicked. For this reason, the children come into the world carrying karma similar to that of their father on account of the similarity of their disposition and past actions. As time goes on, each child's karma manifests in unhappy experiences of the type that one would associate with Mr. Thorn's known wicked ways. It could even happen that at the time the children are reaping the fruits of their own wickedness, the fruits of the father's evil ways are not yet ripe or are not evident, and so the father appears to go unpunished. A person who is unfamiliar with the Laws of Creation and who does not have the knowledge of reincarnation would then erroneously assume that the children were somehow suffering because of their father's iniquities.

But the fact is that a wicked soul (the father) has attracted similarly wicked souls as children, and these children must undergo experiences that one would associate with a person of their father's wicked disposition. If the children retain their father's wickedness into adulthood, they would also attract wicked souls as their own children (Mr. Thorn's grandchildren) who would be similarly burdened with evil karma. Thus, because of the Law of Homogeneity (the Law of Attraction of Similar Species) the sufferings of Mr. Thorn's children and grandchildren may appear to be due to Mr. Thorn's iniquities. But they would all simply be experiencing similar sufferings on account of having similar personal characters and disposition and for having individually committed similar iniquities at some point in time. It is certainly not a question of God punishing anybody.

The process is, of course, the same for a man of benevolent and noble nature. He would attract benevolent and noble souls as children who would in turn bring into the world children of similar character. And the benevolence of the father would appear to be passed on from generation to generation. The reality, however, is that the children and grandchildren are simply the beneficiaries of their own nature, their earlier noble thoughts, words, and actions. Any benefits conferred on children by the circumstances of their birth are consequences of the Law of Sowing and Reaping and the Law of Homogeneity. The Justice and Love of God rest on immutable laws and are perfect.

Why Bad Things Happen to Good People

Two related questions often asked about the Justice of God are why it is that bad things sometimes happen to good people and, conversely, why good things sometimes happen to bad people. The prophet Jeremiah put the second question to God in this way:

> LORD, if I argued my case with you, you would prove to be right. Yet I must question you about matters of justice. Why are the wicked so prosperous? Why do dishonest people succeed? (Jeremiah 12:1, Good News Bible)

As with many of the topics covered in this book, a full treatment would require a whole book. I will here outline an answer only to indicate that the Justice of God is clear and unambiguous. In answer to Jeremiah's question, we should remind ourselves about the purposeful nature of God's Love and Justice; these are geared towards the objective of helping individuals achieve the spiritual purpose of their existence. Earthly prosperity and earthly success do not necessarily lead to spiritual growth; they are not passports to Paradise. Indeed, they may have the opposite effect of keeping the spirits of some individuals earth-bound, that is, trapped in the World of Matter. Without a drastic inner change, such earth-bound spirits might never be able to return to Paradise and might eventually suffer spiritual death.

In corrupt societies, for example, people who have no conscience but who have access to public funds would necessarily be materially prosperous; the more morally bankrupt they are the more 'prosperous' they could become. In such societies, which unfortunately abound in the world today, the really dishonest individual has better chances of earthly 'success' than a noble person. There is no mystery about such prosperity or success. People of conscience would distance themselves from and would certainly not pray for those sorts of success and prosperity. God simply has no hand in corruptly acquired success or prosperity. Moreover, corrupt societies are fertile grounds for miscarriage of earthly justice. Thus, a good man might be punished for crimes he did not commit. God has nothing to do with such miscarriages of justice, which would simply be acts of corrupt judges. Of course, the hour of retribution will surely come for all corrupt and ignoble persons, without exception. And corrupt societies too must eventually fail.

We note from the foregoing paragraph that what some may consider good may not necessarily be good for a given individual. Conversely, it is possible that what appears bad may, in fact, be in the best overall interest of the spirit of the affected person. As an illustration, we may conceive of an apparently good person dying prematurely if that person no longer has any spiritual benefits to derive in this earth-life and if there is, for one reason or the other, the danger of a significant spiritual decline if he had more years. It could also be that the person is destined for an urgent and very important role in the Beyond. There are many reasons why premature death might not be a bad thing for the spirit concerned.

In general, we ought to be very careful when we talk about good and bad people. What counts is the spiritual standing of a person as measured with the yardstick of the Laws of Creation. By that measure, we are certainly poor judges; hence we are admonished *not* to judge. Some people we consider bad may not be so, and those we think are noble may not be. Furthermore, we should always take into consideration the fact that there is an interval between sowing and reaping. The length of the interval depends on the nature of the thought, word or action concerned; it could be rather short or quite long, not appearing until a subsequent earth-life of the human spirit concerned. Therefore, we are not justified in assuming that a person does not deserve a particular experience based solely on what we know of his current outward standing, good or bad.

Enriching the Rich and Impoverishing the Poor

Jesus said: "*For to every one who has will more be given, and he will have abundance; but from him who has not, even what he has will be taken away.*" What does this say of the Love and Justice of God?

The explicit statement of taking away the very little that a person has and giving it to one who already has occurs in four separate passages in three books of the New Testament (Matthew 13:12; Matthew 25:29; Mark 4:25; and Luke 19:26). They were spoken as the lesson to be drawn from the Parable of the Sower in Matthew and Mark, the Parable of the Talents (Matthew 25:14-30) and the Parable of the Pounds, also called the Parable of the Gold Coins (Luke 19:11-27). And in all the cases, the contexts suggest that Jesus concurred with the statement. If interpreted literally, the statement would mean that Jesus saw nothing wrong in deliberately enriching the rich at the direct expense of the poorest. Jesus Christ, as the incarnation of the Love of God, would certainly not support, much less advocate, such a repugnant policy.

The statement is, of course not meant to be interpreted literally. *Jesus was not setting out or advocating a policy. By that* statement, *Jesus was drawing attention to a Law of Creation and its consequence: this is the immutable Law of Movement.* The Law is especially important because all the Laws that manifest the Will of God in Creation operate within the framework of the Law of Movement, as was discussed in Chapter 7.

Motion is a fundamental principle throughout Creation. The closer a realm is to the highest point of Creation, the more pronounced is the motion. And the further away it is the more sluggish is its movement. Thus, movement in Paradise is much more pronounced than on earth. Progress, preservation, and restoration are achieved only through movement of the right kind. It is now widely recognized that we should exercise – which is to say that our bodies should respect the Law of Movement. A body that is exercised stays healthier than one that does not receive any exercise. Moreover, any ability that is used improves; an ability which is not used declines and could be completely lost over time. All these are effects of the Law of Movement. The biological principle of adaptation is a consequence of the Law of Movement; thus, there are birds which can no longer fly because their wings have deteriorated on account of failure to use them over thousands of years.

As a consequence of the Law of Movement, talents and endowments that are used appropriately flourish and get even better; those which are not used degenerate and are finally lost. It is in this sense of a natural law that we should understand and interpret the statement *"For to every one who has will more be given, and he will have abundance; but from him who has not, even what he has will be taken away"*. In other words, a key lesson to be learned from the Parables of the Sower, the Talents, and the Pounds is that human beings must observe the Law of Movement and that there are bad consequences for those who do not conform to this immutable natural law.

The Law of Movement also applies to the acquisition of spiritual knowledge. It is only those who seek seriously, constantly, genuinely and with humility, who will find the knowledge which leads to eternal life as well as happiness on earth, provided the knowledge is applied correctly. Those who indolently proclaim that the Truth cannot be known or that it is all superstition will, alas, never know the Truth. The disciples of Jesus had, through their discipleship, demonstrated their serious and genuine search for Truth. Therefore, in accordance with the Law of Movement, they could expect, as Jesus told them, "to know the secrets (or mysteries) of the kingdom of heaven", secrets or mysteries which are denied to others who had not sought seriously or sought in the wrong manner. But anyone in the audience who heard the Parables told by Jesus and thereafter reflected deeply on their meanings (which would be tantamount to engaging in spiritual movement) would also be able "to know the secrets of the kingdom of heaven". The Law also implies that there should be no stand-still in one's search for truth; Christians who do so, for example, go against the teaching of Jesus!

In the realm of public policy, the Law of Movement implies that people should be rewarded according to their efforts; there should be equity. But governments should not attempt arbitrarily to make people equal regardless of their abilities and their efforts. And those who refuse to contribute to society, even though they could, do not deserve public support.

The Indispensable Factor of Purity

Purity is a difficult concept for us human beings to understand. The childlike attitude and bearing of innocent children give us a notion of purity as it manifests on earth. In thinking about the Love of God, the factor of Purity should be considered. This is because in the Divine Realm, Love and Purity are closely united. God's Love can only reach us on the path of Purity. If we wish to partake of the blessings of God's Love, we must cultivate Purity.

A little reflection should make it obvious to us that Purity and God's Love must be closely connected. If we consider the immutable Law of Homogeneity, the Law that ensures that Like will always attract Like, it becomes clear that only that which is truly pure can attract that which comes from the incomparable Purity that necessarily characterizes whatever comes from or is associated with God. Thus, it is self-evident that to attract the Love of God, we have to make ourselves pure channels; we as individuals on earth should cultivate purity.

In several of his lectures, the author of the Grail Message gave the counsel: "Keep the hearth of your thoughts pure, by so doing you will bring peace and be happy!" He says that this exhortation is the foundation for the building of a new humanity. Once we keep the hearth of our thoughts pure, the radiation of the Love of God enters and true peace and happiness necessarily follow. By the hearth of our thoughts, I understand the fountain from which all our thoughts spring. This means that as a starting point, we have to develop an absolutely sincere and very strong volition for what is good, so that no evil thoughts can arise. The right yardstick for what is good is, of course, God's Will as manifested in his Laws of Creation.

Again and again we must return to the Laws of Creation as the straight path to doing the Will of God. Understanding these Laws and thinking, acting, and speaking according to what they indicate are, in fact, the real way to seek the Kingdom of God. And once we do so, everything beneficial to our spiritual goal and the necessities of life will automatically be given to us. Hence, Jesus said we should strive first for the Kingdom of God and all other things will be given to us as well (Matthew 6:33). Therefore, anyone who harbours evil and from whose heart evil thoughts can still arise has not started to strive for the Kingdom of God. It does not matter against whom the evil is directed. We must, therefore, exert ourselves with all our strength to strive for what is good, and thereby to purify the hearth, the fountain of our thoughts. In doing so, we would instinctively love our 'neighbours' and we would never think of harming them. Moreover, we would no longer seek the faults in others but reflect on what might be our own faults in every disturbance of harmony as well as in great conflicts and disagreements.

Some Remarks on Human Love

We have emphasized the inseparable nature of God's Love and God's Justice. We also stated that God's Love considers only what is of spiritual benefit to us. Reflection on these suggests that we need to redefine love in our relationships with fellow human beings in such a way that we do not exclude justice even in love. Moreover, above all, we must think of what will benefit our loved ones spiritually. It is a fact that some human actions and attitudes as well as ideologies that appear to demonstrate love are unhelpful and wrong when viewed from a spiritual perspective.

In this connection, an ancient Truth Bringer admonished: "Love each other with strong, severe love! It is not love when you remove every stone from each other's path, when you speak in sweet, flattering words, different from your soul's inner perceiving. True love sees the faults of the other, and helps him to overcome them" (cited in *Helping Words* compiled by Herbert Vollmann, p. 26). And the author of the Grail Message wrote:

> Genuine love will take no account of what gratifies the other, of what is agreeable to him and gives him joy, but will only direct itself towards what will *benefit* him, regardless of whether it affords him pleasure or not. That is genuine love and service!

If, therefore, it is written: "Love your enemies", it means: "Do that which will benefit them! Punish them if they cannot otherwise be made to understand!" That is serving them! But justice must prevail, for love cannot be separated from justice — they are one!

Misplaced indulgence would mean fostering the faults of the enemies and thus letting them slide further on the downward path. Would that be love? On the contrary, by acting thus one would burden oneself with guilt! (*In the Light of Truth, The Grail Message*, Volume II, Lecture, "The Religion of Love")

The statement that we should punish our enemies if that is the only way they will understand should be correctly understood. The emphasis is on the *volition* underlying our action. Our volition must be one of love, to *help* the enemy, to set the enemy on the right path of understanding of the Will of God. Such action should neither be due to uncontrolled anger nor stem from the desire to retaliate. People do punish their children purely out of love; therefore, this concept should not be strange. If we merely act out of anger and in the spirit of retaliation, we would be doing evil and thereby open a new cycle of sowing and reaping; thus helping neither ourselves nor the enemy.

The Law of Sowing and Reaping is the mechanism by which the Creator ensures that 'vengeance' and 'recompense' are administered most precisely. That was why Jesus could say: "You have heard that it was said, 'An eye for an eye and a tooth for a tooth.' But I say to you, do not resist one who is evil. But if anyone strikes you on the right cheek, turn to him the other also ..." (Matthew 5: 38-39). The basic principle of the Mosaic Law of 'an eye for an eye' was that whoever harms another person should be punished for it and the punishment should match the offence. This was an improvement on the older Babylonian

Code of Hammurabi in which punishment for a given harm varied according to the relative social status of the offender and the victim. In the primitive society of the time, the Mosaic law was intended to limit retaliation, check aggressive behavior, and yet permit necessary self-defence.

When Jesus spoke about turning the other cheek, He simply meant that we should leave retaliation to the Law of Sowing and Reaping, which manifesting the Will of God, ensures justice with a precision and perfection that is beyond human capacity. Moreover, whatever good we do for others (including our enemies), we do for ourselves because in accordance with the Law of Sowing and Reaping we will reap multiples of it in future. However, it should be emphasized that the teachings of Jesus do not condemn actions taken in self-defence and intended purely to discourage unbridled aggression. One should not give free rein to aggressive behaviour and oppression as one would thereby be unwittingly promoting evil. This is in line with the previous remark that true love sees the faults of the other, and helps him to overcome them. The yardstick for the faults should, of course, be our best understanding of the Laws of Creation. By purposely making individuals or groups see their faults and by taking actions that help them to recognize the self-destructive nature of such faults, we are extending true love to them.

The true love, which we should cultivate, only knows and wishes the spiritual welfare of the beloved one and does not think of oneself. It always wishes what is best for the other, fears for her, suffers with her, but also shares in her joy. It is not demanding, it does not scheme, and has no ulterior motives. In short, whoever harbours true love demonstrates it through idealistic thoughts and actions. And both the beloved and the one who bestows true love are beneficiaries; for in accordance with the Laws of Creation, the one who gives true love must reap multiples of the same at the appropriate future time.

In contrast to true love, earthly love is demanding and one-sided and, therefore, a distortion of true love. For this reason, the problem of love for many people is the need to be loved. They grumble that they are not treated lovingly or that they are not sufficiently loved and the good ones among such people pray that they may find people who love them. The impulse to love never wells up within them. Such earthly love harbours dangerous jealousies and all sorts of evil. Thus, one sometimes hears of various crimes, including even murders, arising from so-called love. Those who are habitually demanding love and ever needing to be loved would never instinctively give love and, therefore, would never receive true love. They certainly would never experience love to their own satisfaction. To be loved, one must love unconditionally. This is the dictate of a Law of Creation: the Law of Balance between giving and taking. And as Jesus explained, it is more blessed to give than to receive; thus giving comes first. By giving true love, we sow true love and must receive multiples of it, and not necessarily from the object of our love!

To conclude, let me note that in the English language, Divine Love and Divine Justice are often used as synonymous expressions for the Love of God and the Justice of God, respectively. As was explained in Chapter 5, the Divine Realm has existed since eternity but only as a consequence of the inevitable reach of the radiation of God. Therefore, the Divine is not the same as God. And God is not Divine; but God is God! Therefore, in the strictest sense, one should not use the adjective 'Divine' to describe that which is directly associated with God.

13 The Omnipresence of God

When most people speak of God, they state that He is omnipresent. This is to say that He is present everywhere at the same time. The idea that God is omnipresent seems straightforward and clear until one starts really thinking about it. In most religious traditions, including Christianity, it is also said that God is 'in heaven'. For example, in the Lord's Prayer, we say "Our Father who art in heaven." And in the Apostles' Creed, there is the following statement about Jesus: "He ascended into heaven, and is seated at the right hand of God the Father Almighty." The question arises: Is God 'in heaven' or is He everywhere as implied by the literal meaning of the word "omnipresent"?

The popular conception of God's Omnipresence is expressed in the following words in the Book of Jeremiah in the Bible:

> I am a God who is everywhere and not in one place only. No one can hide where I cannot see him. Do you not know that I am everywhere in heaven and on earth? (Jeremiah 23:23-24, Good News Bible, Today's English Translation).

In Psalm 139, we encounter a similar conception of the Omnipresence of God:

> Where could I go to escape from you? Where could I get away from your presence? If I went up to heaven, you would be there; if I lay down in the world of the dead, you

would be there. If I flew away beyond the east or lived in the farthest place in the west, you would be there to lead me; you would be there to help me. If I could ask the darkness to hide me or the light round me to turn into night, but even darkness is not dark for you, and the night is as bright as the day. Darkness and light are the same to you. (Psalm 139:7-12, Good News Bible, Today's English Translation).

It is the sense of omnipresence expressed in these two passages that has become popular among religious people. What are we to make of this concept? Does it mean that God is literally present everywhere? If that were so, how are we to envisage Him? In Chapter 6, we noted that pantheism and panentheism are wrong conceptions of God.

Let me state straightaway that if interpreted literally the two passages misrepresent the Omnipresence of God. The two passages become understandable if we interpret them in the sense of emphasizing the fact that we human beings cannot escape the *reach* of God and not that God is literally present everywhere. We are always within God's *reach* because the Laws of God encompass the whole of Creation and Subsequent Creation and there are innumerable species of invisible entities that are active everywhere to ensure the implementation, immutability and inviolability of the Laws. Therefore, wherever we may be, we are subject to the Will of God, which is maintained infallibly by the Laws, as discussed in Chapter 7.

In this book, especially in Chapter 5, we have implied that there is what one may call the Eternal Realm of God that has no beginning and no end. We also stated that next to the Eternal Realm of God is the Divine Realm which has also existed eternally as the consequence of the direct radiation of God. However, it should be remarked that the distance between what we may designate as the Eternal Realm of God and the Divine Realm is far greater than the greatest distance that the human mind can conceive. This is because nothing is in the actual proximity of God, if proximity is measured according to earthly conceptions; "for that which one can call the actual proximity to God is a surging ocean of flames, still without the possibility to acquire form." Thus, it is said: "Before God everything dissolves!" This is why it is so necessary to differentiate between God and the Divine. God is not Divine; God is God!

When we speak of the 'heaven' in which God has existed eternally (as for example in the statement "Our Father who art in heaven") it is to the Eternal Realm of God that we refer. God as the Creator is outside His Creation. In His loftiness and sublimity, God is not one who follows us around or one we may expect to find at the end of our journey. Thus, we must conclude that the popular notion of Omnipresence as applied to God is wrong.

In the next Chapter on "Making Sense of the Trinity", we will discuss Jesus as the Son of God and emphasize that a Son of God means a Part of God. Jesus was heavily cloaked with the substances of the many planes and sub-planes of Creation through which He had to pass before taking on the physical body following incarnation on earth. The earth was thus not exposed to the full radiation of God through Jesus; the earth would have dissolved or become incinerated if it were exposed to a part of God's untransformed radiation. At the end of His mission, Jesus shed all these cloaks and reunited with God as a Part of Him. God cannot be personally and literally present anywhere in Creation or Subsequent Creation.

It follows that the right understanding of the expression "God is omnipresent" must be different from the mundane meaning commonly attached to it. Omnipresence does *not* mean that God is literally everywhere — in every space, every leaf, every stone, etc. It simply means that God is potentially accessible from everywhere. As an illustration, the spirit of one who prays to God earnestly and in the correct manner can be linked with those spheres from which help can be offered; one would, therefore, say that God has heard one's prayer. No matter where he is located, the human being, as a human spirit, can be invisibly linked with the transformed radiation that has its ultimate origin in God through praying aright and through earnest seeking. In other words, we can potentially find the connecting path to God wherever we may be. But God is where He is; He is *not* literally dispersed throughout Creation. And as already stated, the Will of God spans the whole of Creation and Subsequent Creation in the form of immutable Laws, thus ensuring that everything and everywhere is always within God's reach.

This conception of Omnipresence might have been impossible to believe in the past. But it is easily understandable and believable in our time because we have become familiar with all sorts of advanced remote control and guidance systems, such as those installed in cars to guide drivers to their destinations as well as drones sent to far places for surveillance and attack. Awareness of these possibilities should facilitate visualization of a Power (God) that is able to establish mechanisms to oversee and control many things from unfathomable distances.

14 Making Sense of the Trinity

The idea of the Trinity touches directly on the nature of God and must, therefore, be considered when thinking about God. For that reason, it ought not to be contemplated exclusively from the point of view of any particular religion; neither should it be considered of interest only to members of particular sects. However, I will focus almost exclusively on the Christian doctrine of the Trinity only because the Trinity is most prominent and most developed in Christianity. But this should not be construed as an attack on Christianity. I should note, however, that Hinduism has its own form of Trinity – the concept of the Trimurti, composed of Brahma, Vishnu, and Shiva, having the titles of "Creator", "Preserver" and "Destroyer" respectively, and defined as the three highest manifestations of the one reality.

Incomprehensibility is the recurrent theme of most serious discussions of the Trinity, even though it is a core concept for most Christian denominations. Even leaders of Trinitarian churches agree that, as it is traditionally formulated, the Trinity is incomprehensible and even confusing. And yet to be saved members of such denominations are told that they must believe in it. The paradox is striking: one's salvation is said to depend on a mysterious idea whose comprehension is impossible! But true faith, which depends on personal conviction, is impossible where understanding is lacking. In this Chapter, I indicate how the Trinity should be understood and show that it does not have to be the incomprehensible mystery that it has historically been thought to be.

Athanasius and Arius

The most emphatic and explicit expressions of the concept of the Trinity are found in the Athanasian Creed, which has the Latin name *Quicumque Vult*, taken from the opening words of the Creed ("Whosoever wishes"). The Creed has been used since the sixth century and is widely accepted by Christian churches, including the Roman Catholic Church and most Protestant denominations. It was thought to have been written by Athanasius (297-373 AD) Bishop of Alexandria (in Egypt), hence the name. However, the authorship by Bishop Athanasius has been challenged since the last century on several grounds, including the belief that the Creed could not have been written until many years after his death. Most theological scholars are no longer sure of the authorship of the Athanasian Creed.

The attribution of the Creed to Athanasius is not surprising as he was perhaps the staunchest opponent of the anti-Trinitarians – Arius and his supporters (the Arians). Arius (250-336 AD) of Libyan birth was a Church official in Alexandria. Around the year 323 AD, he began to propagate the idea that although Jesus was more than a man, he was not God but was created by God and, therefore, could be described only figuratively as the Son of God. That also meant that Jesus was not co-eternal with God but came into existence only at some point before He was born on earth. His views were condemned as heretical by the Patriarch of Alexandria. And Arius and eleven priests and deacons who supported him were deposed. Arius moved to Caesarea where he continued to propagate his ideas and obtained the support of Bishop Eusebius of Nicomedia (an ancient city in what is now Turkey) and some other prominent priests. At that time Athanasius was the Patriarch's Secretary and he became the Patriarch when his boss (Patriarch Alexander) died in 328 AD.

The ensuing Arian conflict eventually involved bishops, priests, Roman emperors as well as ordinary Christians. The First

Ecumenical Council of Nicaea (in present-day Turkey) was convened by Emperor Constantine I to determine matters of doctrine. Athanasius, as Secretary to Patriarch Alexander, attended the Council meetings and it was that Council that condemned the Arian teaching as heresy and adopted the first Nicene Creed in 325 AD, declaring that Jesus was fully God, just as the Father. But a regional synod at Tyre (an ancient port city in modern day Lebanon) exonerated Arius in 335 and two Roman Emperors, Constantius II (337-361) and Valens (364-378) had Arian sympathies. Indeed, some historians think that at one point there were more Arian Christians than orthodox believers. The doctrine of the Trinity vis-à-vis the Arian teaching waxed and waned depending on the political climate. Largely as a result, Athanasius spent 17 of his 45 years as Patriarch in five exiles ordered by four different Roman emperors. Throughout the period, Athanasius remained the chief defender of the doctrine of the Trinity until he died in 373 AD.

The First Ecumenical Council of Constantinople held in the year 381 AD, after the death of both Arius and Athanasius, reconfirmed Arianism as heretical and officially established the doctrine of the Trinity. Athanasius is venerated by the Roman Catholic Church, Oriental and Eastern Orthodox churches, the Lutherans, and the Anglican Communion.

The Athanasian Creed

While the Athanasian Creed is the most detailed, the other Creeds are not substantially different in terms of what the doctrine of the Trinity is supposed to mean. The Athanasian Creed has two parts: the first part is on the Trinity and the second part on Christology, that is, the nature of Jesus Christ. Both parts are reproduced herewith. The word *catholic* used in the Creed does not refer to the Roman Catholic Church, but it is rather a reference to the *universal* Christian faith.

Whosoever will be saved, before all things it is necessary that he hold the catholic faith. Which faith except everyone do keep whole and undefiled, without doubt he shall perish everlastingly.

And the catholic faith is this: That we worship one God in Trinity, and Trinity in Unity, neither confounding the persons, nor dividing the substance.

For there is one Person of the Father, another of the Son, and another of the Holy Spirit. But the godhead of the Father, of the Son, and of the Holy Spirit, is all one, the glory equal, the majesty co-eternal. Such as the Father is, such is the Son, and such is the Holy Spirit. The Father uncreated, the Son uncreated, and the Holy Spirit uncreated. The Father incomprehensible, the Son incomprehensible, and the Holy Spirit incomprehensible. The Father eternal, the Son eternal, and the Holy Spirit eternal. And yet they are not three eternals, but one Eternal. As also there are not three incomprehensibles, nor three uncreated, but one Uncreated, and one Incomprehensible. So likewise the Father is Almighty, the Son Almighty, and the Holy Spirit Almighty. And yet they are not three Almighties, but one Almighty.

So the Father is God, the Son is God, and the Holy Spirit is God. And yet they are not three gods, but one God. So likewise the Father is Lord, the Son Lord, and the Holy Spirit Lord. And yet not three lords, but one Lord.

For as we are compelled by the Christian verity to acknowledge each Person by Himself to be both God and Lord, so we are also forbidden by the catholic religion to say that there are three gods or three lords.

The Father is made of none, neither created, nor begotten. The Son is of the Father alone, not made, nor created, but begotten. The Holy Spirit is of the Father, neither made, nor created, nor begotten, but proceeding.

So there is one Father, not three fathers; one Son, not three sons; one Holy Spirit, not three holy spirits. And in the Trinity none is before or after another; none is greater or less than another, but all three Persons are co-eternal together and co-equal. So that in all things, as is aforesaid, the Unity in Trinity and the Trinity in Unity is to be worshipped.

He therefore that will be saved must think thus of the Trinity.

Furthermore, it is necessary to everlasting salvation that he also believe rightly the Incarnation of our Lord Jesus Christ. For the right faith is, that we believe and confess, that our Lord Jesus Christ, the Son of God, is God and man; God, of the substance of the Father, begotten before the worlds; and man of the substance of his mother, born in the world; perfect God and perfect man, of a rational soul and human flesh subsisting. Equal to the Father, as touching His godhead; and inferior to the Father, as touching His manhood; who, although He is God and man, yet he is not two, but one Christ; one, not by conversion of the godhead into flesh but by taking of the manhood into God; one altogether; not by confusion of substance, but by unity of person. For as the rational soul and flesh is one man, so God and man is one Christ; who suffered for our salvation, descended into hell, rose again the third day from the dead. He ascended into heaven, He sits at the right hand of the Father, God Almighty, from whence He will come to judge the quick and the dead. At His coming all men will rise again with their bodies and shall give account for their own works. And they that have done good shall go into life everlasting; and they that have done evil into everlasting fire.

This is the catholic faith, which except a man believes faithfully, he cannot be saved.

In some texts of the Creed, the "Holy Spirit" is translated as the "Holy Ghost". A close reading of the above formulation of the conception of God as one in three persons would show why it has remained confusing and truly incomprehensible even among Christians who claim to believe firmly in the doctrine. And this is in spite of the large number of books and innumerable theological and philosophical essays written on the subject over the past several centuries as well as in recent times.

As a general comment, it should be stated that mere belief in a creed, which one does not understand cannot lead to salvation. Only such beliefs, which through understanding and reflection have become convictions and which, therefore, constantly influence one's volition, thoughts, words, and deeds can lead to salvation if they are correct or to damnation if they are wrong.

St. Augustine on the Trinity

St. Augustine (354-430 AD), Bishop of Hippo, spent a long time working on what became his classic treatise on the Trinity, *De Trinitate*. He had to interrupt work on it presumably because of the very difficult nature of the subject and, indeed, he might not have finished the work had not his friends published, without his authorization, the first twelve "books" (each on a different aspect of the Trinity). To avoid an incomplete work in circulation, he finally felt compelled to write the remaining three "books", making *De Trinitate* a 15-volume treatise. In the work, he tried to show evidence of support in the Bible for the doctrine of the Trinity and sought to formulate an intelligible explanation of the Trinity. He defended the idea that Father, Son, and the Holy Spirit were equal as opposed to those who argued that Son and the Holy Spirit were subordinate to the Father. Those opposed to the doctrine of equality in the persons of the Trinity argued that it is said that the Father 'sent the Son'; therefore, the Father must have been superior otherwise He would not be in a position to 'send the Son.'

St. Augustine struggled long and hard in the endeavour to explain the Trinity. He developed his defence of the Trinity on the premise of two principles. The first principle was that the traditional formulation of the Trinity as one God in three persons was consistent with human reason. He was of the opinion that a form of trinity is encountered in human experience. He argued that, for example, in the experience of loving and being loved, there are three entities – the lover, the beloved, and the phenomenon of love. He contended that if one were to love oneself, there would still be three entities – the self; one's knowledge of oneself; and one's love of oneself; in other words, the self, self-knowledge, and self-love form a kind of trinity. Additionally, Augustine stated that in knowing oneself, there is the self remembering itself and that is memory; there is the understanding that one knows oneself; and there is the will to understand. This leads to another triad – memory, understanding, and will.

The second principle that St. Augustine adopted to defend the Trinity was that one should not dismiss an article of faith just because one does not yet understand how it is consistent with reason. Augustine postulated that we do not understand in order to believe; rather we believe in order to understand. Here he makes the crucial point that, whereas faith comes first, reason must follow if there is to be understanding. One should *not* dispense with reason in matters of faith. It seems to me that St. Augustine's position is in line with the reality that the highest spiritual truths cannot be 'thought out' but are *revealed*. Following revelation, the intellect (reason) must then help to facilitate understanding of the truths. But the right faith must ultimately be consistent with refined reason.

I should remark that St. Augustine's illustrations of the Trinity in human experience (the first principle on which his defence of the Trinity is based) seem to me rather abstruse and unconvincing. However, he was right about the spiritual truth of the Trinity. His effort to explain it for earthly understanding was commendable for his time. But it was unsuccessful.

Augustine's struggle with the concept of the Trinity gave rise to the following legend, which, as often happens, has some slight variants depending on who is narrating it. Here is one version. One day Augustine was walking along the beach at Hippo in his diocese (in what is now Algeria) contemplating the Trinity when he saw a small boy running back and forth using a seashell to carry water from the sea to pour into a small hole in the sand. Curious, Augustine approached the boy and asked him what he was doing. With a smile, the boy responded that he was trying to empty the sea into the hole. "But that is impossible, my dear child, the hole cannot contain all that water, however wide you make it," said Augustine.

The boy stopped, looked into the eyes of the Bishop, and replied, "It is no more impossible than what you are trying to do — comprehend the immensity of the mystery of the Holy Trinity with your small brain." Augustine was deeply touched by the child's answer and in contemplation turned his eyes away from the boy for a moment. When he looked back to continue the conversation, the boy had disappeared. It was presumed by some that the boy was an angel sent to instruct Augustine about the limits to human understanding in matters concerning the great mysteries of the Christian faith, such as the Trinity.

Insoluble Mystery?

Joseph Cardinal Ratzinger, later Pope Benedict XVI, addressed the subject of the Trinity in his book (*God and the World*, pp. 266-267). Recalling the legend of St. Augustine on the beach, he stated that the mystery of the Trinity is "in the end insoluble, not just for ordinary people but even for the very cleverest." He remarked that God as "the Wholly Other" (meaning unlike anything we know or can know) remains beyond our comprehension. Other leaders of Catholic religious thought including Cardinal John O'Connor and Pope John Paul II are of the same opinion. Pope John Paul II described the Trinity as an inscrutable mystery that is beyond the capacities of our understanding and can only be known through revelation.   And the Catholic scholars, Karl Rahner and Herbert Vorgrimler, authors of the *Theological Dictionary*, believe that even with revelation, the Trinity is a mystery that cannot become wholly intelligible. In the *Encyclopedia Americana* the doctrine of the Trinity is described as beyond the grasp of human reason.

My explanations in this book so far, especially those of Chapter 5 (Creation and Subsequent Creation) and Chapter 9 (God is Unlike Human Beings) certainly underscore the truth that our comprehension of God must always remain severely limited. But because of such limitations, the official position of the Church ought to stop with an admission of ignorance. And what cannot be understood ought not to be accepted as a doctrine on which salvation depends.

I should point out that some Christian denominations consider the Trinity an erroneous teaching; given its incomprehensibility and its history, this should not be surprising. Such denominations include the Jehovah's Witnesses, the Unitarian Church, the Church of Jesus Christ of Latter-day Saints as well as a few smaller ones. As its name implies, a major doctrine of the Unitarian Church is that God exists in only one person, in contradiction to the popular understanding of the Trinity as three persons in one. Christians opposed to the concept of God as "three persons in one" argue that there are no explicit passages in the Bible in support of the idea and that the earliest Apostles and earliest Christian fathers up until the fourth Century did not entertain such a conception. Moreover, they argue that "three persons in one" smacks of paganism and polytheism (the belief in more than one God).

Judaism and Islam – the two other major monotheistic religions – do not accept the doctrine of the Trinity. They both think the doctrine is a departure from monotheism. Islam repudiates the doctrine of the Trinity and the Koran asserts that God was neither fathered nor did he father a child: "Say, He is God, the One God, the Absolute. He begets not, nor was He begotten. And there is nothing comparable to Him" (Surah 112:1-4).

The Trinity Explained

How should we proceed to find enlightenment on this subject? As I have already noted, some top Church leaders have remarked that the Trinity can only be understood through revelation. I am pleased to state that the revelation has been explicitly made in the work *In the Light of Truth, The Grail Message* by Abd-ru-shin. The first step is to rise above earthly thinking and consider it from purely spiritual perspectives, bearing in mind that God is unlike human beings. When one thinks in an earthly sense about the Trinity as three persons in one, one is bound to form wrong and confused pictures of the concept; pictures which blur and cast doubt on the oneness of God. It should be stated unequivocally, that there is only One God and only One Power and there is None like Him. In His *working*, one can rightly speak of the Trinity, God the Father, God the Son, and God the Holy Spirit. Thus, it is best to say: "It is all *only* God the Father, He works threefold as One!"

It is also absolutely essential that we be clear that Sonship in relation to God is in no way like the relationship between an earthly father and his son. Sonship as should be understood in connection with the Trinity simply means a Part. Thus, the Son of God means a Part of God. And this does not involve the earthly conception of "begetting" or been "begotten".

Before elaborating on the concept of Sonship of God, let me note that the understanding of the "Holy Spirit" has always been vague even outside the context of the Trinity. At the Ecumenical Council of Nicaea in the year 325, there was no consensus on what to make of the "Holy Spirit." It was only at the Council of Constantinople in 381 AD that the Church officially established the doctrine of the Trinity with the Holy Spirit as a full-fledged *Person*.

This means that the doctrine of the Trinity implies that the Holy Spirit is, like Jesus, a personality. Thus, according to current Roman Catholic Doctrine, "The Holy Spirit is the Third *Person* of the Blessed Trinity" and "The Holy Spirit is equal to the Father and to the Son, for *he* is the same Lord and God as they are." (*A Catechism of Christian Doctrine*, p. 20, italics added). It is true that the Holy Spirit is a personality, although this fact is usually not emphasized. Indeed, statements are often made that seem to deny the fact. The situation today is that most Christians and even theologians still do not quite know what to make of the Holy Spirit.

Let me remark that the fact that the Holy Spirit is a personality, just as Jesus was, means that the Holy Spirit does not literally 'come upon' people; neither can anybody 'have' the Holy Spirit. This is in the same manner that Jesus cannot 'come upon' a person. The Holy Spirit as the Creative Will of God *pours out power* into Creation at regularly recurring intervals for the maintenance of Creation. Individuals who are appropriately inwardly prepared for it may receive such power, which takes the form of radiation. It was one such occasion that the disciples of Jesus experienced in what is now called Pentecost. It was not the first occasion and was not brought about especially for the disciples. It happened that their experiences of the last days of Jesus made them especially receptive. Such outpouring of power by the Holy Spirit has recurred yearly since the beginning of Creation. The power, which all human beings have but that is at best poorly developed in most cases, is spiritual power; it is inherent in us as human spirits.

The Holy Spirit is, indeed, a Son of God and His name is Imanuel! Thus, there are two Sons of God: Imanuel and Jesus. Imanuel is the *Creative Will* of God, the Executive Justice of God, also called the "Spirit of Truth". Jesus is the Love of God. Both Jesus and Imanuel (the Holy Spirit) are Parts of God and are inseparable from Him. In the work, *In the Light of Truth, The Grail Message*, the Trinity is illustrated for human understanding in the following words:

> They are like the arms of a body which can act independently but still belong to the body if this is to be complete. Yet they can only carry out independent actions as a part of the whole (Volume II, Lecture "God").

It follows that the Father (God), the Holy Spirit (His Creative Will), and the Son of God (the Love of God) are completely and inseparably one. Whatever the Son of God does can be considered an action of the Father; and the same is true of whatever the Holy Spirit does. The illustration implies that one should not think of the Son or of the Holy Spirit as if they were separate and independent of the Father. One's arms are not separate from one's body, even though they can take seemingly independent actions.

For our further enlightenment, let us contrast the conception of the Sonship of God with the relationship between father and son in the human family. The human father and his son are always two different persons; they can at best become united in carrying out a task. It is the opposite with the spiritual and correct concept of the Son of God. God the Father and the Son of God are one and can only be considered two in their working. One can say that "the two sons of God, Imanuel (the Holy Spirit) and Jesus are one in the Father and only two in the nature of their working". This is analogous to the manner in which both the right and the left arms are one with the body but each arm may act with or without the other; however, they can act always only as part of the body. In a further explanation of the Trinity, the author of the Grail Message wrote:

> Before Creation came into existence God was One! During the process of creating He severed a Part of His Will to work independently in Creation, and thus became two-fold. When later it became necessary to provide a mediator for erring mankind, because the Purity of God did not permit a direct connection to self-enchained humanity, out of His Love He severed a Part of Himself to act as a temporary bridge, in order to make Himself once more understood. Thus, with the birth of Christ, He became a *Trinity!* (*In the Light of Truth, The Grail Message*, Vol. II, Lecture "God").

The severance mentioned in the above quotation was a process of radiation, which could not have been understood in earlier centuries. The radiation process did not involve a "cutting off" or diminution of God in any way. God is eternally complete. When God willed that Creation should come into being, His Creative Will manifested as Imanuel and subsequently as it became necessary to redirect humankind onto the right path, the activity of Love manifested in Jesus. An illustration with human beings on earth might be helpful. We could say that a certain man is a personification of courage. This would mean that the man manifests courage in his activity; courage is a part of his personality. And in manifesting courage, he remains completely himself and is in no way diminished. The same man might also be a personification of humility. Thus, he manifests two distinct virtues, while remaining one personality. Courage and humility are in the person and are inseparable from him, even though they manifest differently.

The activity of the Holy Spirit as the Creative Will of God is hinted at in the first of the two Genesis accounts of the act of creation. Many versions of the Bible speak of the Spirit of God moving or hovering over the surface of the waters. The first three verses of Chapter 1 of the Book of Genesis as translated in the Revised Standard Version of the Bible are reproduced below:

> In the beginning God created the heavens and the earth. The earth was without form and void, and darkness was upon the face of the deep; *and the Spirit of God was moving over the face of the waters*. And God said, "Let there be light"; and there was light. (Genesis 1:2, Revised Standard Version, italics added)

It should be noted that the act of creation recorded in the Book of Genesis is an earthly rendering of something that took place at the highest heights, far above the origin of us human spirits, as I depicted in Chapter 5 on "Creation and Subsequent Creation." The "Spirit of God" in Genesis 1:2 is a hint at the activity of the Creative Will of God, Imanuel.

We find the name Imanuel (variant spellings include Immanuel and Emmanuel) in only two books of the Bible; in Isaiah and in Matthew. Isaiah prophesied that a young woman (or virgin) would be pregnant and give birth to a son who would be named Imanuel, meaning "God is with us" (Isaiah 7:14). In the understanding of the author of the Gospel According to Matthew, Isaiah's prophesy was about the birth of the Messiah whom the Jews were expecting and he sought to link that prophecy with the birth of Jesus (Matthew 1:18-25).

However, in the announcement of the angel who spoke to Joseph in his dream, the son to whom Mary would give birth was to be called Jesus. Objectively, since the son prophesied by Isaiah was to be called Imanuel whereas the one announced by the angel was to be called Jesus, the two sons would not be the same. And it is significant that Jesus is not referred to as Imanuel anywhere else in the Bible. Therefore it was not Imanuel to whom Mary gave birth, nor was her child the one of whom Isaiah prophesied! Jesus is the Son of God, the Love of God. And Imanuel is the eternal Mediator between God and Creation in which man (humankind) dwells, and for that reason, He is called the "Son of Man" (although He is also a Son of God). Imanuel, the Creative Will of God, is also the Executive Justice responsible for the World Judgment – the so-called Final Judgment as well as the institution of the one thousand-year reign of the Will of God on earth.

The Son of God and The Son of Man

In many books of the Bible mention is made of "son of man". The Old Testament Book of Ezekiel is full of the expression but it is used in a literal sense to designate human beings. It occurs extensively in the Gospel of Matthew and less frequently in Mark, Luke, and John. In these Books, the expression is sometimes used as though it were a synonym for the Son of God, Jesus, and at other times the context suggests a different person, one who would return to the earth to judge the world. It would seem that the Gospel writers and the disciples of Jesus were uncertain as to whether or not Jesus regarded Himself as both the Son of God and the Son of Man. But Jesus as a Part of God knew of the Son of Man and sometimes referred to the latter's future coming into the world for the final judgment. However, the author of the Gospel According to Matthew (scholars agree that Levi Matthew was *not* the author) portrays the Son of Man as the judge of the world in the following passages:

> Then will appear the sign of the *Son of man* in heaven, and then all the tribes of the earth will mourn, and they will see the *Son of man* coming on the clouds of heaven with power and great glory; and he will send out his angels with a loud trumpet call, and they will gather his elect from the four winds, from one end of heaven to the other (Matthew 24:30-31, italics added, Revised Standard Version).

> As were the days of Noah, so will be the coming of the *Son of man*. For as in those days before the flood they were eating and drinking, marrying and giving in marriage, until the day when Noah entered the ark, and they did not know until the flood came and swept them all away, so will be the coming of the *Son of man*. Then two men will be in the field; one is taken and one is left. Two women will be grinding at the mill; one is taken and one is left. Watch therefore, for you do not know on what day your Lord is coming. But know this, that if the householder had known in what part of the night the thief was coming, he would have watched and would not have let his house be broken into. Therefore you also must be ready; for the *Son of man* is coming at an hour you do not expect. (Matthew 24:37-44, italics added, Revised Standard Version).

When the Son of man comes in his glory, and all the angels with him, then he will sit on his glorious throne. Before him will be gathered all the nations, and he will separate them one from another as a shepherd separates the sheep from the goats, and he will place the sheep at his right hand, but the goats at the left. (Matthew 25:31-33, italics added, Revised Standard Version).

The Book of Revelation records a vision of the Son of Man as He prepared to pass sentences on the seven churches: Ephesus, Smyrna, Pergamum, Thyatira, Sardis, Philadelphia, and Laodicea (Revelation 1:9-20). The vision was not that of Jesus, the Son of God, but of the Executive Justice of God, the Holy Spirit, Imanuel, the Son of Man who was preparing to pronounce judgment on the seven universes (not mere earthly churches)! If the judgment referred only to the churches in Asia Minor, one would have to ask why the churches in other places were not included. And why would judgment be confined only to churches? How about the rest of humanity and human institutions?

In the Book of Daniel we are told of a Son of Man who was presented to the "Ancient of Days" and to whom was "given dominion and glory and kingdom, that all peoples, nations, and languages should serve him; his dominion is an everlasting dominion, which shall not pass away, and his kingdom one that shall not be destroyed" (Daniel 7:13-14). This was again a vision of the Son of Man, the Part of God who is the Creative Will and plays the role of Executive Justice, while Jesus, the Son of God, is the Love of God. He is called the Son of Man because He is the eternal mediator between the Creator and Creation to which man (the human spirit) belongs.

The Son of God and the Son of Man are not *one* person, but two distinct persons according to *human* conceptions, although they are of one essence and are united with God, in a sense analogous to the manner in which the right hand and the left hand are united parts of the same body that may act independently. A hint about the difference in the manner of working of Jesus (the Love of God) and of the Holy Spirit (the Justice of God) is given by Jesus Himself when He said that all sins and blasphemies could be forgiven men, but never those sins and blasphemies committed against the Holy Spirit (Matthew 12:31-32, Mark 3:28-29, and Luke 12:10). Many thinking readers of the Bible must have wondered why it is that blasphemy against the Holy Spirit cannot be forgiven, even though a sin against Jesus the Son of God can be forgiven. Let me explain. Jesus is the *Love* of God, whereas the Holy Spirit is the *Executive Justice* of God, who is responsible for the World Judgment. The Work of the Holy Spirit lies in the immutable and incorruptible Laws of Creation (discussed in Chapter 7). Jesus Christ *did* forgive sins committed against Him; for example, on the crucifixion cross, He said "Father, forgive them, for they know not what they do." It is clear, therefore, that sins committed against Jesus, the Love of God, can be forgiven.

On the other hand, the Holy Spirit as the *Justice* of God works strictly through the Laws of Creation. Any sin against the Holy Spirit brings about unfailingly the appropriate consequences, in accordance with the Laws of Creation, in particular the Law of Sowing and Reaping as well as through the mechanism of symbolic redemption as discussed in Chapter 11. In short, whereas a sin against Jesus Christ could be forgiven by Jesus Himself, that against the Holy Spirit compels the sinner to go through the mills of the Laws of Creation. The one who sowed the seed must reap it; no one else can reap it for him. In accordance with this Law, Jesus cannot reap the fruits resulting from the sins of others. We certainly can say that, on the authority of Jesus Himself, anybody who sins against the Holy Spirit will not be forgiven and, therefore, Jesus could *not* have died for such sins.

Those who believe that Jesus died as a sacrificial lamb to carry away our sins are for this and many other reasons mistaken. He came to teach us the true Will of God; a coming which involved immense sacrifice. Only those who correctly understand and live according to His true teachings regardless of religion are sure to be saved. Obviously, some of those teachings were brought by earlier and later Truth-Bringers.

The Holy Spirit is the Part of God, which through a radiation process, became distinct when God the Father wanted Creation to come into being with the fiat "Let there be Light!" Jesus is the *Love* of God, the Part of God, which through a subsequent radiation process incarnated on earth as Jesus of Nazareth. Thus, Jesus, the Love of God and the Holy Spirit, the Justice of God both emanated from God the Father and they belong to Him as a unity. This is the Trinity of the One God.

15 Praying and Prayers

Praying is a prominent practice in most belief systems and, therefore, the nature of God's involvement in prayers necessarily comes into consideration in thinking about God. Among those who extol the importance of praying, there are differences in the understanding of what prayer is, how one should pray, what one should expect from prayers, and why some prayers are answered and some are not.

An Activity of the Spirit

Rightly understood, praying should be an attempt to connect oneself invisibly with the holy streams of power that permeates all Creation and whose ultimate origin is God. Once connected, we may then make known our desires, be they gratitude to God, specific requests on our own behalf, or on behalf of other persons. One who succeeds in being linked to the holy streams of power may not even need to utter any words, certainly not many words and the endeavour requires little time. On the other hand, if the attempt at connection does not succeed, one has not actually prayed, no matter how many hours or even days one devotes to petitions and praises, be they in silence, murmurs, or in ear-shattering shouts. In that case, there is no question of the prayer being answered. And, above all, all prayers are subject to the mechanisms that God put in place from the beginning of Creation – the Laws of Creation, which express God's Will. Prayers cannot set aside those Laws. This Chapter highlights these issues.

We may identify two types of prayers depending on how the prayer is initiated. There is the spontaneous prayer, which arises within one without any conscious effort. This happens when one is overwhelmed with unexpected joy, fear, shock, or great pain. Without any prior thinking and before one utters any words, something wells up in one's innermost being, in the spirit, which may then be followed with words. In the other type, one consciously decides to pray, thinks of what to pray, chooses and arranges the words to say and these may then retroactively affect the spirit. We may say that there are prayers without words and prayers with words.

It is necessary to emphasize that formal praying is an attempt to become invisibly linked with the highest heights and thereby to open oneself to holy streams of power originating from God. The holy streams of power flow perpetually throughout Creation, but we can only be connected with them at those moments when we are inwardly open, when our spirits bow down to God in humility and purity. And once we attain a genuine state of humility and purity, the radiations from the Creator automatically envelops and flows into us. One would then personally apply the power that one absorbs and would take appropriate actions according to the guidance and inspiration that flow into one's consciousness. It is wrong to presume that God would somehow personally intervene and fix matters with minimum, if any, action on the part of the person praying (the supplicant).

Thanks to technological advances, we are now in a position to understand the concept of being linked with invisible radiation or power originating from God. We know that our atmosphere has numerous television waves (local and international) floating around all the time and that we can link with them and make their content visible and audible only with the appropriate equipment — television sets, with decoders in some cases. It is the same with radio waves. In an analogous manner, the spirit (the inner self) is the appropriate "equipment" that can absorb the waves of power flowing perpetually in Creation. And this does not at all depend on one's religion! One can also say that the human being, when he prays aright, can become invisibly linked with the Spiritual Realms in the manner that a phone caller is invisibly linked with the person with whom he is speaking.

If our prayers are to have the desired effect, regardless of their kind, we must first gain connection with the spiritual spheres and thus be appropriately placed to absorb the transformed radiations emanating from God. Without such connection, one has not really prayed, regardless of the number of hours, the amount of beautiful words and sycophantic expressions devoted to the effort. Moreover, it is only the spirit that can gain connection with the Luminous Heights (as indicated in Chapter 5) and which can absorb the streams of power that flow from there. Our brain, in which resides the intellect, is capable of producing lots of beautiful expressions of praises and petitions to God. These days, many people around the world present themselves as "prayer specialists" or "prayer warriors" on account of the ease and eloquence with which they utter beautiful expressions of wishes and petitions, praises, and gratitude to God. In most cases, these are mere effusions originating from the brain. The eloquence of such "prayers" is invariably simply the result of practice and habit, with no bearing on the states of the spirits of the persons praying. In other words, 'prayer warriors' often do not actually pray!

In truth, whenever the spirit really gains connection with the Highest Heights (i.e. when it is really praying), it cannot utter many words! Under the pressure of the streams of power from the Luminous Heights, the spirit is simply unable to say more than a few words, if any. Whenever a person who is supposedly praying is able to go on and on (as happens so often) you can be sure that it is the intellectual brain at work, not the spirit. There may have been a great oratorical performance but no praying because the spirit was not engaged and, therefore, there was no connection with the Spiritual Realm! Until the spirit (one's real self) is fully engaged and the intellect is silenced, genuine prayer is impossible! In response to a question, the author of the Grail Message wrote:

> Only *intuitive perception* is the decisive force in prayer, not words, which die away weakly like sound in the wind. Words merely serve us as a help for the soul to become absorbed in the intuitive perception, in order to clarify and to support the direction of the intuitive perception. (Abd-ru-shin, *Questions and Answers*)

When the human spirit is enveloped by the invisible radiation from the Luminous Heights, the spirit expresses itself in its own language, which is a language of pictures (incidentally, not gibberish, not 'speaking in tongue'). Moreover, while the spirit is linked with the lighter realms, all its real needs, including those of which the person praying might not be aware, become evident to the many servants of God's Will. And, in accordance with the immutable Laws of God and in consideration of the human being's best spiritual interest, the needs are addressed with the eventual active cooperation of the supplicant. It is for the reasons indicated above that the Lord Jesus taught:

> And in praying do not heap up empty words as the Gentiles do; for they think that they will be heard for their many words. Do not be like them, for your father knows what you need before you ask Him. (Matthew 6:7-8, Revised Standard Version).

It also follows that we should be quite clear what it is we need before we start praying so that our petitions may be focused and limited. We know that, for example, it does not make sense for a child to go to the father with ten unrelated requests. That would give the father the impression that the child does not really know what he needs. Petitions that are diffuse and endless are less likely to attract help. Whenever possible, one should concentrate on one's most urgent need; the urgency of which moves one's spirit, thereby ensuring an effectual prayer. Indeed, when the spirit is really linked to the luminous spheres, its petitions are likely to be focused, not diffuse and not endless.

The understanding that prayer is an activity of the spirit dictates that praying should be done in an environment most conducive to spiritual unfolding. It is precisely for this reason that the Lord Jesus Christ gave the following admonition:

> And when you pray, you must not be like the hypocrites; for they love to stand and pray in the synagogues and at the street corners, that they may be seen by men. Truly, I say to you, they have received their reward. But when you pray, go into your room and shut the door and pray to your Father who is in secret; and your father who sees in secret will reward you (Matthew 6:5-6, Revised Standard Version).

The Father who is "in secret" refers to the invisible God; and "sees in secret" means knows our volition, thoughts, unstated needs, etc. While we cannot see God, we have, as human spirits, the ability to be connected to His Kingdom by means of invisible radiation. This is an ability that we must actualize through learning to pray aright. The teaching of the Lord Jesus Christ as quoted above is quite simple and clear, and like all His teachings, is intended for all human beings (not just for Christians) and, therefore, for everybody who wishes to pray aright. Unfortunately, the teaching about praying behind shut doors and in few words is routinely ignored these days, especially by those who consider themselves the most knowledgeable and most "anointed". In some religious groups, joint prayer sessions go on for hours, they are loud and raucous and indistinguishable from rock music performances. With loudspeakers blaring, such prayer sessions have become major sources of noise pollution.

In praying, our first concern should be to ascertain that the environment is right and that we are in the right mood to bow our spirit in humility and purity. If we really understand that in praying we are attempting to approach God, we would be able to appreciate how seriously the act should be taken and why *inner preparation* is always required. In cases of joint worship, the inner preparation should ideally start before the beginning of the worship. This suggests that one ought not to be in a situation of having to rush to one's place of worship. In general, there is no point praying when our inward and outward circumstances are not right.

What has so far been said implies that at the time of genuine praying, our gaze is turned towards God and away from this earth; it implies that we have shut off all earthly thoughts and intellectual scheming. Moreover, when it is rightly understood that the purpose of all prayers is to get invisibly linked with God, it becomes obvious why God is the only One to whom our prayers should be directed.

I have stated that pictures are the language of the human spirit and that when one is truly engaged in prayer one is incapable of many words. It is also the case that one can pray in pictures, without uttering any words. By so doing, one bypasses the limitations of human language. This, however, does not mean that words may not be used in prayer. The human spirit in the World of Matter cannot do without prayers that wear the cloak of words, because in the World of Matter the spirit needs varied impressions for its development. In praying with words, we should be aware of the fact that words have formative powers, which are influenced by their inherent nature, how they are arranged in sentences, and how they are pronounced. It is, therefore, very important that we choose our words carefully and mindfully. And we should be mindful of the formative powers of words not only in prayer but also in our everyday speaking; hence we are admonished against habitual bad and abusive language.

Some Truth-bringers have as a help to humanity provided carefully-worded prayers that accord with the Will of God and that arouse the spirit of the person praying. Thus, Jesus gave us the Lord's Prayer ('Our Father'). With the right attitude and frame of mind and in an environment of full attentiveness, the words retroactively affect the spirit and help it to connect with the holy streams of power in Creation. But if the words of the formulated prayer are rattled off (as is often the case), it is as if one has not prayed at all. The Lord's Prayer, for example, was not intended for recitation. Rather, in it Jesus summarized what a person with an earnest volition may request with the certainty of being heard. It contains the foundation for everything which we need for our physical well-being and spiritual ascent, if we penetrate into it deeply and grasp it aright. It was a model for the sorts of things we might ask in prayer – acknowledgement of and vows to God as well as petitions.

The Second of the Ten Commandments says "You shall not take the name of the Lord your God in vain" (Exodus 20:17; Deuteronomy 5:11). This commandment is, unfortunately, frequently and flagrantly flouted, even when we imagine that we are praying. In the course of explaining the Second Commandment, Abd-ru-shin wrote:

Do not dare to pray if you are unable to vibrate with your whole soul in the words, and beware lest you reveal yourselves as thoughtless prattlers before your God; for thereby you would be guilty before Him of misuse of the Name of God.

Before you ask Him for something, consider carefully whether it is urgently needed! Do not become entangled in formal prayers to be rattled off at certain times, as has become the bad habit in *all* religious practices. This is not only misuse of God's Name but blasphemy! (*The Ten Commandments of God Explained to Mankind*, p. 18)

Praying and the Laws of Creation

As discussed in the Chapter on the Will of God, the Creator maintains the whole of Creation, including our earth, strictly through His eternal and unchanging Laws. He does not act arbitrarily. The Creator's strict adherence to His own immutable Laws also applies to the granting of His Grace as well as to His response to our prayers. Prayers operate within the irrevocable and eternal Laws that express the Will of God (see Chapter 7). For example, in order to be linked with the Realms of Light, which true prayer implies, we must rid ourselves of evil thoughts and must not harbour any hatred. This is to say that we must carry a measure of homogeneity with the Realms of Light, which are characterized by goodness and love. In the Lord's Prayer we say: "Forgive us our trespasses as we forgive those that trespass against us"; this clearly means that we reap forgiveness by sowing forgiveness. The purer and the more spiritually open we are, the lighter our prayers will be, and in accordance with the Law of Spiritual Gravity, the higher the prayers will rise in the direction of the Realm of God.

Prayers are answered (or unanswered) only in accordance with the immutable Laws that express the Will of God. This fact should be self-evident in Islam. As Islam means submission to the Will of God, it would be totally illogical for a Muslim to expect his or her prayers to accomplish what goes against God's Will. The same conviction should also be true for Christians, for in His teachings and by His life, the Lord Jesus Christ emphasized that He had come to uphold the laws not to overthrow them. Moreover, He taught humankind that a person must reap what he or she sows. If a person (Jewish, Christian, Muslim, atheist, or pagan) sows rice, he can only reap rice. No amount of prayers, vigils, and fasting can make a planting of rice yield potato.

What I have said implies that, if we align ourselves with the true Will of God in our volition, words, thoughts, and deeds, all our needs will be automatically fulfilled without any specific prayers of petitioning. The help from the Light always lies ready in Creation for the human spirit and as it lives aright in word, thought, and deed, the link to the help is automatically established. The connection is a spiritual happening and as such may go unnoticed by the human brain; that is, the individual may not even be conscious of the connection. If we truly live aright, we would only need to say prayers of gratitude for God's love and infinite goodness as well as for the many opportunities for spiritual growth which earthly existence makes possible.

Fasting

Let me comment very briefly on fasting, since it is often associated with praying. Fasting does not set aside the requirements to pray in spirit, neither does it set aside the Laws of Creation which govern praying. A person whose thoughts, words, and actions are impure while fasting can only attract what is impure and, therefore, the opposite of that for which he may be praying. But if fasting helps an individual to focus in childlike purity on the sublime and to give up his bad habits and unwholesome concentration on purely earthly matters, it would enhance the effectiveness of his praying.

Fasting has the effect of changing one's blood composition and thus the radiation of the blood. Such a changed blood radiation *may* make it easier for the spirit to become invisibly linked with the lighter realms and to attract the various helpful radiations in Creation. Thus the value of fasting lies in the possibility of changing one's blood radiation and disposition in a way that *may* facilitate focus on spiritual matters and turning away from material and mundane issues and thereby purifying one's volition, thought, word, and deed. But in the process of fasting, hunger makes some people quite miserable and so distracted that they cannot concentrate on praying. That is obviously unhelpful. Fasting by itself is not a requirement for effectual prayers.

The practice of fasting during the whole month of Ramadan with the associated voluntary deprivations has the potential for enormous blessing. It means the possibility of continuous upright behaviour and banishing of evil volition, bad thoughts, and wrong actions for a whole month. In accordance with the Laws of Creation, anyone who is able to do so would automatically be continually linked to the radiation from the Luminous Heights that would mature him spiritually and guide him in earthly matters during the period. Moreover, one who genuinely observes the Ramadan fast as a spiritual event and not just as an earthly tradition would be unlikely to go back to his old bad habits; he would thus become an increasingly exemplary person from Ramadan to Ramadan.

Unfortunately, some people cannot possibly benefit from Ramadan fast as much as they could because they in fact feast, eating the most sumptuous meals, between sunset and sunrise. Research in Egypt, for example, shows that the expenditure on food is greatest in the month of Ramadan during which food consumption would be expected to be at its lowest. It may well be that the increased expenditure has more to do with the quality rather than the quantity of food people consume during the period. I do know that many consume much less food during the Ramadan month, for my Muslim friends usually lose weight significantly at the end of Ramadan.

Christians too have a tradition of fasting; it is carried out during the 40-day period of Lent and on some special days. But the tradition is not as formalized as in Islam and the requirements vary from denomination to denomination. In the Catholic Church, for example, to fast simply means 'to eat considerably less food' and to abstain from meat on all Fridays during Lent as well as on other prescribed days. The same spiritual principles, of course, apply to all fasting, regardless of religion.

Petitioning and Thanksgiving
There are, in a sense, two broad categories of prayers with respect to content. There is the prayer of thanksgiving in which we express gratitude to God for the gift of existence, for His Grace, and any specific incidents of His innumerable mercies.

There is petitioning by which we ask for specific help, for clarity and guidance on specific matters as well as the strength to follow any guidance received. Petitioning may be for oneself or for another person (an intercession). Because of the level of our spiritual maturity and the consequent innumerable problems and adverse conditions we have created in the world, praying invariably takes the form of petitioning.

It should be emphasized that a prayer of petition does not take away our obligation to take appropriate actions. And we should not expect fulfilment to accord with our own timetable. Zoroaster, one of the great Truth-Bringers, stated that we should not fold our hands just because we have prayed. But he also cautioned against impatient and impetuous pursuit of personal wishes. He stated:

> There is a great Law that permeates the whole of Creation: He who does not sow shall not reap either. That means he who would like to obtain something shall strive for it. Striving for it, however, does not mean impetuously rushing at it, wanting to force along fulfilment of the wish at all costs. When the wish will be fulfilled, when the harvest is ripe, depends on God's Will. When man has done his part, he must wait. Exactly at the hour decreed by God, he may then receive what he has worked for. (Cited in Herbert Vollmann, *Helping Words*, p. 18)

One sometimes gets the impression that people imagine that once they have asked for help through prayer, their own responsibility is over. They expect that God should then act, while they fold their arms, at times in critical and arrogant expectation.

There is also a misunderstanding of what Jesus meant when He spoke to His disciples about asking in His name. Many people imagine that by ending a petition with the phrase "in the name of Jesus" or its variants, God is obliged to grant the petition. Because of this misunderstanding, many Christians habitually and in good faith conclude their prayers of petitioning with the statement "these we ask in the name of Jesus" or closely similar expressions.

If we consciously do the Will of God as admonished by Jesus and if we truly pray in spirit, as advised by Jesus and indicated above, our prayers will receive the responses most appropriate for our spiritual growth. This is the sense in which the teachings of Jesus with respect to praying should be understood. Only what conforms in word, thought, and deed with the teachings and expectations of Jesus, and therefore accords with the Will of God, constitutes 'asking in the name of Jesus.' We recall that Jesus said that "Not everyone who says to me, 'Lord, Lord,' will enter the kingdom of heaven, but only the one who does the will of my Father in heaven" (Matthew 7:21). "In the name of Jesus" is not a magical incantation that compels God to answer prayers! The teachings of Jesus are much deeper than most Christians realize.

A related matter is what one may call the Pentecostal Churches' formula for being 'born again'. There may be minor variations but basically, it goes thus: "Lord Jesus, I come to you today. I am a sinner. I cannot help myself. Forgive me of my sins. Cleanse me with your precious blood. Today, I accept you as my Lord and Saviour. Thank you, Jesus, for saving me. Now I know I am born again!" It should be noted that the person who says the prayer is presumed to become instantly 'born again'; the person's spiritual condition does not seem to matter. And Jesus is not given a chance to reject the petition, even though He indicated that not everyone who called Him Lord would enter the Kingdom of Heaven. The fact is that to be 'born again' requires a period of sustained working on oneself, including studying and committing to doing the true Will of God, as expressed in the Laws of Creation. By their works (which include thought, words, and deeds), fellow human beings may *guess* who might have been 'born again'. But it is only from higher Realms that it can be seen who is truly 'born again'. No human being is in a position to judge definitively one way or the other. The Pentecostal formula reminds me of 'the wide gate and the easy road' that Jesus explicitly warned us not to take:

> Enter through the narrow gate; for the gate is wide and the road is easy that leads to destruction, and there are many who take it. For the gate is narrow and the road is hard that leads to life, and there are few who find it. (Matthew 7:13-14, New Revised Standard Version)

> Go in through the narrow gate, because the gate to hell is wide and the road that leads to it is easy, and there are many who travel it. But the gate to life is narrow and the way that leads to it is hard, and there are few people who find it. (Matthew 7:13-14, Good News Bible)

Asking, Seeking, and Knocking

Wrong expectations from prayers are also due to wrong interpretations of scriptural passages such as the following: "Ask, and it will be given you; seek, and you will find; knock, and it will be opened to you. For every one who asks receives, and he who seeks finds, and to him who knocks it will be opened." (Matthew 7: 7-8). The passage is meant to teach a deeply spiritual lesson and should not to be taken literally. It should be understood in the sense of the God-given abilities of the human spirit in relation to the Laws of Creation.

A human being has the natural ability to attract automatically what is homogeneous with his volition, attitude, disposition, character, propensities, state of inner maturity, etc. Thus, a truly good person, as judged by the yardstick of the Laws of Creation, automatically attracts to himself what is good. Conversely, a really bad person automatically attracts what is bad. In other words, because of our spiritual nature we are always attracting what is like us, that which is in tune with our own character and with our volition, good or bad. The noble person by his good thoughts, kind and truthful words, and exemplary actions is "asking for goodness", is "seeking goodness", and is "knocking the door of goodness"; and because of Creation's Law of Attraction of Similar Species, the noble person will be given goodness, he will receive goodness, and the door of goodness will be opened for him. This will happen automatically whether or not the person prays in a formal sense.

The converse is, of course, also true. Ignoble persons, by their ignoble nature and ways, "seek" evil, and they find it; they constantly "ask for" evil, and they are given; and they always "knock" the door of evil, and it is opened for them. This is the spiritual principle that demonstrates the Will of God, which Jesus sought to teach humanity. But the principle was not understood and his words were interpreted literally. And, of course, experience shows that things do not happen according to the purely literal interpretation of those words of Jesus.

Joseph Cardinal Ratzinger, who became Pope Benedict XVI, commented on why God often does not seem to answer our prayers despite the biblical statements "Ask, and it will be given you; seek, and you will find; knock, and it will be opened to you." He stated:

> And we know that what we ask is by no means always granted us. In the case of someone for whom it is a matter of life and death, this can become a serious problem. Why has he had no answer, or at least nothing like the answer he had asked for? Why is God silent? Why does He withdraw? Why is it that just the opposite of what I wanted is happening?

> This distance between what Jesus promised and what we experience in our own lives makes you think, every time – it has that effect in each generation, for each single person, and even for me. Each one of us has to struggle to work out an answer for himself so that in the end he comes to understand why God has spoken to him precisely like that.

Cardinal Ratzinger went on to add that the biblical statements "certainly cannot mean that I can call God in as a handyman who will make my life easy every time I want something.

Or who will take away suffering and questioning. On the contrary, it means that God definitely hears me and that what He grants me is, in the way known to Him, what is right for me" (*God and the World*, pp. 40-41).

I have already outlined how the statements Jesus made should be understood. Jesus sought to teach what God has ordained in Creation regarding the natural abilities of the human spirit in relation to the Laws of Creation. Rightly understood, Jesus was definitely not making a literal promise. Therefore, there is no question of a "distance between what Jesus promised and what we experience in our own lives."

And as Cardinal Ratzinger rightly said, it would surely be blasphemous to think of God as our handyman or perhaps a waiter and butler hanging around our dining table to attend to our needs once we ask. First, we should not deceive ourselves into believing that while remaining evil, we can be granted good things just because we have prayed. Incidentally, we should also not be afraid that somebody's evil curses will harm us as long as we are genuinely good and strive to keep the hearth of our thoughts pure. Second, after praying aright, one should be alert and be prepared to act on any inspirations, any ideas suddenly coming into one's consciousness, as well as conversations and happenings in one's environment as they relate to one's desires. Individuals are known to have received solutions to their problems by acting on the conversations among complete strangers; conversations which they overheard as they passed by on the street. To paraphrase the theologian, Joseph Parker (1830-1902), the truly religious man does everything, in thought, word, and deed, as if everything depended upon himself, and then leaves everything as if everything depended on God (Harold Whaley, *Great Men Search for God*, p. 59).

The same principles and mechanisms apply when we pray for others (in prayers of intercession) as when we pray for ourselves. With prayers of intercession, one might wonder how a person who has not prayed can be the beneficiary of a prayer. While praying, the intercessor thinks intensively of the target of intercession and in the process the prayer is first anchored in the targeted person before proceeding on its further course. The response to the prayer returns to the intercessor through the same path, first passing through the targeted person. As outlined before, whether or not there is response depends on whether or not the intercessor succeeded in being linked with the Luminous Heights. Moreover, the targeted person would benefit from the prayer only if he is worthy, through being homogeneous with the effects of the prayer.

In general, only a good person would be able to absorb the benefits of intercession; a bad person would be unable to absorb the benefits because he would repel them in accordance with the Law of Attraction of Similar Species. The effect of genuine intercession may take the form of acting as a signpost to the targeted person. The intercessor's prayer goes forth and points to the one needing help. If in response, help is offered by the Light to the person who has thus been signposted, the possibility of the offer being taken is again subject to the Law of Homogeneity; help would reach the person only if he deserves it.

Memorized Prayers

One implication, among many, of the fact that it is only the spirit that can pray is that memorized prayers that are "rattled off" are unlikely to be effectual. This is because in rattling off formulated prayers, it is the memory part of the brain that is at work. Deep inner feelings are not awakened, and there is no reflection or serious attention to the meaning and significance of the words being regurgitated. Moreover, some people cannot really immerse themselves into such prayers as they struggle to remember the words of formulated and memorized prayers. Therefore, the spirit is not engaged, and the rattled-off prayers, in effect, amount to no prayer!

In general, it can be said that the more spontaneous a prayer is, the more genuine and effectual it is. We usually find ourselves engaging in spontaneous prayers when we are suddenly faced with a grave danger as well as when we experience an unexpected and especially joyful event. At such moments our inner beings suddenly, and without contemplation, open to the Luminous Heights in petition or in gratitude, and usually we find ourselves uttering very few words or even no words at all. However, after the first flash of spontaneous spiritual communion, a person's intellect may take over; he will then embark on a long string of expressions of so-called prayer, as result of the force of religious habit.

One of the five pillars of Islam is five prayers said at specific periods each day. Before each of the prayers, an ablution is performed involving the cleaning of the parts of the body most exposed to dirt. But the ablution is also symbolic of the desire to achieve inner cleanliness by purging oneself of evil thoughts and everything that is contrary to God's Will before one dares to approach God in prayer. The periods of the prayers are so arranged that a human being who adheres to those times and really prays aright will be in a state of humility and inner purity throughout his waking period. He would be incapable of thinking evil, much less deliberately harming others, because his worshipful state lingers from one prayer to the next. The last of the five prayers (the Night Prayer) is to be said as the last thing before one goes to bed, ensuring that the spirit maintains its link with the Luminous Heights while the physical body sleeps.

The five prayers are, of course, of no effect, if they are merely thoughtlessly rehearsed, or said while one is harbouring evil thoughts and planning evil schemes. The prayers do not also have the full desired effect if we say all of them at the same time or even two or three of the five at the same time (because we forget or are too busy during the day). This is because the timing was deliberately determined in order to put one in a prayerful mood and ensure a constant link with the Luminous Heights throughout the day; that objective may be defeated if the prayers are not said at the stipulated times.

In an earlier section of this Chapter, I used the expression 'formal praying'. This is to underscore the fact that good thoughts, words, and deeds as well as a generally good attitude to life are also forms of prayer. In accordance with the Law of Sowing and Reaping, they ensure that good things will come our way at the appropriate future time. We curse ourselves when we do evil, engage in bad gossips, and think evil since the consequent evil harvests are bound to come. Perhaps, in this recognition, Victor Hugo, a famous French literary figure of the 19th century and known by many for the authorship of the play "Les Miserables" wrote: "Certain thoughts are prayers. There are moments when, whatever may be the attitude of the body, the soul is on its knees." Any spontaneous expression of pure joy is a prayer of gratitude to God.

Invalid Investigations

Some researchers have sought to investigate the efficacy of prayers, especially intercessory prayers for hospitalized patients. Some of the studies have found prayers to be definitely helpful while others have concluded that prayers have no effect. Given the mechanisms by which prayers operate, it should be obvious that designing a valid experimental study of prayers is practically impossible. Therefore, the first comment one may make about all the published studies is that their designs are uniformly faulty and their results, positive or negative, are to that extent invalid. One cannot intellectually study a process which is so essentially spiritual.

Take the case of studies of the efficacy of intercessory prayers for hospitalized patients. The intercessors may not pray effectually because they are inwardly unprepared for such intercession or simply don't understand how to pray, even though they may be well-meaning. The intercessors may pray aright but the spiritual states of the patients may be such that they are unable to benefit from the prayers, having regard to the Law of Homogeneity and the Law of Sowing and Reaping. The researcher has no way of telling what is going on. In both cases, one cannot conclude that prayers *per se* are not efficacious.

On the other hand, if the intercessors pray effectually and the patients are inwardly open, the conditions of the patients can be expected to be positively affected. How might this happen? It could be that as a result of the prayers, healing radiations flow towards the patients and such radiations would act just like effective medicines do. Some might then describe the case as one of spontaneous remission. The prayers may influence doctors in such a way that ideas about alternative therapies occur to them. Or it could be the nurses who are influenced to be more loving, more attentive and give better care to patients. In some cases, it could happen that the care-givers (doctors and nurses) are the obstacles to the efficacy of the prayers of intercession by not been inwardly open! Indeed, it is possible that prayers of intercession have the effect of inducing patients or their relatives to decide to change hospitals. It is also conceivable that the positive response to a patient in great physical pain may take the form of early and *natural* release from the physical body (physical death), providing relief from pain as well as spiritual guidance in the immediate Beyond.

Concluding Remarks

I will conclude this Chapter by observing that, in a world increasingly beset by problems of all sorts, religious fervour and multifarious prayer events have increased a great deal. Vigils and special prayer sessions, sometimes accompanied with fasting, proliferate. But in light of the explanations of this Chapter, we may assert that most of such prayers are ineffectual, for the simple reasons that they are in blissful ignorance of the God-ordained Laws that govern praying and prayers. Some individuals, in search of 'prayers that are answered' change their religions, or the sects within their religion, or keep going from one worship house to another. And, invariably, all to no avail.

The greatest service and favour we can all render to ourselves is to take to heart and take the first step repeatedly advised by Abd-ru-shin: *"Keep the hearth of your thoughts pure, by so doing you will bring peace and be happy!"*

Hearth should be understood to mean the fountain, source, or spring from which all our thoughts arise. Once we keep the hearth of our thoughts pure, the radiation of the Love of God enters and true peace and happiness necessarily follow. This means that as a starting point, we have to develop an absolutely sincere and very strong volition for what is good, so that no evil thoughts can arise. The yardstick for what is good must, of course, be God's Will as manifested in his Laws of Creation.

By keeping the hearth of our thoughts pure, by being habitually nice, and by being ever attentive to the demands of the Laws of Creation, we are seeking and asking for everything that will benefit us, give us joy and lasting contentment. And we will find them. And they will be given to us! Moreover, we should always be mindful of the fact that every good word we speak and every good action we take constitute informal but powerful praying.

16 God and Miracles

Miracles are an important element in all religions, especially in Judaism and Christianity. Numerous miracles are recorded in both the Old and New Testaments of the Bible. Islam also believes in miracles. Many passages in the Koran speak of 'signs of Allah', by which miracles are meant. In general, most religions and most religious people are predisposed to believe in miracles. We have by implication already touched on the subject of miracles in Chapter 10 on the Perfection and Omnipotence of God as well as in Chapter 15 on Praying and Prayers. In this Chapter, I explain the fact that some human beings have certain rare but genuine abilities, including that of healing and that, in general, we would all be capable of doing much that would appear miraculous if we did not lag so far behind in our spiritual development. Unfortunately, many charlatans and frauds have made miracles a big money-making business at the expense of gullible and trusting individuals, taking advantage of the fact that unusually gifted people *do* exist.

In the following paragraphs, I discuss some miracles recorded in the Bible to indicate what is possible and what is not. And I stress the fact that *all* the happenings we call miracles do comply with the Laws of Creation. The strictly law-governed nature of Creation makes it impossible for anything to happen in contradiction to the Laws of Creation. What we call or think are miracles are happenings that we are unable to explain only because of deficits in the current state of knowledge. It is also those gaps in human knowledge that make many imagine that some things are impossible, which are in fact permissible within the Laws and mechanisms in Creation. In short, because of deficits in the state of knowledge, we are often not in a position to tell what is or is not possible within the framework of the Laws of Creation.

Definition

The key issues surrounding miracles include first and foremost matters of definition. We cannot tell what constitutes a miracle and whether or not it is possible until we have a clear definition of what a miracle is. Dictionaries usually present two categories of definition. As an example of the first category, the *Oxford Advanced Learner's Dictionary of Current English* defines a miracle as "an act or event that does not follow the laws of nature and is believed to be caused by God." In other words miracles are manifestations of the arbitrary intervention of God in human affairs. Instead of stating that God is the cause of the extraordinary events that do not follow the laws of nature, other dictionaries use the expression 'divine agency'. This is to suggest that the causal agent of miracles may be lesser than God but empowered by God to override natural laws.

The second category of definition of miracle reflects the everyday uses of the word where no divine agency is assumed to be involved. One such definition is: "an extremely outstanding or unusual event, thing, or accomplishment." One might, for example, describe the victory in a soccer game of a team at the bottom of a league over the leader of the league as a miracle without implying that any natural law was overturned. One might similarly describe the performance of a record-breaking athlete as miraculous. And a miracle may simply mean, as the *Oxford Advanced Learners Dictionary of Current English* defines it, "a lucky thing that happens that you did not expect or think was possible." This Chapter will not dwell on this second category of definitions of miracles; it is not what religious people have in mind when they speak of miracles.

We should bear in mind, as I have emphasized in earlier chapters, that the laws of nature are the earthly manifestations of the eternal laws that express the Will of God. The first category of definition of miracles, therefore, implies that God might set aside His own Will, that is, suspend the laws of nature, to bring about certain events. This is impossible, as discussed in the Chapter on the Perfection and Omnipotence of God. It follows that while there may be events that human beings designate as miracles, such events do not in reality contravene the Laws of Creation. The appearance of contravention merely signifies the limitation of human knowledge. Just because an event cannot be readily explained by known natural processes does not necessarily mean that it has no natural cause.

It seems to me that every claim of a miracle should be assessed based on the specific facts of the case. The claims may be fraudulent and aimed at deliberately presenting the alleged miracle-workers as gifted or 'anointed' individuals worthy of followership. We should not be surprised that such false and fraudulent claims abound; after all, there are frauds and charlatans in all human endeavours, including in scientific research. But by the same token, it would be wrong to presume that every such claim is false.

Unusual Abilities

Indeed, some individuals have unusual abilities, such as clairvoyance, clairaudience, as well as the gift of healing. Healing radiation exists in Creation and it can happen that some gifted persons are able to connect to such radiation rather readily and are able to pass it on to sick persons to make cures possible. Genuine healing powers are not cultivated but are a gift to persons with the requisite spiritual qualities. The ability usually manifests at a particular composition and radiation of the blood of the gifted person. For this reason, the healing ability may appear suddenly, and it may also disappear suddenly, if the blood composition changes on account of changes in the diet, temperament, lifestyle, etc. of the person. On account of the nature of this ability, it is possible that the truly gifted person may be initially unaware of the gift. And the gifted person may also not know when the ability has disappeared because of a change in her blood composition. She might then continue to attempt to heal people in good faith and with absolutely no fraudulent intention. It should be remarked that those who have genuine abilities are normally very humble, abstemious, pure-hearted persons and they are generally quite circumspect. They would rather not discuss their unusual abilities. Those who advertise or are most outspoken about their own abilities to heal or to perform miracles are most likely to be the charlatans – the empty barrels that make the loudest noise!

Again, because of the nature of the process, we may envisage that depending on individual disposition, some sick persons may not be able to benefit from such healing power. A patient who is inwardly open and humble is more likely to obtain cure from the healer than one who is cynical; with the latter, the chemistry might just not be right. One might also describe it as a case of lack of homogeneity. In general, humility, simplicity, and trusting faith facilitate absorbing such healing power.

A careful consideration of the complex factors involved would suggest that to test such healing powers in a scientifically valid manner would be quite daunting and perhaps unfruitful, as discussed in Chapter 15 with respect to research on intercessory prayers for hospitalized patients. On this issue, routine scientific methodology should humbly step aside. The point is that such healings do take place and no natural laws are contravened. Such healers presumably utilize the effects of as yet unknown and much finer radiations than those applied in conventional radiation therapy. And the healers themselves do not necessarily understand the mechanisms involved.

X-ray Eyes

Some people possess the very rare ability of seeing through the physical bodies of other people rather like X-ray machines; such people are said to have X-ray eyes. It may be said that they see with the eye of the soul. This means that a person with such ability can help with diagnosing diseases. But the value of the help would depend on the personality of the person, especially her education that would determine how precisely she is able to describe what she sees. Prior academic knowledge of anatomy of internal organs might be helpful but might also excessively influence her 'seeing' and thereby distort her description of the sites of the illness. On the other hand a gifted person who is ignorant of the body anatomy would see clearly but would be unable to describe in a helpful way the sites and nature of the disorder; and that would not be too helpful for the medical doctors in a position to treat the patient.

Obviously, working with a qualified medical doctor, who is genuinely attentive and understanding, would greatly enhance the value of the gift. The doctor would stand by the gifted person and over time would learn to understand precisely the pictures of the illnesses she observes and describes. The doctor would then add his knowledge and experience to the seer's descriptions to arrive at prescriptions for cure. Without careful verification, it would not be advisable to depend completely on the picture of an illness which has been "seen" by a gifted person.

With the so-called eye of the spirit, it is the finer radiation of the illness that is observed and not merely what is physically visible. This *finer* kind of seeing is more valuable and more important because it means that the *seat of a disease,* the actual starting-point, can be recognized very early and it might then be possible to arrest its further development. The seat of a disease consists of fine radiations, which only subsequently leads to effects that become visible to the earthly eye. In the final analysis, everything is radiation.

In rarer cases, the person gifted with X-ray eyes may also be blessed with the additional gift of intuitively knowing the cure for the disorder she sees. In one European case, the gifted person knew a great deal about the curative properties of Alpine herbs and was able to prepare appropriate herbal remedies for the diseases she diagnosed. In that way, she was able to help thousands of people over several decades during the last Century.

Services rendered by such gifted persons should be compensated as required by the Law of Balance. It would be wrong to suppose that the services of spiritually gifted persons should be rendered free of charge. In any case, we should realize that not everyone thus gifted can continually afford to give such help without an appropriate compensation.

Like the healing ability outlined above, the ability of X-ray eyes cannot be cultivated. It may appear in an individual and after some time may disappear. The phenomenon is also closely connected with changes in the blood composition since the ability is induced in an individual by a quite specific radiation of the blood. This possibility of appearing and disappearing of spiritual abilities is also encountered in persons with mediumistic abilities. Thus, it can happen that famous mediums suddenly lose their hitherto outstanding abilities or their abilities become considerably weakened. The explanation lies in the change of blood composition with the consequent alteration of the blood radiation. *It follows that the possession of rare and unusual abilities does not necessarily mean that the gifted person is spiritually advanced or necessarily qualified to hold positions of spiritual or religious leadership.*

The greatest conceivable breakthrough in human physical health and the full unfolding of the human spirit on earth will be knowledge of the effects of the blood radiations and the knowledge of how these radiations can be intentionally and precisely changed. Such knowledge would embrace all that matters for humans on earth and would bring with it happiness and peace.

Miracles and False Prophets

It is a pity that so many people are in search of miracles and that leaders of many religious sects seek to draw crowds with promises of miracles. The clamour for miracles poses the danger that many are actually diverted from the path of spiritual growth and true happiness, which entails trying hard *to understand and to do* the Will of God. Instead, people sheepishly follow self-proclaimed miracle workers through 'the wide gates and easy roads' that lead to perdition. And this is despite the fact that Jesus warned that even false prophets can perform miracles. Speaking about the last days, Jesus reportedly said:

> For false Messiahs and false prophets will appear; they will perform great miracles and wonders in order to deceive even God's chosen people, if possible. Listen! I have told you this before the time comes. (Matthew 24:24-25, *Good News Bible*, Today's English Version).

The warning implies that the ability to accomplish unusual actions, such as healing sick persons, is not a guarantee that the person is a true servant of God. And, of course, a true follower of Christ would not make false miracle claims. Those who claim to perform miracles, even in the sense of contravening the Laws of Creation, sometimes defend their position by referring to the following passage in the Gospel of John:

> Believe me that I am in the Father and the Father is in me; but if you do not, then believe me because of the works themselves. Very truly, I tell you, the one who believes in me will also do the works that I do and, in fact, will do greater works than these, because I am going to the Father. I will do whatever you ask in my name, so that the Father may be glorified in the Son. If in my name you ask (me) for anything, I will do it. (John 14:11-14, *New Revised Standard Version*)

> Just believe it - that I am in the Father and the Father is in me. Or else believe it because of the mighty miracles you have seen me do. In solemn truth I tell you, anyone believing in me shall do the same miracles I have done, and even greater ones, because I am going to be with the Father. You can ask him for *anything,* using my name, and I will do it, for this will bring praise to the Father because of what I, the Son, will do for you. Yes, ask *anything,* using my name, and I will do it! (John 14:11-14, *The Living Bible*)

The text from the *Living Bible* is more explicit on the argument of the 'miracle workers'. On the basis of the passage, they claim that they can perform all the miracles presumed to have been performed by Jesus and even greater ones. Many thoughtful persons find it strange that Jesus would tell His disciples, who were just human spirits, that they could accomplish greater miracles than Himself whose innermost core was a part of God.

In the Chapter on Prayer, I pointed out the widespread misunderstanding of the expression "asking in the name of

Jesus". If we consciously do the Will of God (as discussed in Chapter 7) and as admonished by Jesus and if we truly pray in spirit, our prayers will receive the responses most appropriate for our spiritual growth. This is the sense in which the teachings of Jesus with respect to 'asking in His name' should be understood. Only that which conforms in word, thought, and deed with the teachings of Jesus constitutes asking in the name of Jesus. And all such must also accord with the Laws of Creation because Jesus did not come to overthrow the Laws. All of us should be able to think of many things that Jesus would never do no matter how fervently we ask. You would not, for example, find a million dollars (not even one dollar) under your bed while you sleep just because you asked really fervently in his name. Jesus would not suspend the laws of His Father to bring about a miracle for you!

Moreover, it is certainly not the case that any human being can perform all the genuine miracles of Jesus, much less perform greater ones. There is only one Power and its only source is God and this Power permeates all Creation. As the Power streams down through the various levels of Creation outlined in Chapter 5, it is transformed and also becomes weaker. At their highest level of development, human beings on account of their origin can only exercise spiritual power. Jesus who is a part of God can exercise the much higher Divine Power, which can accomplish a great deal that spiritual power can never accomplish. It follows that human beings are not able to do everything that Jesus could do, much less surpass them, as implied by the statements of the Gospel of John quoted above.

We may also conclude that while some of the miracles of Jesus were beyond spiritual power, they would have been within the possibility of Divine Power. Therefore, even with miracles that are quite beyond the spiritual power of human beings, Jesus did not act arbitrarily but in complete accordance with the Laws of God.

In such cases, He worked in *Divine* Power, not in spiritual power, and naturally the effects far surpassed what human beings can do. It must be stressed, however, that even Divine Power cannot perform miracles that amount to contraventions of the Laws of Creation.

I discuss below some accounts of miracles in the Bible to indicate what is and what is not possible and thereby to deepen our understanding of miracles.

Miracles of Raising the Dead

The raising of the dead through Divine Power does *not* involve a violation of Divine Laws as long as it happens within a certain time after death, the length of which differs for each human being. In Chapter 4 on the human being, we discussed the relationship between the physical body and the soul. The non-physical body (which is a covering of the soul) and the gross material physical body are connected with each other as by a navel cord called "the silver cord." Each individual is responsible for the condition of the silver cord. The more one chains oneself to earthly things the denser and heavier the silver cord becomes. A dense silver cord is more difficult to detach from the physical body, thereby prolonging the process and pains of dying. The more noble and less materialistic a person is, the thinner and more easily detachable is the silver cord and this makes the process of physical death less painful, regardless of the earthly circumstances leading to the destruction of the physical body. The more spiritually mature the soul is when severing itself from the physical body the quicker it will be released, and the shorter will be the time during which the lawful opportunity exists to raise it from the dead. Once the silver cord is detached from the physical body, it is impossible for the person to be raised from the dead. In other words, it was *possible* for Jesus to raise certain individuals from the dead with His Divine Power and in doing so He did not violate the Laws of Creation.

Let us recall the case of the 12-year-old daughter of Jairus, who was confirmed to have died but whom Jesus Christ raised up (Matthew 9:18-19, 23-26; Luke 8:40-42, 49-56; Mark 5:21- 24, 35-43). Jesus kept the wailing crowd away and took with Him to the death-bed only the child's father and mother as well as three of His disciples (Peter, James, and John). The following two verses are highly instructive:

> But taking her by the hand, he called, saying, "Child, arise".
> *And her spirit returned*, and she got up at once; and he
> directed that something be given her to eat. (Luke 8:54-55).
> (Italics added).

The lesson is that when a person dies on earth, what really has happened is that the spirit has abandoned or discarded the physical body. The real person is spirit; the body is only the garment or the cloak. Just as an old or torn coat may be discarded, so does the spirit abandon a physical body that, for one reason or another, is no longer usable. Thus, the process of raising a dead body involves making the spirit repossess the body it had earlier discarded. It can do so if the silver cord is not broken and if the body has not been so badly damaged as to be unusable by the spirit.

To use a somewhat crude analogy: a child takes off his coat and throws it away; but his father makes a timely appearance and commands the child to take the same coat and wear it again. In the miracle of raising the dead, Jesus Christ as the father commands the spirit (the daughter of Jairus) to take up the coat (her body) and wear it again. The Divine Power radiating from Jesus ensured that the soul of the daughter of Jairus obeyed the command, *"And her spirit returned"*. It is the same Power that had shortly before cured the woman, who had been suffering from a hemorrhage for twelve years; full of faith, she touched the clothes of Jesus and she was healed. (Matthew 9:20-22; Luke 8:43-48; Mark 5:25-34). The Divine Power of Jesus radiated through His clothes and could be absorbed by the sick woman because of her great faith.

There are two other instances in the Bible of Jesus raising the dead. There was the case of Lazarus of Bethany, the brother of Mary and Martha and of the only son of the widow of Nain (Luke 7:11-17). The raising of Lazarus of Bethany is reported only in the Gospel of John where it is accorded many verses ((John 11: 1-46) and is tied to the final decision of the Pharisees, the chief priests, and Caiaphas (the High Priest) to get rid of Jesus. Moreover, it was explicitly stated that the miracle was intended to glorify Jesus and to prove that He was truly sent by God. When Jesus asked that the stone covering the tomb of Lazarus be removed, Martha said that the body would already smell since that was the fourth day since he was buried. Thus, one might wonder if the silver cord and the physical body would still be intact.

It can be asserted, however, that Jesus *could* have performed the miracle provided the silver cord had not been broken and the physical body had somehow not been severely damaged. The same would apply to the raising of the son of the widow of Nain. At the call of Jesus with His Divine Power the souls could re-unite with their bodies, which were then compelled to remain on earth until new physical deaths occurred. And the happenings would not have violated the Laws of Creation. But the historical authenticity (as against the *possibility*) of the miracles is another matter.

The Miracle of Calming the Storm

The story of Jesus calming the stormy sea is told in the Gospels of Mark (4:35-41), Matthew (8:23-27) and Luke (8:22-25). Jesus and his disciples were in their boat crossing the sea. While Jesus was asleep at the back end of the boat, a great windstorm arose, setting off waves which beat into the boat almost swamping it. The disciples were afraid fearing that they were about to perish. They awakened Jesus and alerted Him to the danger.

Jesus rebuked the wind and said to the sea, "Peace! Be still!" or, in some translations, "Quiet now! Be calm!" The wind died down and the sea became calm. Jesus asked the disciples, "Why are you afraid? Have you still no faith?" The disciples were filled with great awe and said to one another, "Who then is this, that even the wind and the sea obey him?"

Calming of the storm is possible and may actually have taken place. In the incident, Jesus did not act arbitrarily and His action was not a violation of any Laws of Nature. There are in nature creatures that serve the Will of God and participate in many natural events, such as stormy weather, landslides, earthquakes, etc. These creatures (nature-beings) may be regarded as special natural forces that have acquired form. They are physically invisible but some people may from time to time see them with their inner eyes. Earthly animals are closer to them and it is more common for them to see or perceive them. It is partly for this reason that animals sense natural catastrophes, such as tsunamis, sooner than human beings and seek escape routes. Jesus, who had knowledge of these facts of nature, spoke to the nature-beings who were in action at the time and they obeyed Him. The Divine Power inherent in Jesus on account of His origin and radiating from Him ensured that the nature-beings obeyed His command.

I should remark that we all should become aware of the existence of these creatures and their activities, even though we may never be able to see them. Moreover, we all can potentially communicate with them with our thoughts. Of course, I know that many people consider them as fantasies and figments of the imagination. But let me remind us of the principle of *Adaequatio*, which I discussed in Chapter 2 — The Mystery of Reality. The principle implies that, as E. F. Schumacher put it in his *A Guide for the Perplexed*, "as we are not entitled to assume that we are necessarily adequate to everything, at all times, and in whatever condition we may find ourselves, so we are not entitled to insist that something inaccessible to us has no existence at all and is nothing but a phantom of other people's imaginations."

The Miracle of the Loaves and Fish
Each of the four Gospels of Matthew, Mark, Luke, and John reports the miracle of Jesus feeding thousands of people with a few loaves of bread and a few fish. Matthew and Mark, each report two different miracles of the loaves and fish (Matthew 14:13-21 and Matthew 15:32-39; Mark 6:30-44 and Mark 8:1-10). The accounts in the two Gospels are closely similar. In the first miracle, Jesus blessed and broke five loaves of bread and two fish and gave them to His disciples to distribute to a crowd of 5,000 men (in Mark) or "about 5,000 men, not to say nothing of women and children" (Matthew). They all ate as much as they wanted and there were left-overs that filled twelve baskets.

In the second miracle, the crowd numbering about 4,000 people (Mark) or "4,000 men, to say nothing of women and children" (Matthew) had been with Jesus for three days and had had nothing to eat. Seven (not five) and "a few small fish" (not two) were used to feed the crowd. After the people had eaten to their satisfaction, the left-overs filled seven (not twelve) baskets.

The accounts of Luke and John are similar to the first miracle of the loaves and fish reported by Mark and Matthew. Five loaves and two fish were used to feed about 5,000 men and there were twelve full baskets of left-overs. In the account of John, the five barley loaves and two fish belonged to a boy who happened to be there. There is a twist in the account in the Gospel of John (6:14-15), where it is reported that the people who witnessed the miracle said: "This is indeed the prophet who is to come into the world" and John added that as Jesus realized that the people "were about to come and take him by force and make him king, fled back to the hills alone."

The following day the crowd met with Jesus in Capernaum, where Jesus engaged them in a conversation centered on food and bread 'from heaven'. Jesus told them "Do not work for the food that perishes, but for the food that endures for eternal life, which the Son of Man will give you. For it is on him that God, the Father, has set his seal" (John 6:27). They mentioned the manna that their forefathers ate in the desert and the following conversation ensued (6:32-35):

> Then Jesus said to them, "Very truly, I tell you, it was not Moses who gave you the bread from heaven, but it is my Father who gives you the true bread from heaven. For the bread of God is that which comes down from heaven and gives life to the world." They said to him, "Sir, give us this bread always." Jesus said to them, "I am the bread of life. Whoever comes to me will never be hungry, and whoever believes in me will never be thirsty."

Some questions arise. First, were there really two miracles or a duplication of the same miracle retold differently? A note on the story in *The New Jerusalem Bible* (Standard Edition, 1985, p. 1633) clarifies the issue. There was only one miracle.

The first account is the more ancient one and it is of Palestinian origin. It speaks of twelve baskets – the number of the tribes of Israel. The second account derives from Christians in a Gentile environment and speaks of seven baskets – the number of the Gentile nations of Canaan and of the Hellenist deacons. The note further explains that both traditions depict the event in the light of Old Testament precedents, especially the multiplication of oil and bread by Elisha, the successor prophet to Elijah (2 Kings 4: 1-7, 42-44) and the miraculous provision of manna and quails for the nourishment of the Israelites on their journey to the promised Land.

Elisha allegedly enabled a widow to fill many jars with oil from the one single flask of oil she had and was able to meet her obligations by selling the jars of miraculously produced oil. Elisha asked a man to give twenty loaves of barley bread to a company of one hundred men. The man said he could not serve the twenty loaves to so many men. Elisha urged him to serve them as Yahweh said that they would eat and have some left over. The man served them, they ate, and there were some left-overs. The miracle of the loaves and fish was like a repetition of those of Elisha but on a larger scale. A thoughtful consideration of the comments in *The New Jerusalem Bible* certainly suggests that a literal interpretation of the miracle(s) as reported by the Gospels is not justified.

Moreover, the follow-up account in John's Gospel admonishes against labouring for food that perishes but for food that endures for eternal life and speaks of the bread of God that gives life to the world. These suggest that the event was not a matter of feeding a large crowd with a few physical loaves and fish but rather a case of providing spiritual nourishment, which can be distributed to thousands and thousands of seeking souls.

The objective of the story of Jesus feeding 5,000 (or 4,000) with five loaves and two fish (or seven loaves and a few small fishes) and having twelve (or seven) baskets of left-overs might have been to promote the idea that Jesus was a more powerful prophet than the ancient ones, such as Elisha. And that was indeed true. But Jesus fed the crowd with the *Word* of God, which to the human *spirit* is food and drink. He did not feed them with earthly loaves and earthly fish.

Speaking of bread, we recall that in the story of the testing (temptation) of Jesus in the desert, Jesus was reported to be hungry after fasting for forty days and forty nights. The devil approached Him and asked Him to turn stones into bread if He were the Son of God. In other words, if Jesus could not command stones to become bread, He was not the Son of God. Jesus did not, but cited part of a statement of Moses in the Book of Deuteronomy (8:3):

> And He (God) humbled you (the Israelites) and let you hunger and fed you with manna, which you did not know, nor did your fathers know; that He might make you know that *man does not live by bread alone, but that man lives by everything that proceeds out of the mouth of the Lord.* (Italics added).

Being hungry, Jesus did need bread at that point but it would not have been possible for Him to turn stones into bread, despite His Divine Power; for that is impossible within the Laws of Creation. If He had attempted to do so, His failure would have subjected Him to ridicule; and therein lies the temptation, which by definition was intended to hurt not help His mission. For the same reason, Jesus could not have jumped down from the parapet of the Temple in Jerusalem without hurting Himself; He could not have defied the Law of Gravity. If he tried it, He would make Himself an object of ridicule, which was what the devil or Satan wanted.

Incidentally, we might ask ourselves whether there was in fact a face to face encounter with the devil. Did the devil literally take Jesus to the Temple in Jerusalem and urged Him to jump down? Was Jesus actually taken to a very high mountain and shown all the kingdoms of the world and their splendour? Could it be the case that Jesus, at a stage when the implications of His connection with God were just beginning to dawn on Him, was contemplating the most effective ways to initiate His mission? Is it possible that these temptations were merely thoughts invading the mind of Jesus?

Turning water into wine

According to the Gospel of John, the first miracle of Jesus was turning water into wine at a wedding at Cana in Galilee. The mother of Jesus was there and his first few disciples were also invited. According to John's Gospel, the disciples at that point were Andrew, Peter, Philip, and Nathaniel. The wedding party ran out of wine and the mother of Jesus said to Him, "They have no wine". Jesus responded, "Woman, what concern is that to you and to me? My hour has not yet come." But the mother told the servants at the party to do whatever Jesus told them.

Six stone water jars ordinarily used for the Jewish rites of purification were available, each holding twenty or thirty gallons. Jesus apparently changed His mind following the mother's prompting and instructed the servants to fill the jars with water. After the servants had filled the jars to the brim, Jesus asked them to draw from them and take to the chief steward (or master of ceremony). On tasting the water that had now become wine, the steward declared it the best wine at the party. Thus, a huge quantity of excellent wine (between an estimated 640 and 960 bottles) suddenly became available for the party. The chief steward called the bridegroom and remarked: "Everyone serves the good wine first, and then the inferior wine after the guests have become drunk. But you have kept the good wine until now."

It is noteworthy that Jesus did not say any prayers or make any overt petition to God that the water be turned into wine. But He might have prayed silently or even in pictures, which would also underscore the inadvisability of long-winded and ostentatious praying. Going by the account, only the mother of Jesus, Jesus Himself, his first four disciples, and the servants who filled the jars with water were aware that a miracle had taken place. And the point of the miracle seemed to have been to 'reveal his glory and make his disciples believe in him' (John 2:1-12).

This miracle was recorded only by the Gospel of John. As the *first* miracle, one would have thought that it would be much talked about and would have been reported by more than one Gospel. It would seem reasonable to conclude that the miracle of turning water into wine might not have been a historical event.

John concluded his account of this miracle with the following words: "Jesus did this, the first of his signs, in Cana of Galilee, and revealed his glory; and his disciples believed in him." In other words, the point of the miracle was for Jesus to display his power and strengthen His disciples' belief in Him. This objective seems to be quite important throughout the Gospel of John. Chapter 20 is the second to the last Chapter of the Gospel but its last two verses (20:30-31) is sometimes given the heading 'The Purpose of this Book' or its 'First Conclusion' by some versions of the Bible. In other words, the two verses set out the purpose of the Gospel of John and its first conclusion. These two verses, which are preceded by the post-resurrection appearances of Jesus, state: "Now Jesus did many other signs in the presence of his disciples, which are not written in this book. But these are written so that you may come to believe that Jesus is the Messiah, the Son of God, and that through believing you may have life in his name." John narrated the miracles to serve the purpose of persuasion and conversion. That fact might suggest that one should not be reading them as if they were accounts of strictly historical events. That would in turn mean that they should not be taken necessarily as evidence of what is literally possible.

Miracle of Healing of the Ear of the Slave of the High Priest

The story of the betrayal and arrest of Jesus is carried by the four gospels (Matthew 26:50-56; Mark 14:43-52; Luke 22:47-53; and John 18:3-12). Matthew reports that "one of the followers" of Jesus drew a sword and cut off the ear of the slave of the high priest. Jesus said: "Put your sword back, for all who draw the sword will die by the sword. Or do you think that I cannot appeal to my Father, who would promptly send more than twelve legions of angels to my defence?" Matthew did not say who the follower was who drew the sword and seemed unaware of the miracle of the healing of the ear of the slave.

Mark mentions the incident but did not name the sword wielder and the slave whose ear was cut off and he seemed unaware of any healing. He also did not mention the possibility of legions of angels being sent to defend Jesus. Matthew, Mark, and Luke wrote about Judas kissing Jesus as the sign he had given to those who came for the arrest but John's account indicated that Judas was merely standing with those who came for the arrest and made no effort to identify Jesus. John specifically mentions Simon Peter as the sword-wielder and Malchus as the slave whose ear was cut off: "Then Simon Peter, who had a sword, drew it, struck the high priest's slave, and cut off his right ear. The slave's name was Malchus. Jesus said to Peter, "Put your sword back into its sheath. Am I not to drink the cup that the Father has given me?" John did not mention any healing.

Luke stated that the disciples asked Jesus if they should fight those who had come to arrest him. But without waiting for an answer, "one of them struck the slave of the high priest and cut off his right ear." Luke does not identify the ear slasher and the slave. He wrote: "But Jesus said, 'No more of this!' And he touched his ear and healed him." Only the Gospel of John mentions Peter as the one who wielded a sword as well as the name of the person whose ear was slashed (Malchus). Yet, John did not say that a miracle of healing took place. Only Luke writes of a miracle, which would have been the last of his healing miracles.

Note that only Matthew reported the possibility of a miraculous dispatch of twelve legions of angels to prevent the arrest. Luke (22:47-53) and John (18:3-12) give accounts of the arrest of Jesus but did not mention the possibility of God miraculously dispatching legions of angels. That possibility did not exist; God does not intervene in human affairs in such a manner. It was simply Matthew's imagination.

Did Jesus perform a miracle on the slave (Malchus) as reported by Luke? If so, why is it reported only by Luke? After all, that would have been quite memorable as his last miracle. It is interesting to note that his first alleged miracle (turning water into wine) is also reported by only one of the four Gospels. Jesus might have been able to heal the slashed ear, depending on the nature of the damage. But the question is did He do so? It seems that we cannot unequivocally say that this alleged last earthly miracle of Jesus took place.

Miracles That Could Not Have Happened

Reported claims of miracles that directly violate natural laws include the Old Testament story of the sun standing still at Gibeon and the moon standing still in the valley of Aijalon. This was supposed to have happened after Joshua prayed to God because his army needed extra daylight hours to complete the massacre of the Amorites (Joshua 10:12-15). At the time the story was written, people were ignorant of the motions of the stars such as the sun, the interconnections with the motions of other celestial bodies, and of the multifaceted consequences of any disruptions of those motions. They thought that God could act arbitrarily and against natural laws. Today we know, of course, that the notion of the sun and the moon standing still is unthinkable and impossible. Such a story was conceivable only because of the great level of scientific ignorance of the period. The sun and the moon did not stand still; there was simply no such miracle.

In a related alleged case of violation of natural laws, Prophet Elisha caused an iron axe head to float on water in violation of the Law of Gravity (2 Kings 6:1-7). Elisha had commissioned some servants to build a place for him and his group of prophets. The iron axe head of one of the servants engaged in cutting logs for the building by the river Jordan fell into deep water. The servant was distraught as the axe did not belong to him but was borrowed. When he told Elisha about it, Elisha asked to be shown where the axe fell. Elisha "cut off a stick and threw it in there, and made the iron float" (verse 6). And the servant then simply picked up the floating axe. *The King James Version* in verse 6 used the expression "and the iron did swim". Such violation of a natural law is impossible and we can assert that real iron axes cannot be made to float on ordinary water by *anybody*.

Concluding Remarks

Discussions on miracles are confused on the one hand by the presumption that we already know everything that is possible, the assumption that there are no invisible forces that can act in the material world, and atheistic orientation.

Materialistic convictions do not recognize some of the realities at work in Creation, including the possession of uncommon abilities or powers. People of such convictions take pride in their own ignorance, which they consider as sophistication. On the other hand, there are people of blind faith, who are willing to believe that absolutely anything is possible for God and that God, like an arbitrary earthly potentate, can contravene His own Laws. These are the people behind the cacophonous clamour for miracles in some Christian denominations. Many fraudulent individuals arise to take advantage of such credulous people of blind faith.

We must all come to terms with the reality that we are human spirits on earth for a spiritual purpose and are part of a strictly law-governed Creation about which we are still largely ignorant. If we had not faltered and lagged behind in our spiritual development, we would have been capable of doing a great deal that would appear miraculous. Many more people would have been able to actualize their potentials for uncommon healing and other abilities now encountered only in rare people. I mentioned that healing radiations, which are as yet scientifically unrecognized, permeate our world. Some people do individually benefit from such radiations whenever they are spiritually open and are thus able to absorb them. Some are able to prepare themselves inwardly to absorb the radiations and pass them on to others. As we develop a spiritual outlook on life, 'miraculous' healings will become more common. This process is, in fact, possibly one of the explanations of the rather well-established phenomena of spontaneous remissions or regressions of diseases and of the placebo effect.

Our urgent task and the greatest favour we can do ourselves is to keep our thoughts pure and to develop a strong volition to understand and to do the Will of God in everything and at all times. By so doing, we would be guided to meet our earthly needs (not wants) and to fulfill our spiritual purpose. This is what Jesus meant when He admonished us to strive first for the Kingdom of God and all other things would be given us.

17 God and the Problem of Evil

The problem of evil in relation to our understanding of God has been of interest for millennia and commands so much attention that it constitutes a recognized branch of theology. It is the subject of many books, treatises, and essays in ancient and modern times. Authors of such publications range from academic philosophers and theologians to fiction writers and playwrights. They include leaders and followers of various religions as well as agnostics and atheists of all shades. The fact that catastrophes and tragedies as well as their concomitant human and economic costs are increasing is now well-documented and with each disaster, the same questions are raised. Consequently, the age-old questions are not going away, rather they have become more insistent: How did evil come into the work of a perfect Creator and what sustains it in our world? Why would God, described as omnipotent, not wipe out evil? Why does He allow tragedies? These and related questions shore up support for atheism and agnosticism and shake the faith of many believers irrespective of religion. And it is true to say that the matter of God in relation to evil in the world remains perplexing to even the leading lights of most religions.

Moral and Physical Evil

But first some general comments about evil. What do people mean by evil? Those who study the subject divide evil into two forms – moral and physical. In this classification, moral evils are the atrocities and wrongs which people inflict on other persons. They include such horrific phenomena as genocides, terrorism, and slavery as well as more common acts of immorality like cruelty, corruption, greed, deceit, racism, etc. Among the most infamous moral evils are the fates to which Native American tribes were subjected, the Holocaust in which millions of European Jews were murdered, the genocide committed in Cambodia by the Khmer Rouge, the genocide against the Tutsis in Rwanda, and the ethnic cleansing in Bosnia as the Republic of Yugoslavia disintegrated. The historical list of horrendous acts of moral evil is a very long one and features virtually every country.

Natural disasters due to physical nature such as earthquakes, volcanoes, and landslides as well as those due to unusual weather such as droughts, floods, etc., are classified as physical evil. Physical evil also includes the problems posed by pests and various disease-causing organisms as well as inherited diseases and birth defects.

With technological developments and the increasing intensity of human impact on the physical environment, the dividing line between moral and physical evil has in some cases become blurred. For example, our economic and social activities may affect the environment adversely in a manner that contributes to floods, droughts, famines, forest fires, and human diseases. On the other hand, it is now possible to alleviate considerably the effects of some physical disasters on the affected populations depending on the moral standing of those in a position to help. One might also note that new technologies provide anonymity and possibilities for those inclined to do evil and detection by law enforcement authorities is more difficult; the internet is an obvious example. Technological developments make early warning systems possible, thus reducing the 'evil' caused by natural phenomena like tsunamis, floods, and droughts. Technologies resulting from biomedical research help to reduce the populations of pests and disease-causing organisms and to cure some of the diseases they cause.

But various types of weapons of mass destruction have come into being through technology, thus enhancing the capacity of human beings to commit moral evil.

Thus, we are in a position both to worsen and to alleviate the problem of physical evil, depending on the technologies we develop and how we deploy them. Experience shows that every technology is a double-edged sword; how a technology is used, for good or for evil, depends on the volition and Free Will of individuals and in some cases, the moral tone of society as a whole. This fact already suggests an answer to the questions posed in the opening paragraph of this Chapter: it is that human volition and human Free Will play crucial roles in causing and curtailing evil, both moral and physical evil.

The September 11, 2001 Attack

An incidence of horrific evil took place in the United States on September 11, 2001. It involved planes hijacked by al-Qaida terrorists used in a coordinated series of attacks. Two of the planes were rammed into the North and South Towers of the World Trade Center Complex in New York City. A third was crashed into the Pentagon (the headquarters of the United States Department of Defence) and the fourth crashed near Shanskville, Pennsylvania as the passengers heroically struggled to overcome the hijackers who were heading the plane presumably to the Capitol building in Washington, DC. The two towers in the World Trade Center complex (each 110 story high) collapsed completely. The other buildings within the complex also either collapsed completely or partially due to the resulting fires and debris. Considerable damage was done to the Pentagon complex. The death toll included 246 victims on the four planes (from which there were no survivors), 2,606 in New York City in the World Trade Center and on the ground, and 125 at the Pentagon. In a globalized world, the casualties of major tragedies in urban centres tend to involve many nationalities; more than 90 countries lost citizens in the attacks on the World Trade Center alone. This spectacular act of unimaginable evil understandably shook the United States and the world.

A "National Day of Prayer and Remembrance" was observed in the United States on Friday, September 14, 2001. On the occasion, there was a solemn interfaith ceremony at the National Cathedral in Washington, DC attended by the incumbent President George W. Bush and other prominent citizens. Those who played conspicuous roles at the ceremony included Christians, Jews, and Muslims. Among those who addressed the audience (consisting of those in the Cathedral and the many millions of television viewers in the United States and around the world) was the American evangelical icon, Rev. Billy Graham. In his message, Rev. Graham asked: "But how do we understand something like this? Why does God allow evil like this to take place?" He went on to say:

> I have been asked on hundreds of times in my life why God allows tragedy and suffering. I have to confess that I really do not know the answer totally, even to my own satisfaction. I have to accept, by faith, that God is sovereign, and He is a God of love and mercy and compassion in the midst of suffering. The Bible says God is not the author of evil. It speaks of evil as a mystery.

In Chapter 8 (*Beyond the Scriptural Portrayal of God*), we saw that the Bible does not present a consistent view of God. It is certainly true that God is not the author of evil! He is Love and He is Justice! But contrary to what Rev. Graham said, the Bible is in fact equivocal on the authorship of evil. For example, the authors of the books of Isaiah and of Amos in the Bible thought that God created evil:

I form the light, and create darkness: I make peace, and create evil: I the LORD do all these things. (Isaiah 45:7, King James Version).

I am the one who forms light and creates darkness; the one who brings about peace and creates calamity. I am the LORD, who accomplishes all these things. (Isaiah 45:7, New English Translation).

Is a trumpet blown in a city, and the people are not afraid? Does disaster befall a city, unless the LORD has done it? (Amos 3:6, New Revised Standard Version).

Rev. Graham confessed that he really did not know the answer totally, even to his own satisfaction, to the question of why God allows evil. He is, of course, not alone in expecting that God should somehow be able to prevent moral and physical evil and who fail to understand why God does not do so. Joseph Cardinal Ratzinger (later Pope Benedict XVI), responding to the question of the diverse circumstances of birth of human beings, acknowledged that there are extreme cases of people who are seriously disadvantaged and, therefore, cannot find any way to realize their potential. He stated that it was, yet again, the problem of why there is so much suffering in the world and that we should not suppose that we can ever find an answer to it (Joseph Cardinal Ratzinger, *God and the World*, pp. 117-118).

Most religious people, leaders and followers, as well as most philosophers are in the same boat. The questions persist: If God is all-loving, omnipotent, and omniscient why is there evil on earth? Why can't God simply decree evil out of existence? How did evil come into the Creation of an all-wise God? And they remain unanswered satisfactorily. This is because satisfactory answers require *new knowledge*, which is now available but of which most of the people interested in the subject are yet to take advantage.

I will show in the succeeding paragraphs that these questions can be answered simply and clearly. Indeed, some of the answers should already be evident from several of the previous Chapters of this book. Evil and suffering in the world need not be a mystery. Clarity is possible provided one is armed with the following pieces of knowledge: the immutable Laws of Creation that express the Will of God; the right understanding of the Perfection and Omnipotence of God; the correct conception of the Omniscience of God; and the right appreciation of the Love and Justice of God. In addition we must understand what the Free Will of the human being entails and the havoc that its misuse has caused. All of these pieces of essential knowledge have been presented in earlier Chapters. I will apply them as appropriate in the context of the problem of evil and present additional information on hereditary sin, what it means and how it brought in its wake the evils in the world.

The Spirit and Free Will

The concept of Free Will is central to the problem of evil. It is, therefore, necessary to be clear about it. Free Will is an inseparable part of the human spirit. When we think of a human being on earth, a picture that arises within us includes a head, two legs, two arms, etc. Just as we do not picture a human being without a head, so there can be no human spirit without Free Will. A child's Free Will is dormant and only awakens fully in adulthood. While its Free Will is still dormant, the child has an active imitative instinct; it learns through imitation.

What does Free Will entail? It means simply that the human spirit is endowed with the ability to choose, to decide. It may choose to act or not to act, to do good or evil, to love or hate, to assist or hinder, to obey or break the law. Free Will lies in the freedom of decision and no more. The consequence of each decision rests exclusively on the immutable Laws of Creation; laws that existed before the creation of the human spirit and against which it is powerless.

Some creatures, such as archangels and angels, do not have Free Will. They act strictly according to the Laws of Creation; thus, they never do wrong. Therefore, it is legitimate to ask why the human spirit is endowed with Free Will. All that is spiritual by nature exercises the power of attraction in a manner analogous to magnets. The human spirit would attract indiscriminately if it did not have Free Will. Think of a hypothetical magnet that could attract indiscriminately — paper, iron, wood, soil particles, etc.; such a magnet would be useless for most practical purposes. Similarly, the human spirit's ability to attract would overwhelm and incapacitate it, if it could not control what it draws to itself and distances from itself. Therefore, as a counterpoise or counterbalance to the ability of the spirit to attract, it is given the ability to decide what to attract and what to reject. This is the origin of Free Will and it cannot be taken away from the human spirit. The endowment of Free Will is also a demonstration of a principle that rests in Creation: the principle of balance. The inherent ability of the spirit to attract is balanced with the ability to choose what to attract.

The human spirit, by exercising its Free Will and by being subjected to the consequences of its choices and decisions, acquires the knowledge necessary for its maturing. As it matures, it is increasingly able to make only those decisions that advance the spiritual goal of its existence on earth. And at full maturity, back home in Paradise, it is, like the angels, able to make only decisions that accord with the Will of the Creator.

It is not accidental that human beings generally desire freedom to choose. Political, social and economic systems should make this possible. And, of course, freedom of religion and of thought should be guaranteed. However, as implied above, societies must also ensure that individuals are held accountable for the choices they make through appropriate legislation and policies. By so doing, the *quality* of the exercise of Free Will is enhanced. Many moral evils in the world are due to denial of people's freedom to decide as well as failure to hold people accountable for the decisions they make.

The Law of Sowing and Reaping, which operates throughout Creation, is God's mechanism for influencing the human spirit's use of its Free Will. This Law ensures that we reap multiples of whatever we sow in thought, word, or deed. If the harvest gives joy, one is encouraged to sow more of similar seeds; a harvest of painful experiences dissuades one from sowing more of the same. All the policies of societies should aim at complementing this God-willed process. Since the harvest always indicates the sowing, bad and painful experiences must be seen as reminders of the imperative to change for the better. We do not need to remember specifically what we did wrong or when.

By choice, we inflict evil on fellow human beings. And in accordance with the Law of Sowing and Reaping we have to reap multiples of the evil consequences at the appropriate later time, which means yet more evil. Similarly, societies and their governments make bad policy choices and sometimes refuse to adopt obviously sensible policies. The consequences are again multiple evils. For example, many governments have refused to take necessary measures to preserve the environment and they are doing nothing about climate change because of short-term economic considerations. Such economic myopia must in future lead to natural disasters. And then people, including those who failed to act, would thoughtlessly ask, "Why does God allow natural disasters?"

The Neutral Power of God

There is only one Creator, one God, and only *one* Power. While it is right to speak of heaven and hell, of good and evil, it would be *wrong* to think that there are two powers, a good one and an evil one. The one Power from God flows continually in appropriately transformed states through the whole Creation. This Power is neutral and may, therefore, be used for good or evil.

The world in which we find ourselves is not part of Original Creation but of Subsequent Creation (see Chapter 5). It came into existence through the volition of the Primordially Created Spiritual Beings and it can be influenced by us human spirits developing in the World of Matter. On account of the possibility of human influence, the World of Matter has imperfections that are not to be found in the Original Creation. This implies that imperfections, including evil, exist only in the World of Matter.

The central role of the human being in regard to the problem of evil lies in the fact that the human being is the only creature in the World of Matter which is able to absorb the transformed Power from God. The human being absorbs the Power utilizing a faculty of the spirit. This spiritual faculty is the intuitive volition, the innermost volition, as against the volition generated by the brain. The human being can, through its inmost disposition, control its intuitive volition but it cannot control the products of the union of the volition with the Power it absorbs. Some of the products of the union have independent existence and may do a lot of good or a great deal of havoc according to the nature of the volition from which they were formed. Benevolent beings and so-called demons are some of the products with independent existence. Through this process, human beings consciously and unconsciously influence everything in the World of Matter including the earth and are, therefore, answerable for the condition of the world.

A person, who has no convictions (no principles) or whose convictions are weak, cannot maintain constant good volition and so would use the neutral Power for evil depending on circumstances. I suppose it is safe to say that the majority of human beings today do not have strong convictions for what is good; hence they often direct the neutral Power of God to evil purposes. Thus, we should not really wonder about the prevalence of evil in the world.

A person whose convictions for good are so strong and pure that they have become his instinctive guide will always use for good the transformed Power of God that he absorbs. Such convictions can only come from knowledge borne of experience. In this regard, we should note that indolence, both intellectual and spiritual, is an enemy of conviction; for conviction comes only through uncompromising weighing and careful examining of all sides.

The Fall of Man, the Brain, and Hereditary Sin

The question arises as to why human beings through exercising their Free Will so frequently misuse the neutral Power of God in a manner that has led to so much evil in the world. This has, indeed, been the case for perhaps millennia. Simply put, the answer lies in the disruption of the God-ordained structure of the human physical body caused by neglect of our spirituality, as I explain in the following paragraphs.

Many people have acknowledged that there is something wrong with the human being, which probably accounts for the problems of the world. Bertrand Russell (1872-1970) was a renowned philosopher, Nobel Laureate in Literature, and social activist. He might have been hinting at this when he made the following statement in his book *Authority and the Individual*: "In the world in which we find ourselves, the possibilities of good are almost limitless and the possibilities of evil no less so. Our present predicament is due, more than anything else, to the fact that we have learnt to understand and control to a terrifying extent, the forces of nature outside us, but not those that are embodied in ourselves."

Joseph Cardinal Ratzinger (later Pope Benedict XVI) stated that reflections about man indicate a fault line and "a certain disorder within man in that he is not the person he ought to be able to be." He says that the disorder is presented to us in the Book of Genesis and that "awareness developed with increasing clarity that men always incline toward evil." Cardinal Ratzinger quoted the Biblical God as saying: "I see that they are but flesh; they are weak; they incline toward evil" (Joseph Cardinal Ratzinger *God and the World*, pp. 85-86). According to him, these were hints at the idea of 'original sin', which St. Augustine subsequently systematically set out as a Church doctrine. Cardinal Ratzinger asserted that original sin was not banished by the death of Jesus on the Cross. On this last point, I would remark that if individuals live according to the true teachings of Jesus, they would, in the purity of their thoughts, increasingly overcome the propensity for evil. Finally, Cardinal Ratzinger stated: "The great question really is exactly how we are to understand this word "original" and the continuing presence of the disorder. We certainly get stuck here in trying to formulate an answer." (p. 87)

This leads me to a consideration of the human spirit, the brain and hereditary sin. The human spirit has its origin in the Spiritual Realm as described in the Chapter 5. For this reason, even while it is on earth, it is drawn upwards to the spiritual heights as a matter of course. But it would be unable to achieve its purpose of existence on earth if it is not adequately anchored so that it can experience the earth meaningfully. To prevent the spirit from only floating in spiritual heights, the human being on earth was endowed with the intellect to act as a counterpoise pulling downwards to balance the upward-striving spirit. Working harmoniously with the spirit, the intellect is also intended as a facilitator of success in all purposeful aspects of life on earth. First and foremost, the intellect is meant to anchor on earth the spirit's absolutely natural longing for what is uplifting and noble, pure and perfect. In other words, the intellect should be the tool and the servant of the spirit in bringing about on earth the conditions that characterize the Spiritual Realm. It should take dictations from the spirit and help implement on earth the decisions of the spirit. If the intellect operated in this manner, it would help bring about a truly 'wonderful world' and humanity would experience the peace of Paradise, even here on earth.

Since the intellect was designed as a counterweight, in other words, as a means 'to keep the spirit's feet on the ground of the physical world', it can only lead away from spirituality if left on its own. Thus, we can say that the intellect is valuable and constructive only when it is under the direct domination of the spirit. Otherwise, it can only be destructive as far as the spiritual purpose of human existence is concerned. Even its role of facilitating life on earth would be misdirected and would ultimately achieve the opposite.

An oversimplified process of communication between the spirit and its physical body as ordained by the Creator goes through a chain involving the solar plexus, which is situated just below the diaphragm, the cerebellum (also called the back brain or the small brain), and the cerebrum (also called the frontal or large brain). The solar plexus is the point of the invisible connection between the spirit and its physical cloak. The cerebellum is the spiritually receptive part of the brain while the cerebrum is the seat of the intellect. Communication from the spirit hits the centre of the solar plexus in the form of waves of energy and from thence to the cerebellum. The cerebellum, acting like a photographic plate, forms pictures corresponding to the impressions received from the spirit and transmits them to the cerebrum. The cerebrum in turn processes what it receives from the cerebellum and generates thoughts and with the collaboration of other organs of the physical body, gives rise to words and specific actions. The experiences of the physical world are meant to reach the spirit through the same channel in the reverse direction. They are communicated from the cerebrum through the cerebellum to the solar plexus and finally reach the spirit.

The proper functioning of this system ordained by the Creator depends on the health of, and maintenance of appropriate relationships among, all parts in the chain of communication. But this system has for a very long time ceased to function properly. This is because human beings for millennia have busied themselves almost exclusively with earthly pursuits utilizing the intellect which is produced in the cerebrum. The excessive use of the cerebrum over thousands of years led to its overdevelopment in accordance with the principle that whatever is used develops, whereas that which is not or only infrequently used atrophies. And the cerebellum, the instrument of the spirit that was underutilized, became relatively stunted. Thus, the spiritually receptive part of the brain (the cerebellum) became stunted relative to the intellectual part (the cerebrum). This was the 'Fall of Man.'

Through the biological process of genetic inheritance, the disproportionate overdevelopment of the cerebrum (the intellectual brain) relative to the cerebellum (the spiritual brain) was passed on to subsequent generations and became the "hereditary sin". The frontal brain was supposed to take instructions and guidance from the back brain on the basis of the impressions received from the spirit. With the overdevelopment of the cerebrum and the concomitant stunting of the cerebellum, the intellect was practically on its own and got little or no guidance from the spirit. The result has been a focus on the material world and a loosened connection with the spiritual world. As a result, the Free Will is often exercised based exclusively on earthly considerations and without the input and direction that should come through the cerebellum to the cerebrum (the seat of the intellect).

As implied above, once the ordained communication chain is disrupted and there is no or inadequate guidance from the spirit, the intellect ceases to be valuable and constructive; rather it can only be destructive as far as the spiritual purpose of human existence is concerned. The human being is thus cut off from the source of eternal and uplifting values that can only come from the Spiritual and higher Realms. In the absence of those values, the floodgates to all sorts of evil are opened.

Let me emphasize the fact that the earthly intellect becomes an antagonist of the spirit *only* when it is elevated above it. It is a valuable and faithful servant as long as it remains under the dominion of the spirit in accordance with the original design. These days, many who consider themselves sophisticated have turned the intellect into an idol and given it free rein and even doubt the existence of the spirit. By its nature, the intellect focuses on and can only understand the material world. Therefore, people who practically depend exclusively on their intellect cannot have any understanding for what is spiritual; for them a spiritual outlook on life is meaningless and amounts to mere superstition. Such people are not really sophisticated but are victims of the distorted brain, of hereditary sin.

The assertion about the overdevelopment of the cerebrum relative to the cerebellum is supported by research on the evolution of the brain. Human evolution is characterized by a dramatic increase in brain size and complexity and a prominent trend in the evolution of humans is the progressive enlargement of the cerebrum. Francisco J. Ayala, a prominent evolutionary biologist and a 2001 recipient of the United States National Medal of Science, wrote: "Humans have a very large brain relative to their body size, and a cerebral cortex that is disproportionately large and complex even for their brain size" (Francisco J. Ayala, *The Big Questions: Evolution*, p. 79). Research shows that the size of the human cerebellum compared to the rest of the brain is less than would be expected of an ape of human size; humans have large cerebral cortices relative to their cerebella. The frontal brain is the structure that exhibits the most remarkable increase in relative size with increasing brain size and has become, in terms of size, the predominant structure amounting to 84 percent in the human brain, while the back brain is only about 10.3 percent.

Even though the cerebrum is so much larger than the cerebellum, it is found that the vast majority of brain neurons (80 percent) are located in the cerebellum. Neurons are cells that carry information within the brain and between the brain and other parts of the body. This should suggest that the cerebellum might have as yet un-deciphered roles in the human body. I suggest that such roles would include a spiritual one. Recent research shows that the cerebellum is much more important than traditionally assumed. It was thought that the cerebellum only plays a part in a person's timing, coordination, and precision of movement by connecting with the body's system of sensory organs and in collaboration with other parts of the nervous system. Brain scientists now recognize that the cerebellum and cerebrum work in conjunction and they are paying more attention to the behavioral and cognitive functions of the cerebellum, in addition to its traditional motor and sensory functions.

Furthermore, one might note that the cerebellum includes the "arbor vitae", a tree-shaped, white-coloured component. In Latin, "arbor vitae" means "tree of life". The phrase, "tree of life", may remind some readers of the "tree of knowledge of good and evil" in the biblical story of the Garden of Eden and is thus faintly suggestive of a spiritual function for the cerebellum and of the true meaning of the Fall of Man.

In the biblical story, the woman, incited by the serpent, offered the apple to the man. The man took and ate it. The offering of the apple by the woman is a figurative expression of the woman's becoming conscious of her charms and her intentional exploitation of the charms in her relationship with the man. The acceptance and eating of the apple by the man symbolizes his response, which involved the awakening of the urge to draw and hold the attention of woman only to himself. This he did by accumulating earthly treasures, power, and various material things that would make him desirable to the woman. Success in such an endeavor required all manner of scheming, greed, falsehood, and oppression. Thus began the cultivation of the intellect whose natural field of activity is the earth. The struggle for woman's attention (eating of the apple) eventually led to the overcultivation of the intellect and the distorted brain as described above. With the domination of the intellect, man could no longer understand whatever is beyond the earthly concept of space and time, which amounts to his *severance* from spirituality, from the real Paradise.

Consequences of Hereditary Sin

As would be expected, there are individual differences in the extent of distortion of the brain. And for a given level of distortion, the effective damage would be less for those who make conscious effort to pay attention to the non-material aspects of life and to listen to their inner voice and conscience.

In some people, obviously rather few, the spiritually receptive cerebellum and the cerebrum harbouring the intellect cooperate harmoniously to some extent. Such people rise above the ordinary level and distinguish themselves in different ways. Some display special artistic talents while some are responsible for great inventions. For some people, the harmonious working of the back and frontal portions of their brains is reflected in an amazing reliability to perceive intuitively, which enables them to grasp complex ideas that would be impossible for most other people. The people with relatively undistorted brains remind us of what the normal, ordinary human being was meant to be as well as of the high levels of uplifting accomplishments that the world would have experienced if we had lived as willed by God.

Albert Einstein is acknowledged as perhaps the greatest scientist of the 20th Century. The way he went about his work, his lifestyle, and the values that he espoused suggest to me that he was one of such people. In the last paragraph of a speech about his credo, which he gave to the German League of Human Rights in Berlin in the autumn of 1932, he stated:

> Although I am a typical loner in daily life, my consciousness of belonging to the invisible community of those who strive for truth, beauty, and justice has preserved me from feeling isolated. The most beautiful and deepest experience a man can have is the sense of the mysterious. It is the underlying principle of religion as well as all serious endeavours in art and science. He who never had this experience seems to me, if not dead, then at least blind. To sense that behind anything that can be experienced there is a something that our mind cannot grasp and whose beauty and sublimity reaches us only indirectly and as a feeble reflection, this is religiousness. In this sense I am religious. To me it suffices to wonder at these secrets and to attempt humbly to grasp with my mind a mere image of the lofty structure of all that there is. (Michael White and John Gribbin, *Einstein*, p. 262)

On another occasion, Einstein wrote: "The ideals which have lighted me on my way and time after time given me new courage to face life cheerfully, have been Truth, Goodness, and Beauty. Without the sense of fellowship which men of like mind, of preoccupation with the objective, the eternally unattainable in the field of art and scientific research, life would have seemed to me empty. The ordinary objects of human endeavor — property, outward success, luxury — have always seemed to me contemptible." The point is that while Einstein might not have been religious in the traditional sense, spiritual values and spiritual orientation were the driving force in his work; a connection with the spirit that might have resulted from a back brain working harmoniously with the intellectual brain. We can only imagine the number of giants of science and of related endeavours with which humanity would have been blessed if we had not one-sidedly cultivated the intellect at the expense of the spirit.

We have already noted that the distorted brain (as the hereditary sin) has severely undermined our connection with the Spiritual Realms. With the loss of the associated spiritual values and needed guidance, development in all spheres of life was largely misdirected. And moral evils proliferated in the world. One specific consequence is the confusion in dreams. With normal development, dreams should be the *experiences* of the spirit received and reproduced by the cerebellum while the cerebrum is at rest during sleep. These would constitute specific guidance, warnings and other clear information for the individual to use on awakening. On account of its dominant development the cerebrum, even in sleep, still exercises a strong influence on the cerebellum through its strong radiation. Because of the influence, the cerebellum in its present weakened condition absorbs the radiation of the cerebrum simultaneously with the experiences of the spirit, creating what the author of the Grail Message described as "a mixture like a double exposure on a photographic plate." The product is the confused dreams we often have.

It follows that we no longer routinely receive instructions and revolutionary ideas through the channel of dreams and when we do, they tend to be vague and inadequate. Therefore, positive developments in all spheres of life on earth are slower than they would have been. And more directly pertinent to the subject of this Chapter, we fail to receive spiritual warnings of impending dangers of natural disasters. We are, therefore, needlessly exposed to the effects of earthquakes, tsunamis, landslides, volcanic eruptions, floods, forest fires, etc.

Those natural phenomena, to the extent that human activities are not contributory factors, are associated with the continuous development and evolution of the physical world and are, therefore, not at all evil. And they need not take human toll and need not entail suffering. If we human beings had developed along the God-willed path, there would always have been many reliable and trustworthy people with fore-knowledge of such events, ensuring that people are relocated in time. Unlike human beings, animals are often aware of the coming of such events, and those which are in a position to move *do* relocate.

The so-called warfare in nature and, in general, the struggles of animals do not constitute evil. On the contrary, they are a necessity for development. The struggles in nature keep animals alert and active outwardly and inwardly and they ensure that their senses do not atrophy. They are the means of ensuring compliance with the Law of Movement in this world, which is relatively sluggish on account of its immense distance from Primordial Creation. All the Laws that manifest the Will of God in Creation operate within the framework of the Law of Movement.

Therefore, the natural struggles of animals and humans on earth should not be seen as evil but a requirement for the necessary compliance with the Law of Movement. In the Chapter on the Love and Justice of God, we noted that Jesus hinted at this fundamental Law in some of His parables, including the Parable of the Talents.

In compliance with this Law of Movement, human beings on earth must be *awake* not only spiritually but must also be alert in an earthly sense. If a person here on earth lives only for his spirit and ignores the realities of his earthly surroundings, he exposes himself to harm and suffering in the hands of ill-disposed fellow-men. Our spiritual wakefulness should go hand in hand with the necessary earthly alertness and vigilance. By being awake in an earthly sense, we can prevent much evil through ensuring that ill-disposed people are not able to carry out their evil intentions.

Recapitulating

Through the overcultivation of the intellect (the so-called hereditary sin) human beings curtailed their access to spiritual influences and higher values. They became enmeshed and engrossed in the World of Matter, resulting in a situation in which millions today proudly but sadly call themselves "sober materialists". Human beings exercised their Free Will without reference to the Will of God, which is expressed in the immutable and eternal Laws of Creation. Consequently, their volition, thoughts, words, and actions were mostly contrary to the Will of God. The intuition, the voice of the spirit, became inaudible to most people. Spiritual warnings about activities in nature that could lead to catastrophes were no longer heard. The few who hear are derided, are not taken seriously and they often stop talking. The generally misguided and misdirected development opened the floodgates of evil in the World of Matter.

God's Perfection and God's Omnipotence are inseparable and they preclude all arbitrary interventions or actions. As explained in previous Chapters, God relates to Creation and Subsequent Creation only through his perfect Laws, which on account of their perfection cannot be changed. All that God does is to permit His Laws, their applications, and implications to be brought to the attention of human beings dwelling on earth and in other parts of the material world. This is the role that various true prophets and spiritual teachers have played over the ages. The closest to what might be called God's direct intervention takes the form of permitting on very rare occasions a part of the Trinity (as explained in Chapter 14) to incarnate on earth with the mission of bringing about an intensification of spiritual radiation in our world, reminding us of His Will, and further clarifying It.

But God does not at all personally and directly intervene in the small and great cares of human beings on earth. The common expectation that God would intervene routinely in human affairs amounts to insulting His Omniscience. For example, in the light of the Law of Sowing and Reaping, why should we expect God to intervene in order to prevent people from reaping whatever good or evil they have sown in previous earth-lives or in the present one? From the very beginning, God has woven into Creation His perfect Laws, which carry out His Will automatically, immutably and irresistibly. Therein lies His Omnipotence. Hence, evil can only be wiped out and will be vanquished through the mechanism of the Laws of Creation and not through any arbitrary actions on the part of God.

Mission Karma

With respect to the victims of catastrophes and mass evil, I should emphasize that the Law of Sowing and Reaping is not the whole story. Not all misfortune is due to some *existing* karma. This is because karma itself must have a beginning. In addition to existing karma, new karmic threads are being woven for each individual and others are being severed continually. To illustrate this point, let me remind you of the phenomenon of Mission Karma, which was discussed in Chapter 7. One may voluntarily take on a mission which involves evident danger. Any harm arising in the course of that mission is "mission karma". Thus, Jesus suffered crucifixion, not because of any existing karma but on account of mission karma. Jesus undertook His mission out of love despite the full knowledge of the dangers involved, given the spiritual state and disposition of the people, especially the religious people, of that time.

Mission karma explains the misfortune of the firemen who got trapped and died in the Towers at the World Trade Center on September 11, 2001. They had acted courageously and out of love to save the lives of other people. The same was true of some of the passengers on the flight that crashed in Shanskville, Pennsylvania; those people consciously and voluntarily decided to sacrifice their own lives to save the lives of other people targeted by the terrorists. These people as well as the hundreds of firemen demonstrated superhuman love. They sowed love and they will, in their continuing existence, definitely reap multiples of the love they sowed.

However, we should not on account of the phenomenon of mission karma, delude ourselves into becoming vainglorious. We stand in the period of harvest of the consequences of our millennia of wrong-doing; the increasing incidence of human-made and avoidable natural disasters confirms it. Each of us has incarnated on earth many times before our current earth-life and none of us may claim to be innocent of deviations from the true Will of God. Tragedies and suffering are the consequences of the wrong and bad choices we human spirits as individuals and members of groups have made during thousands of years of continuous existence that involves many incarnations in different parts of the earth and as members of various races, ethnic groups, and communities. Causal factors also include what we have neglected or failed to do.

Hell

Let me make a brief remark about hell. Hell is solely the work of human spirits. God did not create hell, just as he did not create evil. Hell has arisen through the automatic coming together of people who have engaged in similarly awful volitions, thoughts, words, and actions. Such gatherings are the consequence of the Law of Attraction of Similar Species, the Law of Homogeneity.

Thereby, the murderous are forced to associate with the murderous, the greedy with the greedy, etc., and they mutually inflict their propensities on one another. If nobody did evil or carried evil volition, there would be no gathering of the evil; that is, there would be no hell. As a soul in hell improves, it is automatically drawn to other souls who have similarly improved. Those who improve sufficiently and in time can escape from hell; all those who don't will eventually suffer spiritual death or disintegration. Thus, hell and the evil ones they harbour would be effaced from Subsequent Creation.

I should mention the fact that realms of perfect peace, joy and beauty also exist; these are the automatic gatherings of noble human spirits in accordance with the Law of Homogeneity. And we could bring about such communities on earth by adjusting our volitions, thoughts, words, and actions to accord with the Laws of Creation.

The Imperative of New Knowledge

The events of our time, especially the multiplicity of evil and catastrophes associated with this period of final reckoning, are strong pointers to the inadequacy of the prevailing religious ideas, doctrines, and philosophies. We must now have the courage and humility to embrace new knowledge, particularly the knowledge of the Laws of Creation and of the right conception of God. The Ten Commandments given to humankind through Moses were intended as a guide to help humanity adapt to the Laws of Creation. But the Commandments were not (and are not) well understood and are often misinterpreted.

Abd-ru-shin, the author of the Grail Message, has revealed how the Ten Commandments were meant to be understood and interpreted. The explanations convey the depth, significance, and sublimity of the Commandments (*The Ten Commandments of God (and) The Lord's Prayer*, pp. 8-55). Take the fourth Commandment (Exodus 20:12). It is rendered more or less uniformly in different versions of the Bible, as indicated below:

> Honour thy father and thy mother, that thy days may be long upon the land which the Lord thy God giveth thee. (Authorized King James Version)

> Honour your father and your mother, that your days may be long in the land which the Lord your God gives you. (Revised Standard Version)

> Honour your father and your mother so that you may live long in the land that Yahweh your God is giving you. (The New Jerusalem Bible)

Anyone who really reflects on this Commandment must be touched by some troubling concerns. Why, for example, would God demand that a morally upright person honour his father who is an unrepentant criminal and who is a constant source of embarrassment and shame? Should children honour their fathers and their mothers even if they are patently unworthy of honour? Does God expect children to be hypocritical? Or is the Commandment really, first and foremost, about how fathers and mothers must comport themselves? In the translated words of Abd-ru-shin:

> How can a child honour the father who degrades himself to the level of a drunkard; or a mother who grievously embitters the hours of the father and the entire household through her caprices, through her unrestrained temper, lack of self-discipline and so much else, making a peaceful atmosphere quite impossible!

> Can a child honour its parents when it hears them roundly abusing and deceiving each other, or even coming to blows? How many a conjugal incident has often made the Commandment a torment for the children, rendering it impossible of fulfilment. (*The Ten Commandments of God and The Lord's Prayer*)

Indeed, the right conception of God is one who would not command us to honour another (regardless of relationship) who does not deserve honour. Moreover, as it stands, the Commandment is one-sided – making a demand on children without any corresponding obligation on parents. And this contradicts the eternal Law of Balance between giving and taking. In its present form the Commandment refers to particular, specific persons, whose character cannot be foreseen and which may be honourable or ignoble. The word "thy" or "your" was interpolated in error in the Commandment, thus making it personal. The Commandment should simply read: "Honour father and mother".

In other words, the fourth Commandment is about the *idea or principle* of fatherhood and motherhood and not about honouring particular individuals. It is addressed in the first place to parents and demands that they maintain fatherhood and motherhood as concepts of honour, of utmost dignity and high responsibility. By so doing, they would fully deserve honour from their children as well as from others. If this commandment is obeyed, fathers and mothers become enduring and exemplary role models for their children throughout the entire earthly existence of those children. And children would truly honour such parents in every sense and as a matter of course.

In connection with the subject of this Chapter, let me remark that if this Commandment had been rightly understood and obeyed, there would be much less evil in the world. On account of their moral carelessness and irresponsibility, some mothers and fathers provide opportunities for ignoble souls to incarnate on earth, thereby increasing the types and extent of evil on earth. Truly dignified, responsible, and honourable couples would automatically block the incarnation of souls with evil dispositions. And they would be more successful in bringing up children who would be more likely to fight evil rather than contributing to it.

Evil Exists Only in the World of Matter

God is Primordial Light, eternally radiating and generating heat to such an extent that nothing can take on form or be conscious in God's proximity. What can be called the proximity of God is a surging ocean of flames. Thus, it is said: "Before God everything dissolves!" The Divine Sphere is not in the true proximity of God but forms at an appropriate distance at which considerable cooling has taken place. This explains why we should not equate God with the Divine. In the Divine Sphere and in Primordial and Spiritual Creations, no volition contrary to the Will of God can develop and no deviation from His Will is possible. It is, therefore, clear that no iota of evil, no jot of impurity is possible or even conceivable in such spheres.

Impurities and evil only develop in the World of Matter – in Ethereal Matter and in Gross Matter, which are unimaginably distant from the Spiritual Realms. Therefore, in thinking about God and the problem of evil, we should be mindful of the fact that evil exists only in the World of Matter, which despite its astronomical vastness is but a speck when compared with the direct Creation of God. And it is the after-effects situated at the remote periphery of God's Creation.

The World of Gross Matter consists of seven universes, each of which in turn consists of billions of galaxies comprising billions of star systems. Our earth is in the Universe Ephesus, located in one of its many billion galaxies – the Milky Way. The Milky Way includes our solar system as one of its billions of star systems and in which the earth is a planet. Thus, considering just the World of Matter alone, our earth is no more than a tiny spot formed only 9 billion years after the Big Bang. The point is that the reality is such that we should not make conclusions about God based on our observations of the current state of the earth.

Finally, it should not be presumed that there will always be evil on earth. That is not the case. There is an ongoing intensification of spiritual radiation in the World of Matter and this drives everything (good as well as evil) into greater activity. Whatever accords with the Will of God will be strengthened and will blossom, whereas that which goes against It (i.e. that which is evil) will wear itself out and will eventually destroy itself. At this time of spiritual purification, all types of evil including previously unknown types are frantically rearing their heads. Through their activities, the forces of evil will willy-nilly bang their heads against the invisible but indomitable walls formed by the ever-increasing Pressure of the Light and will be destroyed. The spiritual pressure will also make it increasingly difficult for souls with evil dispositions and propensities to incarnate on earth. Through these and other processes, evil will eventually be wiped out and the Kingdom of God in which only what accords with the Will of God can exist will be established. Thus, one can say that evil is not a permanent feature of the world.

References

Abd-ru-shin. *In the Light of Truth, The Grail Message*. Vomperberg, Tyrol, Alexander Bernhardt Publishing Co., 1979. 3 volumes.

Abd-ru-shin. *Questions and Answers, 1924-1937*. Vomperberg, Tyrol, Alexander Berhhardt Publishing Co., 1972. (232p).

Abd-ru-shin. *The Ten Commandments of God* (and) *The Lord's Prayer, Explained to Mankind*. Vomperberg, Tyrol, Alexander Bernhardt Publishing Co., 1979. (71p).

Ayala, Francisco J. *The Big Questions: Evolution.* London, Quercus Publishing Plc, 2012. 208p.

Baker, Joanne. *50 Ideas You Really Need to Know: Universe.* London, Quercus Publishing, 2010.

Borg, Marcus J. *The God we never knew: Beyond dogmatic religion to a more authentic contemporary faith*. San Francisco, HarperSanFrancisco, 1997. ix, 182p.

Buddha: Life and Work of the Forerunner in India. Received in the proximity of Abd-ru-shin through the special gift of one called for the purpose. Vomperberg, Tyrol, Alexander Bernhardt Publishing Co. 1987. 273p.

A Catechism of Christian Doctrine, third edition. London, Catholic Truth Society, Publishers to the Holy See, 2013. 88p.

Collins, Francis S. *The Language of God*: *A Scientist Presents Evidence for Belief.* New York, Free Press, 2006. viii, 294p.

Darwin, Charles. *On the Origin of Species by Means of Natural Selection*. London, John Murray, 1859.

Dawkins, Richard. *The God Delusion*. New York, Houghton Mifflin Co, 2006. x, 406p.

Dawkins, Richard. *The Magic of Reality*. London, Black Swan, 2012. 267p.

Eagleton, Terry. *Reason, Faith, and Revolution: Reflections on the God Debate.* New Haven and London, Yale University Press, 2009. xii, 185p.

Eccles, John C. *How the Self Controls Its Brain.* Berlin, Springer-Verlag, 1994. 216p.

Fuller, R. Buckminster. *Intuition*, 2nd ed. Luis Obispo, Calif., Impact Publishers, 1983. 223p.

Geim, Andrew K. "Random Walk to Graphene." Nobel Lecture, December 8, 2010.

Hawking, Stephen. *A Brief History of Time.* New York, Bantam Press, 1998.

Hermanns, William. *Einstein and the Poet: In Search of the Cosmic Man.* Wellesley, Massachusetts, Branden Books, 1983. 151p.

Hoyle, F. and Lyttleton, R.A. "The internal constitution of the stars." *Occasional Notes of the Royal Astronomical Society* 12:89-108, September 1948.

Karger, Friedbert. *The Consequences of Non-Material Environmental Pollution*, Manuscript of a Lecture, Vomperberg, Tyrol, 1991. 11p.

Lampe, Stephen. *The Christian and Reincarnation*, Legacy Edition. Ibadan, Millennium Press, 2008. x, 257p.

Lewontin, Richard. "Billions and Billions of Demons", *New York Review of Books*, January 9, 1997.

Matthews, W. R. *God in Christian Thought and Experience.* London, Nisbet & Co. Ltd, 1930. xix, 283p.

McGrath, Alister and McGrath, Joanna Collicutt. *The Dawkins Delusion? Atheist fundamentalism and the denial of the divine.* London, Society for Promoting Christian Knowledge (SPCK), 2007. xiii, 78p.

Nadler, Steven. "Why Spinoza was excommunicated." *Humanities*, Vol. 34, Number 5, September/October 2013.

Past Eras Awaken. Received in the proximity of Abd-ru-shin through the special gift of one called for the purpose. Volume III. London, Grail Acres Publishing Co. Ltd, 1998. 417p.

Penfield, Wilder. *Mystery of the Mind: a critical study of consciousness and the human brain*. Princeton, New Jersey, Princeton University, 1975. 152p.

Prophet, Elizabeth Clare with Erin L. Prophet. *Reincarnation: The Missing Link in Christianity*, Corwin Springs, MT, Summit University Press, 1997. xviii, 412p.

Ratzinger, Joseph Cardinal. *God and the World: Believing and Living in Our Time. A Conversation with Peter Seewald*. Translated by Henry Taylor. San Francisco, Ignatius Press, 2002. 460p.

Reyes, Benito F. *Scientific Evidence of the Existence of the Soul*. Wheaton, Ill., The Theosophical Publishing House, 1970. 259p.

Schumacher, E. F. *A Guide for the Perplexed.* New York, Harper & Row, 1977. 147p.

Sheldrake, Rupert. *The Science Delusion: Freeing the Spirit of Enquiry.* London, Coronet/Hodder & Stoughton, 2013. 392p.

Stapp, Henry P. "Compatibility of contemporary physical theory with personality survival". (http://www-physics.lbl.gov/~stapp/Compatibility.pdf).

Tabbarah, Afif A. *The Spirit of Islam: Doctrine and Teachings* 3rd revised edition translated into English by Hasan T. Shoucair and revised by Dr. Rohi Baaalbaki. Beirut, Lebanon, Dar El-Ilm, 1993. 479p.

Templeton Jr., John M. Statement at the Templeton Prize Press Conference, New York City, March 9, 2005. (www.templetonprize.org/pdfs/Templeton_Prize_Chronicle_2005.pdf).

Townes, Charles H. Statement at the Templeton Prize Press Conference, , New York City, March 9, 2005. (www.templetonprize. org/pdfs/Templeton_Prize_Chronicle_2005.pdf).

Townes, Charles H. Statement at the Templeton Prize Luncheon Media Briefing, London, May 3, 2005. (www.templetonprize.org/ pdfs/Templeton_Prize_Chronicle_2005.pdf).

Townes, Charles H. Question and Answer session with Prof. Charles H. Townes at the Templeton Prize Luncheon Media Briefing, London, May 3, 2005. (www.templetonprize.org/pdfs/ Templeton_Prize_Chronicle_2005.pdf).

Van Zeller, Hubert. *Prayer and the Will of God*. Manchester (New Hampshire), Sophia Institute Press, 2009. viii, 156p.

Vatican International Theological Commission. *The Hope of Salvation for Infants Who Die Without Being Baptised.* April 2007. 41p. (http://www.vatican.va/roman_curia/congregations/cfaith/ cti_documents/rc_con_cfaith_doc_20070419_un-baptised-infants_en.html)

Vollmann, Herbert. *A Gate Opens.* Stuttgart, Stiftung Gralsbotschaft Publishing Co., 1985. 394p.

Vollmann, Herbert. *Helping Words: Selected Texts from the Book Series of the Grail Message Foundation*. Vomperberg, Tyrol, Alexander Bernhardt Publishing Co., 1976.

Whaley, Harold. *Great Men Search for God.* Mount Vernon, New York, The Peter Pauper Press, 1975.

White, Michael and Gribbin, John. *Einstein*. New York, Dutton, Penguin Books USA Inc., 1994

Younghusband, Sir Francis. *Modern Mystics,* 1st edition. New York, E.P. Duttton and Company Inc., 1935. 316p.

Index

www.ingramcontent.com/pod-product-compliance
Lightning Source LLC
Chambersburg PA
CBHW021038090426
42738CB00006B/138